# Dreamweaver CS5 and Web Developn HTML5, CSS3, and jQuery

Harness the cutting edge features of Dreamweaver for mobile and web development

**David Karlins**

BIRMINGHAM - MUMBAI

# Dreamweaver CS5.5 Mobile and Web Development with HTML5, CSS3, and jQuery

First published: September 2011

Production Reference: 1160911

Published by Packt Publishing Ltd.
Livery Place
35 Livery Street
Birmingham B3 2PB, UK.

ISBN 978-1-84969-158-1

www.packtpub.com

Cover Image by Asher Wishkerman (a.wishkerman@mpic.de)

# Credits

**Author**
David Karlins

**Reviewers**
Chad Adams

Nelson Therrien

**Acquisition Editor**
Wilson D'souza

**Development Editor**
Neha Mallik

**Technical Editors**
Kavita Iyer

Azharuddin Sheikh

**Project Coordinator**
Srimoyee Ghoshal

**Proofreader**
Mario Cecere

**Indexer**
Rekha Nair

**Graphics**
Valentina D'silva

**Production Coordinator**
Shantanu Zagade

**Cover Work**
Shantanu Zagade

# About the Author

**David Karlins** is a consultant, writer, and teacher on digital graphics and interactive design solutions. He has written or co-authored some fifty books, professional instruction videos, and apps on web design, vector graphic design, digital photography, sports photography, project management, digital video, and animation.

David Karlins' consulting clients have ranged from Hewlett Packard to the Himalayan Fair, from AAA Health Insurance to the Association of Alternative Newsweeklies.

David Karlins is the author of *Adobe Creative Suite 5 Web Premium How-Tos: 100 Essential Techniques*, (Adobe Press), *Adobe Dreamweaver CS4 How-Tos: 100 Essential Techniques* (Adobe Press), *Adobe Illustrator CS4 How-Tos: 100 Essential Techniques* (Adobe Press). He is also the author of *PC Magazine Guide to Printing Great Digital Photos* (PC Magazine Press), *Build Your Own Web Site* (McGraw Hill), *Adobe Illustrator Gone Wild* (Wiley), *and Enhancing a Dreamweaver Web Site with Flash Video: Visual QuickProject Guide* (Peachpit).

Thanks to Wilson D'souza, Srimoyee Ghoshal, Priya Mukherji, and the entire management and staff at Packt Publishing. I would also like to thank my agent Margot Maley Hutchison.

# About the Reviewers

**Chad Adams** is a graduate of University of Central Missouri with a B.F.A. in Commercial Art in Graphic Design, and has been a professional web developer and user experience designer for over seven years. He has developed websites and mobile applications for iOS, Android, and Windows Phone 7 as well.

In order to know more about Chad, visit his website at: `http://chad-adams.com/`.

My amazing wife, Heather, was always so patient with my late nights studying and working and I want to thank her for her faithful support during my career. Lastly, I offer my regards to my friends, family, and thanks to all those who have supported me in any respect during the completion of the project.

**Nelson Therrien** has computer degrees in both multimedia and programming. He is an **ACE** (**Adobe Certified Expert**) with Dreamweaver and has many Brainbench certifications (HTML, XHTML, Dreamweaver, Flash, Web design, Photoshop, and so on).

Most of his time is spent in teaching and developing web applications and dynamic forms. He is teaching at Eliquo, Canada's biggest Apple and Adobe authorized training center. He is responsible for everything that revolves around the Web at the Montreal office.

You could see him if you take a course on Dreamweaver, Flash, ActionScript, Flex, ColdFusion, HTML5, CSS3, XML, JavaScript, jQuery, PHP, LiveCycle Designer, or accessibility and standards on the Web. He also touched some ASP, .NET, Java, SQL, Photoshop, Fireworks, and Illustrator.

He also gave a conference for the launch of Adobe CS5 and CS5.5 in Canada as an Eliquo representative.

He is the father of three young children.

As a way to relax, he is constantly reading and searching to improve his skills and knowledge, and he can find some time to play Canada's national game: hockey! He is a goaltender on his own and coaches his two sons.

I would like to thank Craig Boassaly, Eliquo's president, and the entire team at Eliquo for making my teaching job so much fun.

I would also want to thank my wife, who has the job of taking care of our three angels when I am too busy to help her. Moreover, I would like to thank my three kids, Josué, Isaac, and Kaïla for putting so much sunshine in my life.

# www.PacktPub.com

## Support files, eBooks, discount offers and more

You might want to visit www.PacktPub.com for support files and downloads related to your book.

Did you know that Packt offers eBook versions of every book published, with PDF and ePub files available? You can upgrade to the eBook version at www.PacktPub.com and as a print book customer, you are entitled to a discount on the eBook copy. Get in touch with us at service@packtpub.com for more details.

At www.PacktPub.com, you can also read a collection of free technical articles, sign up for a range of free newsletters and receive exclusive discounts and offers on Packt books and eBooks.

http://PacktLib.PacktPub.com

Do you need instant solutions to your IT questions? PacktLib is Packt's online digital book library. Here, you can access, read and search across Packt's entire library of books.

## Why Subscribe?

- Fully searchable across every book published by Packt
- Copy and paste, print and bookmark content
- On demand and accessible via web browser

## Free Access for Packt account holders

If you have an account with Packt at www.PacktPub.com, you can use this to access PacktLib today and view nine entirely free books. Simply use your login credentials for immediate access.

# Table of Contents

# Preface

Dreamweaver is the most powerful and industry-leading web design software that utilizes innovative web technologies such as HTML5, CSS3, and jQuery for web and mobile development. These technologies have radically reconfigured the process of designing the web content and function in the widest possible range of browsing environments ranging from desktops to mobile devices.

For experienced Dreamweaver designers and for designers who are new to Dreamweaver, this book explains in detail how to take advantage of the new features available in the latest releases of Dreamweaver that add support for HTML5, CSS3, and jQuery. In addition to this, the book also contains detailed systematic directions for building mobile applications in Dreamweaver CS5.5.

This book starts off by teaching you to create web pages in Dreamweaver using the latest technology and approaches—HTML5, CSS3, and JavaScript. It demonstrates how to create or customize pages with HTML5 layouts and add multimedia to these pages with HTML5 elements. Then, you will learn to add various CSS3 effects to web pages. This book also covers different techniques of adding interactivity to web pages. The later chapters show how to optimize web pages with Dreamweaver for display in various browsing environments. You will also learn to build jQuery-based mobile apps from scratch in the later chapters. By the time you finish reading this book, you will have learned several techniques to use the latest features of Dreamweaver for web and mobile development.

## What this book covers

*Chapter 1, Creating HTML5 Pages in Dreamweaver*, begins with the exploration of creating HTML web pages with Dreamweaver CS5.

*Chapter 2, Customizing HTML5 Layout—Content and Look*, provides information about customizing both the content and the look of HTML5 pages generated with the HTML5 Layouts in Dreamweaver.

*Chapter 3, Customizing HTML5 Layout Elements,* provides an exploration of using new HTML5 layout elements, including `<header>`, `<nav>`, `<article>` and `<section>`, `<aside>`, and `<footer>`.

*Chapter 4, Building HTML5 Pages from Scratch,* guides you through the process of building modern standards-complaint pages relying entirely on HTML5 layout tags.

*Chapter 5, Defining and Implementing Multiscreen Previews and Media Queries,* guides you through the process of providing media-sensitive content for a variety of viewports, ranging from large-screen projections of websites to hand-held devices.

*Chapter 6, Applying CSS3 Effects and Transforms,* highlights the importance of using CSS3 to format effects such as drop-shadows, rounded box corners, and opacity (transparency) along with transforms that change the shape, location, rotation, and size of objects.

*Chapter 7, Embedding HTML5 Audio in Dreamweaver,* guides you through the process of embedding native (browser-based, not plugin-based) audio to web pages using Dreamweaver CS5.5 tools for HTML5 media.

*Chapter 8, Embedding HTML5 Video in Dreamweaver,* provides information about embedding a variety of HTML5-compliant video formats to web pages using HTML5 and Dreamweaver CS5.5.

*Chapter 9, Creating Mobile Pages with jQuery,* guides you through the process of creating jQuery Mobile-based pages — accessible, inviting, animated pages that work particularly well in mobile devices.

*Chapter 10, Adding jQuery Mobile Elements,* provides information about building jQuery Mobile-based pages from scratch with layout grids, and collapsible blocks.

*Chapter 11, Generating Apps,* guides you through the process of publishing mobile apps for iOS (iPhone, iPod Touch, and iPad) and Android devices using new tools in Dreamweaver 5.5.

# What you need for this book

In order to work through this book most effectively, you need access to Dreamweaver CS5.5 or higher. However, the book includes asides and notes to enable designers using earlier versions of Dreamweaver, back to Version 3, to take advantage of Adobe-provided tools for creating HTML5 and CSS3-based websites.

# Who this book is for

This book is geared towards experienced Dreamweaver web designers migrating to HTML5 and jQuery. It also targets web designers new to Dreamweaver who want to jump with two feet into the most current web design tools and features. While focused primarily on Dreamweaver CS5.5, the book includes content of value to readers using older versions of Dreamweaver with directions on installing a version of Adobe's HTML5 Pack that updates those packages.

# Conventions

In this book, you will find a number of styles of text that distinguish between different kinds of information. Here are some examples of these styles, and an explanation of their meaning.

**New terms** and **important words** are shown in bold. Words that you see on the screen, in menus or dialog boxes for example, appear in the text like this: "Doing this opens the **Select Image Source** dialog".

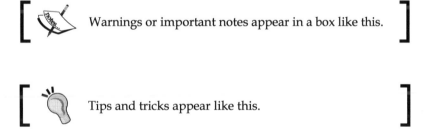

Warnings or important notes appear in a box like this.

Tips and tricks appear like this.

# Reader feedback

Feedback from our readers is always welcome. Let us know what you think about this book—what you liked or may have disliked. Reader feedback is important for us to develop titles that you really get the most out of.

To send us general feedback, simply send an e-mail to feedback@packtpub.com, and mention the book title via the subject of your message.

If there is a book that you need and would like to see us publish, please send us a note in the **SUGGEST A TITLE** form on www.packtpub.com or e-mail suggest@packtpub.com.

If there is a topic that you have expertise in and you are interested in either writing or contributing to a book, see our author guide on www.packtpub.com/authors.

# Customer support

Now that you are the proud owner of a Packt book, we have a number of things to help you to get the most from your purchase.

## Errata

Although we have taken every care to ensure the accuracy of our content, mistakes do happen. If you find a mistake in one of our books—maybe a mistake in the text or the code—we would be grateful if you would report this to us. By doing so, you can save other readers from frustration and help us improve subsequent versions of this book. If you find any errata, please report them by visiting http://www.packtpub.com/support, selecting your book, clicking on the **errata submission form** link, and entering the details of your errata. Once your errata are verified, your submission will be accepted and the errata will be uploaded on our website, or added to any list of existing errata, under the Errata section of that title. Any existing errata can be viewed by selecting your title from http://www.packtpub.com/support.

## Piracy

Piracy of copyright material on the Internet is an ongoing problem across all media. At Packt, we take the protection of our copyright and licenses very seriously. If you come across any illegal copies of our works, in any form, on the Internet, please provide us with the location address or website name immediately so that we can pursue a remedy.

Please contact us at copyright@packtpub.com with a link to the suspected pirated material.

We appreciate your help in protecting our authors, and our ability to bring you valuable content.

## Questions

You can contact us at questions@packtpub.com if you are having a problem with any aspect of the book, and we will do our best to address it.

# 1

# Creating HTML5 Pages in Dreamweaver

This chapter begins our exploration of creating HTML5 web pages with Dreamweaver CS5. The focus here, and throughout this book is on unleashing the exciting, powerful HTML features for page layout, animation, media, and design using HTML5. At the same time, we will of necessity, take a concentrated looks at basic techniques involved in setting up Dreamweaver websites and basic editing and formatting tools in Dreamweaver.

After briefly introducing HTML5, CSS3, and Dreamweaver CS5, and the way they work together to create websites, the focus of this chapter will be generating page layouts in Dreamweaver that avail themselves of HTML5 layout tools. By the end of this chapter, you will be able to create basic, attractive web pages that use the improved HTML5 page layout elements. In addition, you will be in a position to customize those pages with your own content, and formatting, in the next chapter.

In this chapter, we will:

- Survey the evolution of HTML5 and understand how it simplifies the web page design
- Explore key HTML5 elements used in web page layouts
- Understand how Dreamweaver CS5 generates HTML5 web page layouts
- Install the HTML5 Pack as an Extension (for Dreamweaver CS5 and older versions as well)
- Create Dreamweaver CS5/HTML5 sites and files
- Generate new pages from layouts using the HTML5 templates
- Control views
- Generate HTML5 page layouts in Dreamweaver
- Create a 3-column HTML5 page layout in Dreamweaver

# HTML5 and Dreamweaver CS5 in the world of web design

We will be working with a few key acronyms in this book and they stand for things, which are essential to creating innovative websites. So, let's start with introductions:

- HTML5 is the latest and most powerful version of the HTML (**HyperText Markup Language**). It is the newest and the most powerful language for creating the basic elements of a web page.

- CSS3 is the latest and the most powerful version of CSS (**Cascading Style Sheets** — or **Style Sheets** for short). CSS handles how web pages and elements on them look.

- Dreamweaver CS5 is the most widely used, powerful, and flexible tool for creating the web page content, including HTML5 and CSS3. Thus, the basic flow of this book will be exploring the key powerful features of HTML5 and CSS3 and generating those features using Dreamweaver CS5.

> Limited CS4 and CS3 functionality: Some, but not all of the features explored in this book are available in older versions of Dreamweaver with the HTML5 Pack installed. In general, you can follow the same steps indicated here for Dreamweaver CS3 and CS4 and take advantage of those elements of the HTML5 Pack supported by older versions of Dreamweaver.

# HTML5—the cutting edge of web design

I like to describe HTML5 concisely as solving the 3s: simplifying, standardizing, and styling. Those terms don't embrace everything new in HTML5, but they highlight key new features and help break down what HTML5 is all about into digestible chunks.

HTML5 simplifies the web design by taking frequently used features, such as the page layout elements we will explore in this chapter, and defining elements (previously known as tags) for them. Therefore, for example, instead of every page designer needing to invent a special batch of code to define a page header — a common element in many web pages — HTML5 has added a standard, pre-set `<header>` element.

HTML5 is an attempt to standardize how browsers interpret the page layout code. Now, an obvious question is, who sets the standards and how standard are they? The answer in this case is complex, contradictory, and a work in progress. However, suffice to say that an alignment of the most powerful players on the Web, in particular the makers of all the major browsers (Safari, Firefox, Chrome, Opera, and Internet Explorer starting with version 9) have all embraced HTML5, to the point that a critical mass is either now in place, or emerging quickly. That said, it would be a long time before everyone browsing the Web is doing so in an HTML5-compliant browser. Therefore, in the course of this book, we will explore approaches for providing alternative content for visitors using non-HTML5 browsers.

HTML5 also expands what can be done in web design style, without resorting to plugins (such as JavaScript or Flash). Many of these additional features are accessed through CSS3 — the latest version of Style Sheet formatting that is an enabling, co-dependent partner (in a good way!) with HTML5.

# HTML4.1, XHTML, and HTML5

HTML5 was preceded by XHTML, and before that, HTML 4 (in various versions). In some ways, HTML5 is not a continuation on that evolutionary line, but a new synthesis that stands on both HTML and XHTML.

There is no great need here to clutter our heads with the ways in which HTML5 addresses non-standardization in different previous versions of HTML and browsing environments, but such housekeeping and standardization is a significant contribution of HTML5.

The new features in HTML5 (and the related features in CSS3) are of more interest for designers.

HTML5's <video> and <audio> elements provide a much simplified approach to presenting the online video and audio, without resorting to different and competing media players (such as Windows Media Player, QuickTime player, or Flash Player). The new canvas elements open the door to an exciting array of possibilities for presenting images, interactivity, and media.

Moreover, as we will focus on in this chapter, HTML5 introduces a set of elements that standardize and simplify the page layout.

# Compatibility issues with HTML5

As HTML5 is new, and emerging, designers obviously want to know whether elements they create using it (such as video, or page design elements) are supported in different browsers.

The answer is more complicated than you might think. Different HTML5 elements are supported in different browsing environments and in different ways. For example, many (but not all) browsers support HTML5's new VIDEO element, but within that grouping of browsers, there is support for different video formats.

In other cases, older browsers support the HTML5 elements, but some of the features don't work. In general, these elements still work in older browsers and visitors simply forego nice but non-essential features. For example, an HTML5 e-mail will be easier to fill out in an HTML5-complaint browser, but will still work as a plain text field in older browsers.

This might sound like a messy situation. In some ways it is. However, as I say in almost every session of my live web design classes, "welcome to the experience." Compatibility issues with HTML5 are, however, an eminently manageable challenge that we will address from different angles and with different problems in mind throughout this book.

Each time we introduce HTML5 elements, we will also look at how to provide alternatives for visitors viewing the page in a browser that does not support HTML5.

Sometimes, the HTML5 features not supported in non-complaint browsers limit available features, but do not cause harm. For example, the following screenshot illustrates the PLACEHOLDER attribute in HTML5 that displays a "hint" text in a form field that vanishes when a visitor begins typing in that field.

HTML5 allows a placeholder text, in this case, **Enter search text here**:

In the case of HTML5's placeholder attribute, when this is not supported in a browser, the form field simply appears without the placeholder text, as shown in the following screenshot.

Viewed in a non-complaint browser, the HTML placeholder text simply disappears, but the form still works:

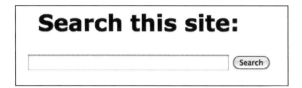

In some situations, we will address compatibility issues exploring, on the spot, and creating an alternative content for older browsers. We will also explore more radical approaches to provide alternative formatting for different browsers using techniques such as Media Queries (see *Chapter 5, Defining and Implementing Multiscreen Previews and Media Queries*) to provide alternate page layouts for different browsers.

However, the bottom line is, in one way or another, we will take into account and build into the process by providing alternative content for non-HTML5 environments.

# HTML5 and Dreamweaver CS5.5

Having briefly surveyed HTML5, we will now step back and see how Dreamweaver fits into the whole picture of creating websites using HTML5.

Dreamweaver is the premiere tool for generating web content and design. We will parse that a bit: First, Dreamweaver produces a range of web content. Dreamweaver generates HTML (including, as we shall explore in a moment) HTML5. HTML is the foundation of web pages, but Dreamweaver also generates two other critical elements of Web design: CSS (Style Sheets) and JavaScript.

Dreamweaver's capacity to generate interactive (objects that interact with visitor actions) is somewhat limited. We will see these features at times in this book, but in the main, we will focus on Dreamweaver's very powerful tools for managing CSS, the styles that control how content appears in web pages.

# Dreamweaver generates code

Let's define what we meant when we say Dreamweaver generates HTML, CSS, and (in a more limited way) JavaScript. Dreamweaver generates this content in three basic ways that work together.

The first way Dreamweaver generates code is when you edit and format content in the Design view of the Document window. Second, Dreamweaver generates CSS and JavaScript using panels such as the CSS Styles panel and the Behaviors panel (respectively). Finally, you can write HTML and CSS in the code view and Dreamweaver will assist with code hints.

Dreamweaver's Document window has three views, which we will explore shortly. However, the most intuitive is the Design view—an environment that approximates those in other Adobe Creative Suite applications such as InDesign, Photoshop, and Illustrator. The Design view is used to format text, images, design containers, media, and other elements. As you use intuitive editing and formatting tools, including the utilitarian and context-sensitive Properties Manager panel, Dreamweaver generates HTML, CSS, and JavaScript to match the content and formatting attributes you create in the Design view. In the following screenshot, for example, the selected image is having attributes such as an associated link edited in Dreamweaver CS5.5's Properties inspector and the code (on the left) is updated automatically.

Defining a link in Dreamweaver's Design view, while the code updates in the Code view (on the left):

The second way Dreamweaver generates code is through panels. There are several panels which generate different kinds of code. In this book, we will focus on the CSS Styles panel which generates the critical CSS that controls the page formatting.

Finally, the Dreamweaver's Code View provides code hinting and completion tools that make writing of the code easier. As much as possible, we will rely on the Design view and Panels to generate all the code we need to maximize the HTML5 page design in Dreamweaver. We will resort to the Code view when necessary and take full advantage of the Dreamweaver's code hinting features.

# Dreamweaver—catching up to HTML5

We will begin with a candid assessment: Dreamweaver CS5.5 (and even more so CS4 and CS3) is racing to catch up with HTML5. Why? The answer is a complex mix of technical factors (HTML5 is, after all, still something of a work-in-progress and has not been adopted by all browsers), as well as business and what might be called economic and political factors, including the competition between Adobe and Apple.

This later element involves contending visions for how to implement media on the Web in particular. Just as Creative Suite 5 was being released, Apple consolidated its position that **Adobe's Flash Video (FLV)** and **Flash animation/interactivity (SWF)** formats would not be supported on iPhones, iPads, and other Apple mobile devices. Instead, Apple has backed HTML5's audio and video tools. Without going into this in any more detail, or "choosing sides," this level of background helps contextualize the release of Dreamweaver CS5.5 without support for HTML5.

That said, Adobe responded quickly with the release of the HTML5 Pack to add HTML5 tools to Dreamweaver CS5. The HTML5 Pack represented a significant upgrade to Dreamweaver. The HTML5 Pack is actually available in a limited edition for Dreamweaver CS4 and in an even more limited edition for CS3. However, in order to implement the HTML5 functionality completely, designers will find the most powerful set of tools in the combination of Dreamweaver CS5.5 and HTML5. In this chapter, you will learn to test for and—as necessary—install the HTML5 Pack.

In this context, our exploration of the HTML5 design in Dreamweaver will require a bit more time spent in the Code view than might be usual for a basic-to-intermediate book like this. However, we will work hard to make those forays in the Code view as effortless as possible. Moreover, I promise to leave "no stone unturned" to utilize the friendly Design view and more accessible Dreamweaver panels whenever possible.

# An introduction to HTML5 layout elements

It is often helpful, in understanding something new, to have a sense of where it came from. The evolution of different versions of HTML and accompanying versions of CSS (style sheets) has been marked in a fundamental sense by the need to create more attractive, complex, and creative page designs.

Web page design has evolved radically, but HTML in one version or another remains the foundation for web page design. HTML pages are the basic containers in which text, images, media, and animation are packaged. Moreover, HTML5 is the up-and-coming version of HTML that, as it gradually is adopted and unified across browsing environments, opens up vast opportunities for more easily creating web pages that are more inviting.

In the course of this book, we will explore how to use Dreamweaver to create page layouts, interactive elements, embedded media, and creative design with HTML5. However, we will start with one of the most basic, and substantial, new improvements in HTML5: the creation of a set of elements dedicated to the page layout. These elements ("tags" in earlier incarnations of HTML) are used to define regions of a page common to many, if not most, web page layouts.

HTML5 elements (like all HTML elements) are enclosed in "<>" characters in the HTML code. Therefore, for example, in coding books, the `footer` element is often written as `<footer>`. Even though Dreamweaver generates HTML and HTML5 code, we will use "<>" when referring to elements to make it easier to identify and work with them, once generated, in Dreamweaver.

# The evolution of HTML layout elements

The earliest versions of HTML did not provide for any real page design tools. Web pages were envisioned as pages to hold very basic content, with some images and text formatting, but without any real page layout.

## Phase 1: Tables

Inventive designers forged a way to use tables—a feature originally created to present data in columns and rows—as a page design tool. Table columns were used to layout vertical blocks of content, whereas table rows were used to layout horizontal bands of content.

Tables are still available as a tool for page design and a large percentage of older websites that were built using tables still rely on tables for page design. Moreover, Dreamweaver, including Dreamweaver CS5.5, still provides tools for designing pages with tables. The following screenshot shows a web page design in Dreamweaver. The properties inspector (shown in the following figure) identifies the selected table as having three columns (merged in the top and bottom rows) and three rows.

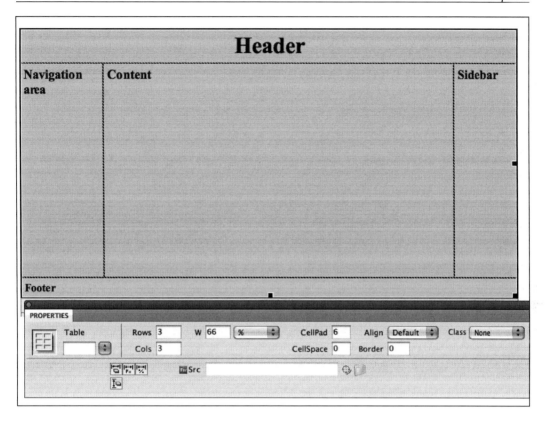

## Phase 2: CSS DIV tags

Tables had (and have) two great limitations as page layout tools.

The first was that they were (and are) a clunky way to design pages. Creative and unique page layouts with tables required contorting what was essentially a checkerboard of squares into desired headers, footers, sidebars, navigation spaces, and so on. Placement of images and text was awkward, requiring unstandardized combinations of table, row, column, and cell attributes, mixed and matched with attributes like those that margins assigned to text and images.

The second problem was that it was nearly impossible to orchestrate the *global* page designs across a website. The page design was embedded in *individual* pages—and thus if a designer wanted to tweak the layout of dozens of pages across a website, this generally required changing each page layout, one by one.

There is a third; it is a less recognized problem with using tables as page layout tools: They are not compatible with special reader software that allows vision-impaired people to experience web pages.

The solution that emerged to these challenges was just as creative and out-of-the-box as the original invention of using tables for page layout. Designers began relying on external (separate) CSS files to control both the attributes of text and images, but also to define blocks that could be used for the page design. Designers took and expanded the vaguely defined HTML DIV tag, and used it as a page layout tool. By attaching rules (attributes) defined in the CSS file to uniquely named DIV tags, designers concocted a work-around to the lack of real page layout elements in HTML. This situation existed through all the versions of HTML and XHTML (an updated, enhanced version of HTML that preceded HTML5).

Working with these blocks was (and is) awkward. There is no uniform or standardized set of DIV tags for page design, each designer creates and defines his or her own. This means that designers working in collaborative environments, or with content created by other designers, have to create their own sets of defined DIV tags for page layout. Editing other designers' work often requires far too much unproductive time and energy decoding the unique set of DIV tags used for page layout in an inherited design.

Therefore, DIV tags provided more flexibility than tables and allowed global editing (by changing the CSS file, all DIV tags across a site are updated). However, DIV tags are not standardized and are a clumsy and unnecessarily anarchistic approach to defining page layout elements.

The following screenshot shows a page designed with DIV tags in Dreamweaver. The Properties inspector reveals a non-standard DIV tag defining the selected container on the left side of the page (sidebar1, displayed in the **Class** pop up):

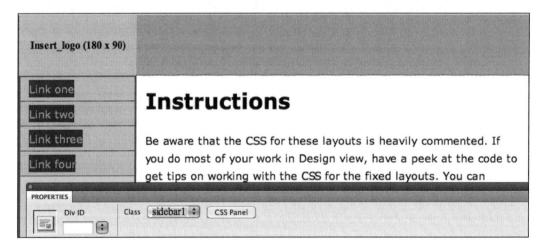

# Phase 3: HTML5 layout elements

From this set of demands and constraints, HTML5 evolved a standardized set of page layout elements. Sections of a web page such as Header, Footer, <nav> (for navigational elements), or <aside> (sidebars) come pre-named.

Like DIV tags before them, HTML5 layout elements can be updated across a website quickly and easily.

In addition, like DIV tags before them, HTML5 elements rely on CSS styles to define their location, size, and other appearance attributes (such as the background color or padding). Therefore, in the course of this, and following chapters, we'll be using Dreamweaver to orchestrate a dynamic relationship between HTML5 layout elements and CSS styles.

# Meet the HTML5 layout elements

As alluded to in our journey thus far, HTML5 comes with pre-set elements for commonly used components of a web page design. Once we have briefly surveyed the main HTML5 layout elements, we will explore how they are generated and modified in Dreamweaver with the HTML5 Pack.

Some of these elements are more adapted to laying out particular kinds of web pages. For example, the <article> and <section> elements are particularly useful for online periodicals or other publications that have articles, with (sub)sections within them. The <aside> element defines boxes for sidebars associated with articles.

The intuitively named <header> element, as you would expect, holds the content at the top of web pages. The <footer> element holds the content at the bottom of a page.

The <nav> element is used to layout the navigational content—links to other pages or locations on the Internet.

The following diagram illustrates a typical page layout using the `<header>`, `<nav>`, `<article>` and `<section>`, `<aside>`, and `<footer>` HTML5 elements:

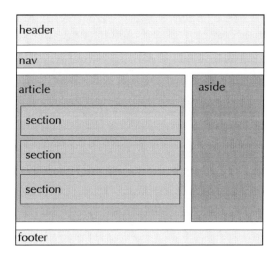

# Dreamweaver's HTML5 Pack and design elements

Now that we have introduced the key design elements of HTML5, we are almost ready to generate pages that use those elements in Dreamweaver. Before we do, however, it will be helpful to preview briefly, conceptually, how Dreamweaver generates HTML5 layouts.

The first thing to emphasize is that HTML5 elements such as `<header>`, `<footer>`, `<article>`, `<section>`, `<aside>`, and `<nav>`, do not really do much if anything "on their own." Like their DIV tag evolutionary precursors, they are more or less empty vessels. HTML5 elements take shape, literally, when connected with CSS styles.

For example, a web page might have a `<header>` defined as stretching the entire width of the page, at the top of the page, with a set background color, and spacing that keeps it from bumping into other page elements. All of these attributes (size, location, background color, and spacing) are defined in a CSS style sheet that includes a specific CSS style associated with the `<header>` element. Moreover, this symbiotic relationship between HTML5 layout elements and CSS styles is required for each HTML5 layout element.

Therefore, when Dreamweaver generates page layouts using HTML5 elements, it also generates a CSS file that has already built-in style rules for all the HTML5 elements used in the page.

Of course, you can change how HTML5 elements appear. You can edit the generic content that Dreamweaver provides with the HTML5 layouts. Alternatively, you can change the appearance of the HTML5 elements by editing the CSS styles. We will do both of these things in the next chapter of this book. Here and now, we will focus on setting up Dreamweaver so that it can generate HTML5 pages and then we will actually create those pages.

With the basic understanding of HTML5 layout elements and the way they interact with CSS under our belts, the time has come to launch into Dreamweaver and begin to create HTML5 layouts.

# Detecting or installing the HTML5 Pack in Dreamweaver

If you are working with Dreamweaver CS5.5, then you have the HTML5 editing features automatically installed. Therefore, you can skip this section of this chapter.

If you are working with an earlier version of Dreamweaver, then you may need to install the HTML5 Pack separately.

Depending on how recently you have installed Adobe-supplied updates to your version of Dreamweaver, you may have to install the HTML5 Pack to access Dreamweaver's new HTML5 tools. A quick test will determine whether the HTML5 Pack is installed in Dreamweaver CS5 (the following test won't work for earlier versions of Dreamweaver, as the HTML5 Pack features for those versions are much more limited).

Here it is. Launch Dreamweaver, and choose **File | New** from the main Dreamweaver menu (you can do this whether or not the Welcome Screen is visible). The **New Document** dialog appears.

In the **New Document** dialog that appears, choose the **Blank Page** category in the far left column. In the **Page Type** category, choose **HTML**. At the bottom of the **Layout** column, you should see two layouts that begin with HTML5, as shown in the following screenshot. You can see previews of these layouts if you click (once) on them in the **New Document** dialog:

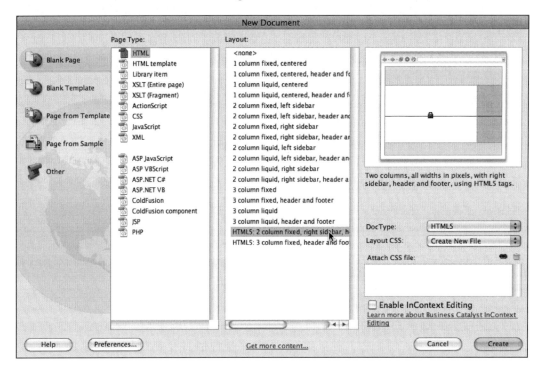

If your New Document dialog does display the two HTML5 layouts, hit the pause button (figuratively speaking) while we catch up readers who do not have the HTML5 Pack installed.

If you do not have the HTML5 layouts available in the **New Document** dialog, then your installation of Dreamweaver CS5 has not been updated for HTML5 and you will have to install the HTML5 Pack. In order to do that, use your web browser to go to `http://labs.adobe.com/technologies/html5pack/` and follow the instructions to update your installation of Dreamweaver CS5 to add the HTML5 Pack.

 **Older versions of Dreamweaver**: In order to add the HTML5 Pack to older versions of Dreamweaver, follow links to the **Dreamweaver Exchange** at the preceding URL.

With your installation of Dreamweaver CS5 updated (or if you have upgraded to CS5.5), or with the HTML5 Pack added as an extension to an older version of Dreamweaver, you are ready to roll. You now have Dreamweaver enabled to access HTML5 tools.

# Creating a Dreamweaver site

Most of the features associated with creating HTML5 content in Dreamweaver require that you first define a Dreamweaver site. Dreamweaver sites organize and manage all the files you create as you generate the content in Dreamweaver. Moreover, that kind of careful file management is essential in order to make sure that your HTML5 content works the way it is supposed to. For example, very shortly we will create web pages using HTML5 page layouts in Dreamweaver CS5.5. Those page layouts are dependant on CSS files that control how the HTML5 elements look. By defining a Dreamweaver site, and managing all files through this, you will ensure that the linked CSS file meshes properly with the HTML file that holds the page content.

In addition, let me emphasize this: Always work within a Dreamweaver site. Again, the more complex (and interesting, attractive, and inviting) your HTML5 pages, the more important it is that Dreamweaver is working its magic to orchestrate how all the generated files synch up with each other.

In order to create a Dreamweaver site, carry out the following steps:

> **Planning and Designing a site**: With our focus on implementing HTML5 elements in Dreamweaver, a full exploration of approaches to aesthetic, content, and audience issues is beyond the scope of what we can explore. However, as a general point of departure, you will want to sketch out in some form the pages you wish to create, prepare and organize text, images, and media content, and define basic thematic elements such as fonts and a color scheme either before, or during the process of creating your site. A wide range of online resources can provide perspectives and advice on web planning and design.

1. Copy and paste all the content you have prepared for your website (text files, images, and media) into a folder on your computer.

2. From the Dreamweaver CS5 or CS5.5 main menu, select **Site | New Site**.

3. The **Site Definition** dialog opens. With **Site** selected in the category list on the left, type a name for your site in the **Site Name** field. This name can contain spaces, upper and lowercase characters, and special symbols.

4. Click on the **Browse for folder** icon (the little gray folder) at the right of the **Local Site Folder** field and browse to, and select the folder in which you copied the content that will be used in your website, as shown in the following screenshot:

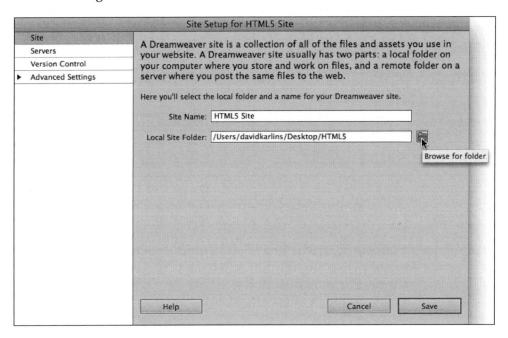

5. There are advanced options available, but the default settings will work fine. Click on **Save** to complete the process of defining your site.

**Connecting to a remote site**: In order to publish your website on the Internet, you have to define a remote site in Dreamweaver. The techniques explored in this book do not—overwhelmingly—require a remote site. If you are creating a remote site as you work through this book, then you will contract with a web hosting service that will provide you with an FTP address, a username, and a password. Enter this information in the **Servers** tab of the **Site Setup** dialog to connect your local site to the remote site. In order to upload files from your local site to your remote site, choose **Site | Synchronize Sitewide**, and choose upload options from the intuitive **Synchronize** Files dialog. For a more detailed discussion of creating and managing remote sites in Dreamweaver CS5, see *Adobe Creative Suite 5 Web Premium How-Tos: 100 Essential Techniques*, by David Karlins.

# Generating new pages from layouts using the HTML5 templates

Now that you have defined a Dreamweaver site, you are ready to generate new page layouts using HTML5 elements. In subsequent chapters, you will learn to customize the content, size, shape, colors, fonts, and other elements of these HTML5 elements. However, the first and foundational step is to generate pages.

In order to do that, choose **File | New**, and select **Blank Page** from the categories in the **New Document** dialog. Click once on the **HTML5: 2 column fixed, right sidebar, header and footer** layout to see a thumbnail preview of that layout in the **New Document** dialog and read a description of it, as shown in the following screenshot:

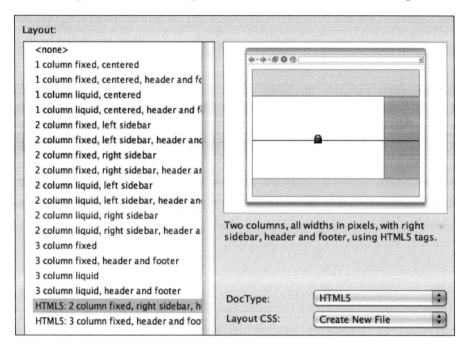

Similarly, you can click once on the **HTML5: 3 column fixed, header and footer** layout to see a preview thumbnail of that layout, and read a description of it.

The **DocType** pop up in the **New Document** dialog allows you to choose a file format other than (older than) HTML5 to save your file to. However, choosing any option other than HTML5 effectively negates the HTML5 elements essential to the layout (this option is more useful for page layouts using pre-HTML5 elements).

The **Layout CSS** pop up presents an important set of three options. The default, **Create New File**, sets up a new CSS file that will hold all the formatting information for this page. The **Add to Head** option is not considered best practice because it embeds styles within the HTML page. CSS files are much more powerful when they are saved externally—as distinct files—that can be applied to unlimited web pages, not just one. The final option, **Link to Existing File**, is used when you already have a CSS file ready to use with your generated page layout. If you are starting out on the process of exploring HTML5, then you won't yet have such a page. Later in this book, we will examine situations where it is useful to link a generated HTML5 layout to an existing CSS file.

After you have selected one of the two HTML5 layouts, click on the **Create** button in the **New Document** dialog. If you elected to generate a new style sheet, then the **Save Style Sheet File As** dialog appears, with a suggested file name as shown in the following screenshot. By default, if you first created a Dreamweaver site (and you should have!), the CSS file will be saved to your site folder. It works just fine to accept the default filename and folder and click on **Save** in the **Save Style Sheet File As** dialog:

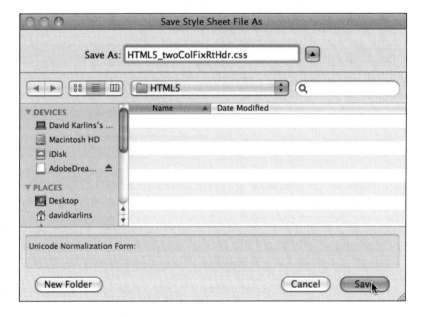

**Why we are saving a style sheet**: The HTML5 layout generated by Dreamweaver includes HTML5 elements (tags) that, very roughly, demarcate sections of the page. The formatting of those HTML5 elements is controlled by CSS styles, saved in an external (separate and distinct) Style Sheet file.

# Examining the generated HTML5 layout

Carefully examining a generated HTML5 introduces HTML5 elements and enables editing the content of the layout.

Dreamweaver CS5 and CS5.5 provide a wide array of views and combinations of views with which we can examine the generated HTML5 layout. Here, we will survey the most important and useful of those views and the way they work in various combinations to make it easier to edit the content.

You can view the page content in ways that provide access to the code that display how the page will look in a browser, or both. You can edit the page content or lock out the editing features to see how elements, such as links, will appear in a browser. In addition, you can explore related files that affect the way an open web page appears.

# Toggling between related files

The first component of the page display to be aware of is the related files tab. This set of tabs provides access to all files related to the main HTML page. When you generate either of the two available HTML5 layouts, a separate, distinct, but related (linked) CSS file generates. Both the HTML file and the CSS file are displayed in the related files tab, as shown in the following screenshot. You can toggle between them by clicking on either tag.

Toggling between an HTML page (the **Source Code** tab) and a related CSS file (indicated by the .css filename extension):

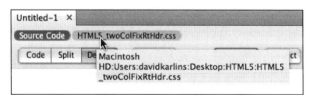

As you create more complex HTML5 layouts, being aware of what related files affect the appearance of that page opens the door to powerful design techniques. For now, simply note that the appearance of your generated HTML5 layout is defined by both the basic HTML web page and the related (linked) CSS file.

# Code, Split, and Design views

Your HTML5 page can be viewed in the Code, Split, or Design view. You can toggle between these views from the **View** menu, or by using buttons in the Document toolbar (if the buttons are not visible, choose **View** | **Toolbars** | **Document** to display it).

Code view reveals the HTML code that defines the basic page content. The Design view shows, roughly, how the page will look in a browser. The Split view splits the screen between the Code view (by default on the left) and the Design view (on the right).

> **Only the Code view for CSS pages**: CSS pages that are related to HTML pages are only displayed in the Code view. This is because CSS pages are just code—they define how the HTML page displays, but these files themselves are not normally viewed in a web browser and if they are, they simply appear as lines of code.

The Design view functions in two modes—with the Live View on or off. With the Live View on, you cannot edit most of the page content, but you can preview how interactive elements, such as links, will appear in a browser. The following screenshot shows a link being tested in a Split mode, with the Live View on.

Testing how a link will appear in Split view, with Live View enabled. Note that the mouse cursor is interacting with a link as it would in a browser:

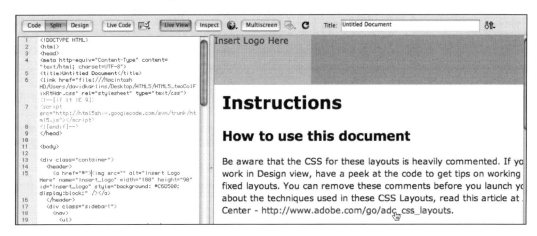

# Dissecting design elements with the Inspect Mode

The **Inspect** button in the Document toolbar turns on a feature that makes it easier to identify HTML5 (and other) elements that control how a page looks.

When you hover over any element on a page in the Inspect mode, elements such as padding (space within an HTML or HTML5 element) appear in purple and spacing created by margins (spacing outside of an HTML or HTML5 element) displays in yellow.

The Inspect mode is also of a particular relevance in working with HTML5 elements. When you place the mouse cursor over any part of a web page created from HTML5 layouts, you can click on the left-arrow key on your keyboard to "work backwards" in the list of elements that appears in the tag bar at the bottom of the Dreamweaver window.

The generated HTML5 layouts include elements such as `<header>`, `<nav>`, `<section>`, `<aside>`, and `<footer>`—new HTML5 elements that make page design simpler. In the following screenshot, the `<header>` element is identified in the Tag bar.

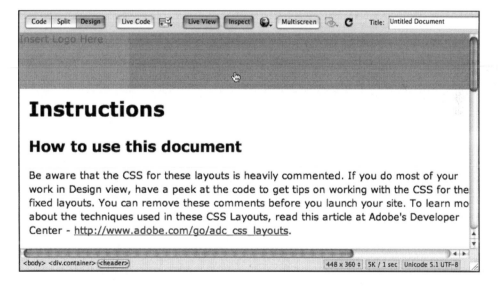

**Other workspace settings for the Inspect mode**: When you click on the **Inspect** button, Dreamweaver prompts you to change other workspace settings as well. Those other workspace changes are not essential, except for one—do work in the Live View when using the Inspect mode.

# Saving a layout as a web page

After you generate an HTML5 layout, the next step is to save the generated web page as an HTML file. However, before you do that, enter a page title in the **Title** box in the Document bar in Dreamweaver. File names should not have spaces, special characters (such as "?," "/," or "!"), but page titles should be descriptive. The following screenshot shows the **Title** field in the Document bar:

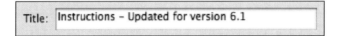

Title: Instructions – Updated for version 6.1

In order to save the file, choose **File** | **Save**. The **Save As** dialog opens, with a default file name assigned, and an HTML filename extension.

Here, it is time to revisit my earlier admonitions in order to be sure to create a Dreamweaver site, and work within it. One simple way to make sure you are saving your web page in the proper folder in your Dreamweaver site is to click on the **Site Root** button in the **Save As** dialog. This will ensure that your file is saved at the proper location.

Having ensured that you are saving your page to a folder defined in your Dreamweaver site, you can customize the filename for your page. Whatever filename you select, you should retain the `.html` filename extension. This is one of the acceptable filename extensions for web pages. The filename itself should have no spaces or special characters. In addition, while this is not a requirement for web page filenames, I recommend keeping filenames all lowercase to prevent confusion in file management (much of the Web is case sensitive when it comes to filenames).

 **The Unicode normalization form pop up**: The default "C" setting in this pop up is the most widely supported way of coding characters used in different languages (such as o, ó, ò, ô, ö, õ) for the World Wide Web. Dreamweaver allows you to save in other, less widely supported systems of coding characters, but this is only useful in very specialized situations.

After entering a filename in the **Filename** (Windows) or **Save As** (Mac) field in the **Save As** dialog, click on the **Save** button. The **Save As** dialog with a valid filename is shown in the following screenshot:

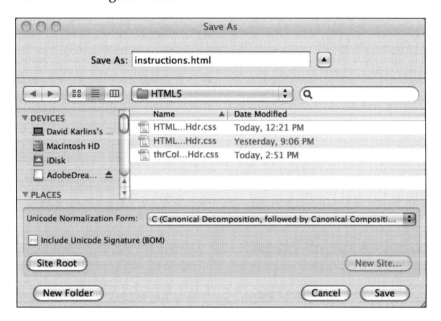

# Recipe: Creating and saving a 3-column HTML5 page

This recipe will walk you through the process of generating and saving a 3-column web page using the key HTML5 Layout elements. We will assume that you have created a Dreamweaver site (see the section named *Creating a Dreamweaver site* in this chapter).

1. Select **File | New** to open the **New Document** dialog. Select **Blank page** on the left-hand category column. Choose **HTML** in the **Page Type** column. Moreover, select **HTML5: 3 column fixed, <header> and <footer>** in the **Layout** column.

2. Note that HTML5 is now selected in the DocType pop up and Create New File from the Layout CSS pop up.

3. Click on the **Create** button. The **Save Style Sheet File As** dialog appears.

4. Click on the **Save** button and if prompted to replace an existing file, click on **Replace**. A generated HTML5 layout opens in Dreamweaver Document window.

5. Click on the **Inspect** button in the Document toolbar to more easily detect and identify HTML5 Layout elements. With the **Inspect** button enabled, hover over different sections of the page, and look for HTML5 Layout elements such as `<header>`, `<footer>`, `<aside>`, `<nav>`, `<article>`, and `<section>` in the tag bar at the bottom of the Dreamweaver window, as shown in the following screenshot:

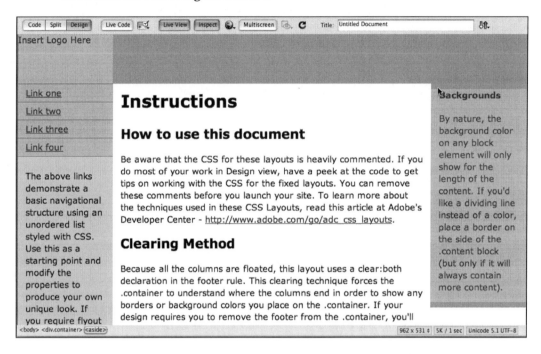

6. Enter a page title in the **Title** box in the Document toolbar.

7. Choose **File | Save**. Replace the default filename with your own filename—all in lowercase, no spaces, or special characters. Leave the HTML filename extension in tact. In order to work through the recipe in *Chapter 2*, save your file as: `chapter1.html`:

8. Click on the Site Root button to ensure the file is correctly managed by Dreamweaver and then click on the **Save** button.

This is, of course, only the first step in creating a web page using the HTML5 layout elements in Dreamweaver. The next steps are to customize the content and look of your page. We will do that next!

# Summary

In this chapter, we explored how to verify that the HTML5 Pack is installed in Dreamweaver CS5.

We have focused on generating web pages using the two available HTML5 Layouts that are part of the HTML5 Pack. We have explored both the HTML (HTML5) file that is generated from either of these layouts and noted that the formatting of the HTML5 elements (and other HTML elements) is dependent on a related (linked) CSS (style sheet) file.

Finally, we began to acclimate to some of the most useful views in Dreamweaver CS5 that will be of great value as we detect and change the attributes of HTML5 elements in future chapters.

# 2
# Customizing HTML5 Layout–Content and Look

In the previous chapter, we learned to generate HTML5 Page Layouts using Dreamweaver's HTML5 Pack. By the end of this chapter, we will have walked through the first phase of customizing both the content and the look of HTML5 pages generated with the HTML5 Layouts in Dreamweaver.

Customizing the content and look of pages generated from Dreamweaver HTML5 Layouts is best digested as a two-course meal. The first course is customizing the content, as well as the HTML tags that define the overall look of the page. We will do that in this chapter.

The second course, which we will see in the next chapter of this book, involves identifying and customizing the size, shape, location, background, type, and other attributes of HTML5 Layout elements.

In the course of all that, we will:

- Further explore the HTML and CSS tabs of the Properties inspector
- Explore the CSS Styles panel
- Identify and edit basic HTML tags that define the appearance of text on the page
- Customize page content

# Customizing layouts – An overview

Customizing page layout content in Dreamweaver is not particularly simple. Is that a bad thing? It depends. If you are not fussy about how your pages look, or if a "customized" blog with your own font color and logo is sufficient, then the course we have embarked on is overkill and you can use a WordPress blog for your content.

However, if your content really requires customization, unique page layouts with your own artwork, media, fine-tuned colors, and interactivity, then the price of working with Dreamweaver is probably good value.

# Embedding content where it belongs

Here is the challenge in conceptual terms: the page designs you generate in Dreamweaver are actually generated code. Specifically, they are HTML (in our case HTML5) and CSS (Style Sheets) code. Moreover, the challenge, or the trick, is to be sure that content you add falls in the proper place within the coding.

Doesn't Dreamweaver's Design view manage this? Kind of. For relatively simple page design projects, all you need to do is click on the Design view of Dreamweaver's Document window and type text, embed an image, or place a media file. However, more complex page layouts, involving the kinds of containers we are generating with Dreamweaver's HTML5 tools.

All this is highly manageable, and the challenges it poses are eminently solvable. However, it helps to go into the process with the approach of Sherlock Holmes (or his modern counterpart, TV's Dr. House). I will walk you through techniques and tools for making sure your content fits nicely and neatly into Dreamweaver-generated containers, and with the right élan and attitude, you will be able to both place content cleanly, and clean up messes when content doesn't quite fit into containers like it is supposed to.

Styles can be defined within a document (embedded or inline styles), or they can be defined in a separate (external) style sheet file. If all this seems a bit vague, or even ominous, don't worry. Again, we will hold hands as we walk through this together in the course of this chapter.

# Dissecting format

Doing the diagnostic work to identify why an element on your web page looks the way it does is even more of a challenge than getting content placed properly in containers.

That is because there are all kinds of ways to define and apply formatting to elements on a page. Formatting can be defined and applied via a style sheet (a set of CSS rules) that is embedded within a single page. Another way to define and apply is through an external style sheet—a distinct CSS file that is linked to the page.

When CSS styles are defined both within a page, and through a linked external CSS style sheet file, the local embedded CSS rules (the ones defined in the page itself) trump those applied via the external style sheet. In this book, we will simplify the challenge of sorting through which set of styles is doing what by adopting a simple, best practice. We won't do any CSS style definition within a page. We will do all our CSS style definitions through external, linked CSS style sheet files. That will simplify our exploration of formatting HTML5 elements, and it is—for a whole range of reasons, a full exploration of which is beyond the scope of this book—the best way to format websites in almost every situation.

However, there is more. Even when all styles are applied through external style sheets, it is still often complicated to determine where the formatting for an element comes from. When there are several style sheets attached to a single page, they can issue conflicting "instructions" as to how a page should look. The best way to deal with this kind of challenge is to avoid having such conflict within a web page. However, in the course of this book, we will encounter and surmount situations where such conflicting style sheets are attached to a page.

Finally, and with direct applicability to the more basic dimensions of page formatting that are the focus of this and the following chapter, there can be conflicts between style definitions within a single style sheet. For example, in this chapter we will learn to apply basic, page-wide styles to manage features such as background color and font type. However, those basic page-wide styles will come into conflict with styles associated with specific page design elements created by Dreamweaver's HTML5 Layouts in some cases. In that case, the general rule is that the more specific the style, the higher priority it has. For instance, a style that defines the font and font color for an entire page will be overridden by a font definition that is applied to a specific container within that page. In the following figure, elements in many HTML files are defined by a single style sheet.

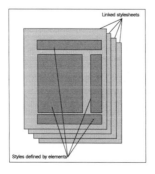

These formatting and styling challenges will all make more sense as we work through specific challenges, but it will be helpful to keep the conceptual big picture in mind, and return to it as needed, as we solve specific formatting challenges one-by-one.

 **Formatting HTML5 Layout Elements**: In the next chapter of this book, building on the foundation we establish here, we will work through the specific HTML5 page layout elements that are generated by Dreamweaver's HTML5 Pack.

# Editing content in HTML5 page layout elements

Obviously, the point of generating HTML5 page layouts is to replace the generated dummy content with your own, real content! Having explored in a bit of depth the conceptual challenges of properly embedding custom content in HTML5 page layouts, we are ready to walk through the specific techniques for embedding your own real-live content into HTML5 layouts.

In the following discussion, I will be building on the tools and techniques covered in the previous chapter in this book. I will assume you are familiar with the HTML5 layouts generated using the HTML5 Pack in Dreamweaver. Moreover, I will be zooming in on specific aspects of those layouts, and how to customize them.

 While our focus here is on embedding your actual text and other content in web pages, if for some reason you need to generate pseudo-Latin type to use as a place-holder for design wireframing or mockup purposes, you can generate Lipsum type at `http://www.lorem-ipsum.info/generator3`.

## HTML text tags versus HTML5 layout elements

When you copy and paste text into the generated HTML5 layouts that come with the HTML5 Pack, you have to be aware of two things: What HTML5 layout element are you placing content in

What HTML tag is applicable to that content

Uncovering what elements and tags are in effect does not require us to memorize HTML code or syntax, but it does require us to figure out what HTML code is operative for selected text.

# Organizing content in containers

Both the 2-column and 3-column HTML5 layouts generated from the HTML5 Pack come with header, footer, article, section, and content boxes. These boxes (and there can be more than one of each on a page) hold text and other content.

The first step in customizing pages is to replace the generic placeholder content with your own content. This requires selecting content in a box, and copying and pasting, or typing your own content into the box, or, embedding images or media.

Some of that process is obvious and intuitive. To replace the logo, for example, that comes with the 3-column layout; double-click on the placeholder **Insert_logo (180x90)**, as shown in the following screenshot:

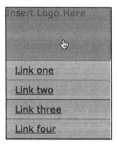

Doing this opens the **Select Image Source** dialog. Navigate in that dialog to select your own image and click on Choose.

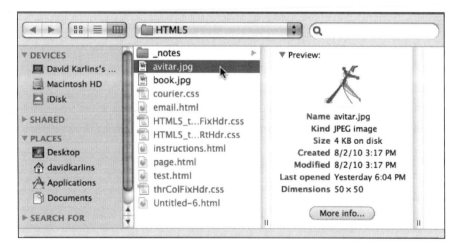

Similarly, you can simply select text in a container, and replace it with your own text, as shown in the following screenshot:

# Utilizing Split view for editing content

Sometimes all that is required to replace template content that comes with the HTML5 layouts with your own content is to delete the existing text, and copy and paste (or type) your own text.

However, sometimes the process is more complicated because within the fairly clearly defined HTML5 layout elements, there are different HTML text tags. Therefore,, different text within an HTML5 element appears differently.

This is where Dreamweaver's Split view becomes particularly valuable. Split view is a useful way to sort out which tags and elements are defining how different text looks. Let's take an example. To replace the first section of text in the 3-column HTML5 layout generated by the Dreamweaver HTML5 pack (the full name of the layout is the **HTML5: 3 column fixed, header and footer** layout), we can replace either the <p> (paragraph) content, or the <h2> (heading 2) content. In the following screenshot, the Heading 2 content is selected:

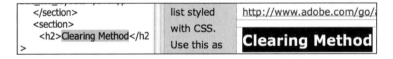

We can determine which HTML tag (paragraph, or Heading 2) is applied to the selected text by looking at the highlighted code in the Code side of Split view in the Document window. In the following screenshot, both the Heading 2 content, and the paragraph content have been edited, separately.

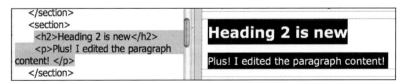

Understanding how HTML tags like the paragraph tag, or heading tags (<h1>... <h6>) intersect with HTML5 layout elements, like <article>, <section>, <aside> and so on is the key to customizing content. Appreciating and distinguishing between these two things—layout elements and text tags—opens the door to understanding and controlling how your pages are customized.

Moreover, you need not be in Split view to manage this. You can also identify which HTML tags and elements apply to selected content in the tag bar on the bottom of the Document window. We explored this tag bar in the previous chapter. Particularly, as you become more comfortable working with HTML5 layouts and HTML in general, you will be able to rely on the tag bar in Design view. In the following screenshot, for example, the tag bar reveals that the selected text is within the <section> HTML5 element, and, within that, governed by rules for the <h2> tag.

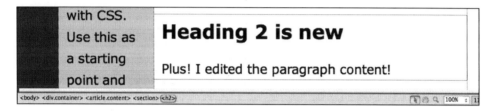

# Adding articles and sections

On the foundation established up to this point, we can walk through the process of adding articles and sections to the set that come with the HTML5 layouts. Both layouts come, by default, with one article box, and three section boxes.

Your page content, however, might well contain more than one article, and your article(s) may well contain more or less than three sections. Deleting sections is easier than adding them, but even that takes a bit of technique. Let's look now at how to add, or delete articles and sections.

The first step in adding an article, or a section, is to select an existing article, and then copy and paste it. That's not quite as simple as one might expect.

# Identifying and selecting HTML5 layout elements

Dreamweaver CS5.5 (and CS5) has three Visual Aids intended to make it easier to identify page layout elements (mdash)CSS Layout Backgrounds, CSS Box Model, and CSS Layout Outlines. All three can be turned off and on from the Visual Aids popup in the Document toolbar (if that toolbar is not visible, choose **View | Toolbars | Document**). In the following screenshot, all three are turned on.

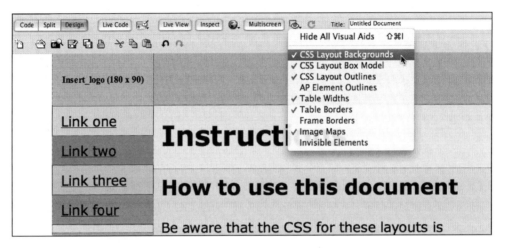

Enabling CSS Layout Backgrounds makes it easier to determine where margins and spacing are defined for elements on a page. We will look at that piece of the puzzle in the next chapter of this book, but in the following figure, you can see ten pixels of padding associated with the `<aside>` element indicated with diagonal shading.

Finally, and most critically, the CSS Layout Outlines visual aid is very useful in identifying and selecting HTML5 and other layout elements. In the following screenshot, a `<header>` element is selected.

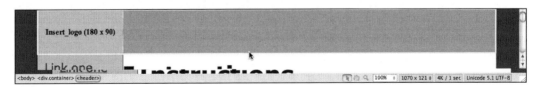

# Copying, pasting, and deleting HTML5 Elements

In later chapters in this book, we will explore, from different angles, different ways to build pages from scratch using HTML5 layout elements. However, even when we do that, copying and pasting plays a big role in quickly and easily duplicating already existing design elements.

Even with Dreamweaver's visual aid, there is a dimension of trial and error in selecting distinct HTML5 layout elements in Design view. The reason is that the borders between elements are a hair's breadth, and it often takes a bit of clicking to select the element you wish to copy and paste. However, finding and selecting elements is exactly how you duplicate them.

If, for example, you need to add an `<article>` container to your page, the easy way to do that is to start by locating, selecting, and copying to the clipboard an existing article container, as shown in the following screenshot:

Alternatively, take another example (because this can be a bit confusing until you practice a bit), to copy an article section you would click on the border of the section itself and you could double-check in the tag bar (or triple-check using the Code section of Split view) to be sure you had a single section selected. The following screenshot shows all three of these methods for confirming that a section is selected, plus the popup code hint to be absolutely, positively sure a section is selected.

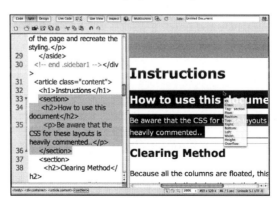

Once you have selected and copied any HTML5 layout element, the next step is to locate the spot to which you want to copy it. This requires some precision, and at least until you get comfortable with relying on the tag bar at the bottom of the Design window; you may want to work in Split view.

The trick here is to position your cursor just past the container that precedes where you wish to position the copied container. Again, particularly until one becomes comfortable with doing this, it is helpful to rely on the Code in split view. For example, the following screenshot shows a cursor positioned, both as identified in the Code side of Split view and in the tag bar, as being just beyond one article `<section>` tag and just before the next one. This is the position where it is possible to paste a copied section, inserting it between the two existing sections.

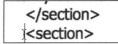

# Identifying style rules

Now that we have explored on how to work with the content of generated HTML5 layouts; let's turn to formatting those pages.

To review, there are two main components of this: formatting the regular HTML tags that define the look of the page overall; and formatting the HTML5 elements themselves. In the remainder of this chapter, we will learn to do the former, which is a substantial part of page design with or without HTML5.

Remember back when you first generated an HTML5 layout? You were asked to save an associated CSS file with a long name either `HTML5_twoColFixRtHdr.css` or `HTML5_thrColFixHdr.css`.

That supplied CSS file, is what applies formatting to the HTML5 elements and other layout features of your web page. You can see that attached style sheet in the CSS Styles panel. In the recipe at the end of this chapter, you will save that CSS file with your own file name as you customize it.

# HTML5 layout elements require styles

Without the CSS style definitions in those linked style sheets, the HTML5 layouts wouldn't be layouts at all. Don't believe me? Good for you! A healthy dose of skepticism can be part of critical thinking. So, to see for yourself, try this:

Generate either of the HTML5 layouts (review last chapter if you forgot how). If the CSS Styles panel is not visible, choose **Window | CSS Styles** to display it. Note that the CSS Styles panel indicates that one of the two CSS files listed above is linked to your page (unless you renamed the CSS file in the course of generating the layout).

Now, with that CSS file selected in the CSS Styles panel, click on the Unlink CSS Style sheet icon, as shown in the following screenshot:

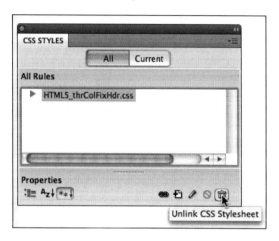

What happened to all the blocks that defined sections of the page? What happened to all the page formatting? Gone with the style sheet, that's what happened to all that formatting! Your "naked" page, with the HTML5 and other elements in tact, but the styles stripped from them, appears as something like an outline, as shown in the following screenshot:

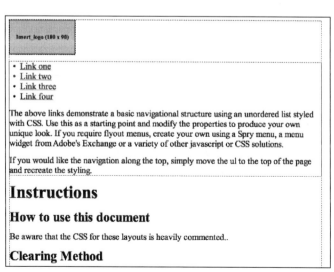

To relink the CSS file, click the **Attach Style Sheet** icon at the bottom of the CSS Styles Panel, as shown in the following screenshot:

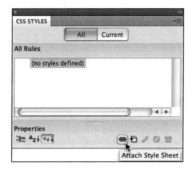

Doing that opens the **Attach External Style Sheet** dialog. Use the **Browse** button to navigate to the root folder for your site (if you are not sure what is meant by "site", hit the pause button and review the discussion of *Creating a Dreamweaver site* in *Chapter 1*). Select the CSS file you just unlinked, and then click on **OK** on the **Attach External Style Sheet** dialog to relink the style sheet file and restore formatting to your page.

# Examining CSS associated with HTML5 layouts

We can examine the CSS styles that come with Dreamweaver's HTML5 layouts by expanding the attached file in the CSS Styles panel (do that by clicking on the triangle next to the CSS file name until a list of styles displays. Select the **All** tab at the top of the panel to view styles as shown in the following screenshot:

Stretch the CSS Styles panel so you can see the whole list of styles. You can adjust the division between the top of the dialog (that lists the styles) and the bottom (that displays style attributes) by dragging on the divider between them.

The CSS styles associated that come with the HTML5 page layouts include all the main types of styles:

- HTML5 layout elements like `<header>`, `<section>`, `<footer>`, `<aside>`, `<nav>`, and `<article>`

- Regular HTML tags like `<body>`, `<h1>`, `<h2>`, `<h3>`..., and `<p>`

- Class styles that can be applied to any element, and can be used multiple times on a single page. The class styles begin with a period, like `.container` or `.navbar1`

- Compound styles that are used for formatting content that includes more than one element or tag, and are used to define links and link states, such as `a:link` or `a:visited`.

 **Using styles for page layout**: For an overview on the evolution and role of styles in page layout, see *Chapter 1*.

We will reserve working with the HTML5 layout elements for next chapter. However, here and now, we will lay the basis for that with a compressed survey of designing pages with CSS.

# Customizing HTML tag rules

To situate ourselves in the process of customizing HTML5 layouts, it's helpful to review once again that the properties of these pages are defined by the content (which we have just learned to customize), and the CSS properties applied to different HTML tags.

Moreover, to review a bit, those HTML tags include both HTML5 layout elements, and traditional HTML tags such as Headings (1-6), the paragraph tag, along with other tags like those for numbered lists and bullet lists.

In *Chapter 3*, we will focus on the particular challenges of redefining the HTML5 layout elements. Here we will jog through a quick, compressed overview of defining CSS styles for other HTML tags.

# Making quick changes to styles in the CSS styles panel

To define the formatting of any HTML tag, select that CSS rule icon in the CSS Styles panel. As you do, the properties associated with that tag appear in the bottom half of the CSS Styles panel. For example, in the following screenshot, the attributes of the Body tag are displayed, most importantly the font color (black), and the font (the Verdana family of fonts).

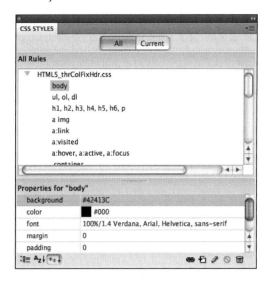

The attributes for a selected tag can be edited in the bottom half of the CSS Styles panel. For example, in the following screenshot, the attributes of the <body> tag have been changed so the background is now black, the font Times, and the font color gray.

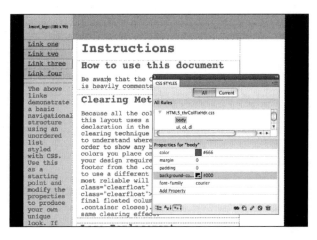

Basic changes to tag attributes can be made using the color picker swatches in the bottom half of the CSS Styles panel or by simply typing new attributes (such as "courier" in the **font-family** attributes box).

# The CSS rules definition dialog

Another way to make changes to the styling rules applied to an attribute is to click the **Edit Rule...** icon at the bottom of the CSS Styles panel (it looks like a pencil). Doing so opens the **CSS Rule Definition** dialog for the selected attribute, as shown in the following screenshot:

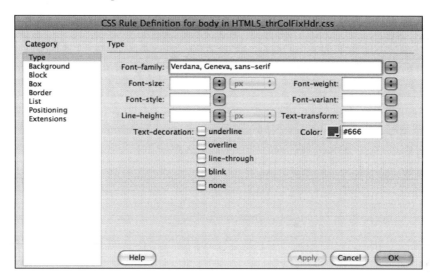

Throughout this book, we will be returning to the CSS Rule Definition dialog. This may well be the most powerful element of Dreamweaver. At this stage of the trip, however, the most important categories to note are the **Type** category (that opens by default as shown in the preceding screenshot), and the **Background** category.

# Editing type styles

In the **Type** category, the **Font Family** popup allows you to choose a group of fonts to assign to paragraph text. The **Font Size** popup defines font size, font weight, and other features such as boldface and italics. You can assign values and units of measurement (like 12 points, 10 pixels, or 1 em) or relative sizes ranging from xx-small to xx-large.

You can change the default values for **Line Height** to create additional space between lines of type. The **Text Decoration** checkboxes are most useful for defining font links, something we will look at shortly.

# Editing backgrounds

The **Background** category of the CSS Rule Definition dialog is where you choose a background color or background image. The **Background-color** picker opens a palette to select a background color. Use the **Browse** button next to the **Background-image** box to browse to an image file on your computer to use as a background.

Backgrounds can be applied to tags associated with text headings, for example, you might apply a background to a heading. However, more typically, backgrounds are assigned to the <body> tag and to an entire page. By default, such background images tile repeat, as shown in the following screenshot:

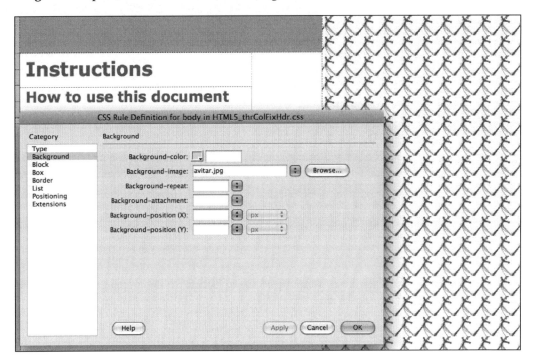

# Preview with apply

As noted earlier, we will be returning to the Rule Definition dialog repeatedly throughout this book, and in the course of doing so, we will visit all the categories and push the limits of how HTML5 elements can be formatted.

The most important thing to be aware of at this stage of the journey is that you can use the **Apply** button to preview how the CSS rule you are defining will look when applied to content on the open web page in Dreamweaver's Document window.

# Saving customized HTML5 layouts

Up to this point, as we have generated pages using Dreamweaver's HTML5 layouts, we have attached the CSS style files supplied with those pages by Dreamweaver.

Moreover, as we have edited the CSS on those pages (by making the kinds of changes just discussed to the <body> tag and so on), we have simply saved those changes to the default CSS file supplied by Dreamweaver.

In real life, however:

- We would want to keep our own, customized CSS file distinct from the generic one generated each time by Dreamweaver, and

- We would want to attach our customized CSS file to the generated HTML5 layouts instead of the one supplied by Dreamweaver.

Let's walk through how this works:

First, as soon as you generate your first HTML5 layout, you will note the Dreamweaver-supplied CSS file is open in an associated file, displayed in the associated files bar in the Dreamweaver document window. You can open that file in its own window by right-clicking (Windows) or Control-clicking (Mac) on the file, and choosing **Open As Separate File** from the context menu that appears, as shown in the following screenshot:

With the CSS file open in its own window (it will appear as a page full of CSS code), choose **File | Save As**. The **Save As** dialog appears. Replace the default file name with your own file name (avoid upper case characters, spaces, or special characters such as "!" or "#"), and click on **Save**.

Choose design view to return to the HTML document you are working on. In the CSS Styles panel, unlink the default CSS styles file, and use the link icon to link your own CSS styles file.

From now on, as you generate HTML5 layouts, you can use your own CSS styles file to apply formatting to those generated pages. Do so when you generate a new HTML5 document by clicking on the attach style sheet icon in the **New Document** dialog as shown in the following screenshot:

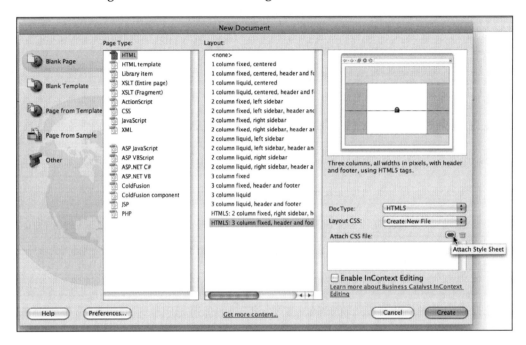

Navigate and select the customized CSS file you saved, and attach it to the generated HTML5 layout.

# Recipe: Customize content and look of an HTML5 page

This recipe will walk you through creating a page with customized content and formatting from an HTML5 layout. The assumption, and it is a critical one, is that you have created a Dreamweaver site. If you do not have a Dreamweaver site already defined, refer back to *Chapter 1* and create one.

1. Select **File | New** to open the **New Document** dialog. Select **Blank Page** in the left-hand category column. Choose **HTML** in the **Page Type** column, and select **HTML5: 3 column fixed, header and footer** in the **Layout** column. Select **HTML5** from the **DocType** popup, and **Create New** File **from** the **Layout CSS** popup. Click on **Create**. The **Save Style Sheet File As** dialog appears.

2. Do not click on **Save** yet! Change the CSS file name to your own file name (like `mystyle.css`). Then click on **Save**.

3. A generated HTML5 layout opens in Dreamweaver Document window. Choose **File | Save** and save this file as `index.html` to make it the home page for your website. In the **Title** box of the Document toolbar, enter a descriptive title for your page.

4. Double-click on the **Insert_logo (180x90)** box in the upper-left corner of the page. The **Select Image Source** dialog opens. Navigate to your own logo artwork and click on **Choose** in the dialog to place your own artwork.

5. Select the text, **Instruction** at the top of the page, and replace it with your own page content. Replace other text on the page with your own text, or select and delete it.

6. Select the **Link one** text on the page. Enter a title for your own link.

7. In the Properties inspector, enter the URL in the **Link** box, as shown in the following screenshot. Include the `http://` part of the URL.

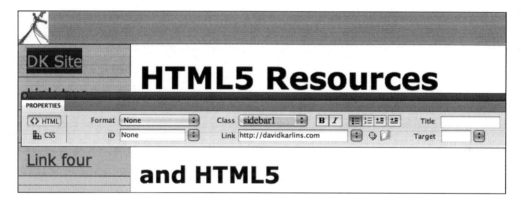

8. In the CSS Styles panel, expand your linked CSS file by clicking on the triangle. Click on the now-visible body tag in the top half of the CSS Styles panel, and click on the edit rule icon at the bottom of the CSS Styles panel. The CSS Rule Definition for the body tag dialog opens.

9. In the **Type** category, choose a type group from the font family popup. Choose a relative font size (such as small, medium, or large) from the font-size popup. Choose a font color from the color picker.

10. In the **Background** category the **Background-color** color picker, choose a color for your page background.

11. Click on **Apply** to test your changes, as shown in the following screenshot. When you are satisfied with your settings, click on **OK**.

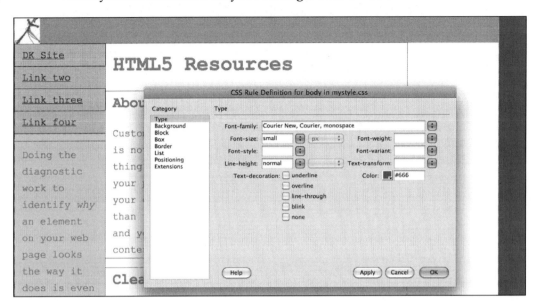

12. Choose **File | Save All** to save both your HTML5 page and your CSS file.

The final phase of customizing HTML5 layouts is to custom format the HTML5 layout elements such as the header, footer, and content containers. We will do that next!

# Summary

In this chapter, you learned to use HTML5 layouts provided by Dreamweaver's HTML5 pack to create customized pages. Don't think of these layouts as "templates". They are highly customizable tools to create really unique page layouts. By the time you are done customizing content, CSS styles—and by the end of next chapter—HTML5 layout elements, there will not be anything "templatey" about your page design.

Along the way, we quickly surveyed the basic HTML tags that define how text looks on a page, as well as the `<body>` tag, which controls the basic attributes of page appearance including page background. And, we replaced placeholder images and links with our own content.

# 3
# Customizing HTML5 Layout Elements

In this chapter, we will continue our journey exploring HTML5 layouts in Dreamweaver CS5.5 (and CS5). In the previous chapter, we customized the content of the HTML5 layout elements that are generated with the two HTML5 layouts that come with the HTML5 Pack. In this chapter, we will examine and customize HTML5 layout elements — `<header>`, `<nav>`, `<article>`, `<section>`, `<aside>`, and `<footer>`.

This chapter, and the following one, will together form a double-edged attack on digesting how HTML5 layout elements are used to design pages. In this chapter, we will work through something the HTML5 layout elements generated in the Dreamweaver HTML5 Pack elements in more detail and depth, examining both specific uses of elements in combination with different kinds of CSS styles and the logic behind those techniques. In the next chapter, we will build something closer to an "ideal" HTML5 layout page, relying more consistently on HTML5 layout elements. By the time you have worked through both of these chapters, you will have had a chance to assimilate both the art and science of HTML5 layouts to the point that you can build best practise pages and deconstruct and work with more typical sites that tend to be a mishmash of HTML5 elements and other components.

What will we accomplish by critically dissecting the two HTML5 layouts provided by Dreamweaver?

First, the two HTML5 layouts that come with the HTML5 Pack are thoughtfully put together and a very flexible foundation on which to build all kinds of page designs. If I can editorialize for just a moment: I have been writing books, articles, and so on about Dreamweaver since before you were born and in the past, I have not had such positive things to say about the sample layouts included in previous versions of Dreamweaver, including pre-HTML5 Pack Dreamweaver CS5. That, to be fair though, has not mainly been the fault of Dreamweaver or the developers at Adobe. The problem has been with HTML itself. Lacking any standardized page layout tags, HTML lent itself to anarchy, chaos, and confusion—and I don't mean that in a good way.

Secondly, in part because Dreamweaver's HTML5 layouts are quite complex, deconstructing them in rather tenacious detail is a good way to master HTML5 page design with Dreamweaver.

As fair warning, I will alert you to the fact that, more than in previous chapters, the "recipe" at the end of the chapter will constitute a good chunk of the experience here. The layouts come with useful documentation, but that documentation assumes quite a bit of perspective, which we will arm ourselves with before dissecting the layouts.

However, don't skip to the end of the chapter. We will prepare for the excursion through the layout with some conceptual and specific exploration of formatting HTML5 elements, including a survey of compatibility challenges presented by browsers that do not support HTML5 and the ways in which HTML5 layout elements fit into other layout tools such as the `<div>` tag and older HTML tags.

In this chapter, we will learn to:

- Understand and implement the ongoing need for `<div>` tags as layout elements within a framework of HTML5
- Identify and address browser compatibility issues for HTML5 layouts
- Explore and adapt CSS styles applied to HTML5 layout elements
- Understand and manage the **class** CSS styles to apply formatting across multiple HTML5 layout elements
- Control the element background, margins, padding, float, and other attributes applicable to many HTML5 layout elements
- Manage CSS styles and additional HTML5 elements specific to a particular layout elements (for example, using the `<address>` element within footer)

# HTML5 layout and browser compatibility challenges

Ready for a not-news flash? Ready or not, here it is, HTML5 is a work in progress.

What does that mean? In historic terms, it means that the standards for HTML5 are still being systematized, although a critical mass has been reached where the meaning and effect of most HTML5 terms is widely agreed on and browsers either support HTML5, or they are evolving in that direction in finite terms.

For developers, it means that as we exploit time and stress saving features of HTML5 to build web pages, we have to be aware of and compensate for the fact that some browsers will not support some aspects of HTML5.

We have addressed this in general terms in previous chapters, but in this chapter, we will examine exactly how this plays out in relation to HTML5 layout elements. Moreover, we will inspect and learn from how the HTML5 layout elements in Dreamweaver address compatibility problems.

## Which browsers support HTML5 layout elements?

As noted, the list of browsers that support HTML5 layout elements that we are exploring in this chapter is growing. Currently (2011) browser environments using the Webkit engine are the most fully compliant. Those browsing environments include Google Chrome, Safari (both the desktop and the mobile versions), Dreamweaver CS4 and CS5's own Live view, the Android mobile browser, and the Palm webOS browser.

Firefox, Opera, and Internet Explorer do not completely support HTML5 layout elements. Overwhelmingly, with exceptions, we will note in the course of this chapter, those compatibility issues are resolved fairly simply by relying on CSS styles that provide these browsers with all the information they need to present the content in HTML5 elements as it should appear.

## Using CSS to solve browser issues

We will examine an example of a compatibility issue with the HTML5 layout elements in Dreamweaver's layouts, and how to solve it. Moreover, in the process, pick up some valuable trouble-shooting and problem solving methods.

The case in point can be illustrated by looking at the `<header>` element that is used in both of the HTML5 layouts. With either of the HTML5 layouts open in the Design view, the header, with its default *kaki-ish green* background appears at the top of the page. As an HTML element, it occupies a full horizontal swath across the top of the page where it has been placed.

However, browsers such as Firefox and Internet Explorer do not recognize `<header>` as an element. They can appreciate that there is something called a "header" on the page, and they can associate attributes (like that green kaki-ish background) with that object. However, as they don't appreciate that `<header>` is an element, they don't reserve an entire horizontal line for the content.

If we look at the CSS Styles panel for the CSS file that comes with either of the Dreamweaver HTML5 layouts, then we can see that the background color (defined by default with the **#ADB96E** hexadecimal code) is assigned to the `<header>` element as shown in the following screenshot:

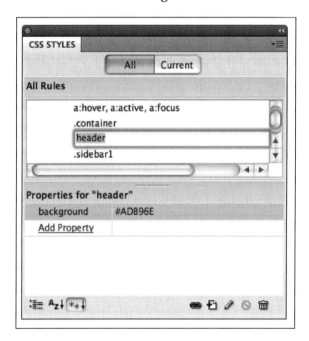

# The magic of display:block

In addition to a background color, the `<header>` element has another CSS attribute, which is assigned to it and all the rest of the HTML5 layout elements in the HTML5 layouts. That is found in the CSS Styles panel by examining the CSS rules for **header, section, footer, aside, nav, article, figure**, as shown in the following screenshot:

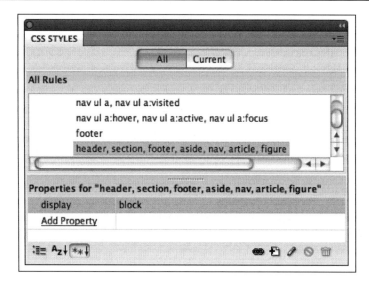

The **display:block** property assigned to all these HTML5 layout elements in the CSS Style sheet linked to the page instructs non-HTML5 browsers that this box of content should be handled as a block—it should fill the entire horizontal row in which it is placed.

## Disabling a CSS rule

We can see how this works by disabling the **display:block** property in the CSS Styles panel for the set of HTML5 layout elements. In Dreamweaver CS5.5 (and CS5), we can temporarily disable any defined CSS attribute by clicking to the left of it, as shown in the following screenshot:

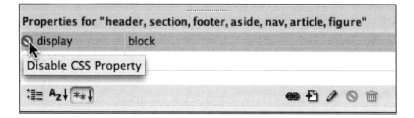

Clicking to the left of an attribute in the CSS Styles panel disables the attribute by turning it into a comment in the CSS code (indicated by /\*). Such disabled attributes display with the international "no" symbol in the CSS styles panel. Both the CSS code and the CSS Styles panel with **display:block** disabled are shown in the following screenshot:

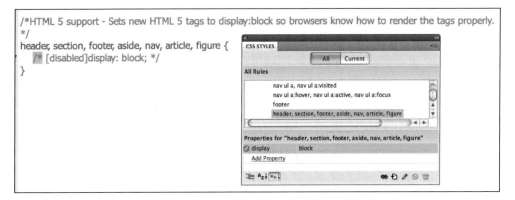

 **Disabling CSS Attributes**: The technique of temporarily disabling CSS settings in the CSS Styles panel has a wide applicability in testing web page layouts and in experimenting with different looks for web pages.

We can see how with the CSS style **display:block** disabled (for the moment), the header formatting collapses when the page is viewed in the Live view in the Document window. Moreover, it collapses when viewed in Firefox. If you have Firefox installed on your computer, then you can test this by selecting **File | Preview in Browser | Firefox**. Alternatively, preview in Internet Explorer. In either case, the header does not appear at all, as it is supposed to, as shown in the following screenshot:

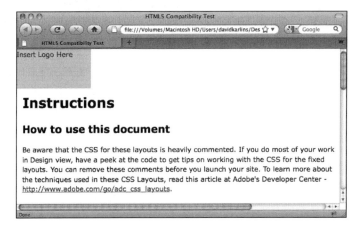

By contrast, even with **display:block** disabled in the CSS Styles panel, the header displays as it is supposed to in Safari, as shown in the following screenshot:

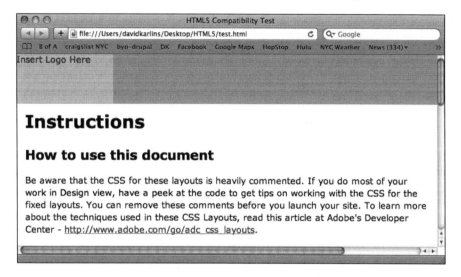

By the way, if you tried this at home, you may have noticed that the footer content also collapsed in Firefox, Internet Explorer, or other non-HTML5 browsers.

Again, the reason that the `<header>` element is handled correctly in Safari and not in Internet Explorer or Firefox is that we have disabled the CSS style that helps those non-HTML5 compliant browsers understand how to handle the header content.

If we re-enable the **display:block** attribute for all the HTML5 layout elements (by clicking again to toggle the international "no" sign off), then the header and footer content and formatting appears as intended in non-HTML5 browsers, as shown in the following screenshot:

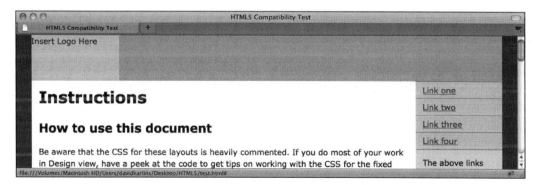

# Global HTML5 layout element attributes

We just examined how the Dreamweaver HTML5 layouts adjust for non-HTML5 compliant browsers with supplemental CSS formatting. However, in the process, we identified another key piece of the puzzle of understanding how HTML5 elements acquire formatting attributes—this is done by defining CSS styles that are associated with those elements.

In order to move on and apply that technique to formatting all the HTML5 elements on our page, it will be useful to explore the following three essential CSS attributes that can be applied to nearly all the HTML5 layout elements:

1. Backgrounds

2. Size, margins, and padding

3. Positioning

While there are many attributes that can be assigned to layout elements, a conceptual handle on these three will prepare you with a foundation from which to dissect, learn from, and be able to adapt Dreamweaver's HTML5 layouts.

# Working with backgrounds

The rules for `<header>`, `<section>`, `<footer>`, `<aside>`, `<nav>`, and `<article>` design elements all, at times, have backgrounds applied to them. While an examination of aesthetic and accessibility aspects of applying backgrounds to design elements is beyond the scope of this book, it would be irresponsible not to note them at all.

Very briefly, colors (and even more so images) can pose serious accessibility issues. One of the most widely noted accessibility problems for websites is the high percentage of people, whose color-blindness makes it impossible to distinguish text when placed on top of various colors, including when those colors appear in photos or other images or artwork. If accessibility is an issue for your web pages, then do sufficient research into dos and don'ts for mixing background colors and foreground text. Inexplicably, **The Dreamweaver accessibility validation report** feature has been deprecated as of Dreamweaver CS5. However, you can find multiple sites online that test your site for color accessibility issues.

While less potentially troublesome, aesthetic concerns are obviously something to consider when defining colors (or patterns) for layout elements. You will find valuable resources for creating color schemes at Adobe's Kuler site (http://kuler.adobe.com/) shown in the following screenshot:

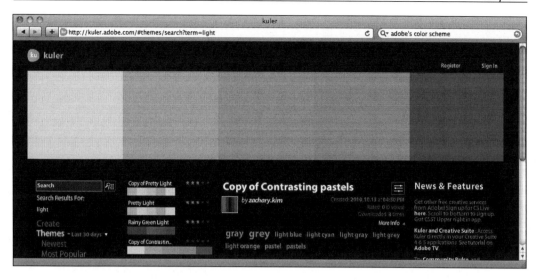

With that ultra-compressed survey of aesthetic and accessibility issues down the hatch, let's look at how to change the background color of any HTML5 layout element in the CSS Styles panel.

The most reliable and flexible way to change the background color is to open the **CSS Rule definition** dialog for any selected style using the **Edit Rule** icon at the bottom of the CSS Styles panel. For example, in order to open the **CSS Rule definition** dialog for the style associated with the `<footer>` element, select that element in the CSS Styles panel, and click on the **Edit Rule...** icon, as shown in the following screenshot:

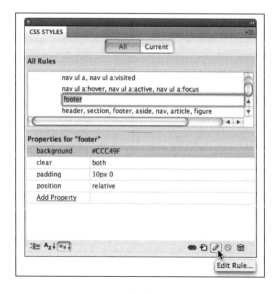

In the **CSS Rule definition** dialog, the background category displays options for defining color and pattern background. Colors are selected from the background color picker. You can enter a hexadecimal value in the **Background-color box**, or use the eyedropper tool to select a color from the palette that appears when you click on the color picker box.

Alternatively, you can select a background image using the **Browse** button to navigate to and select that image from your computer or a connected drive. By default, background images tile, that is, they repeat horizontally and vertically to fill the assigned space. In the following screenshot, a tiling image has been applied to the <header> element and clicking on the **Apply** button displays how that tiled image will appear when applied:

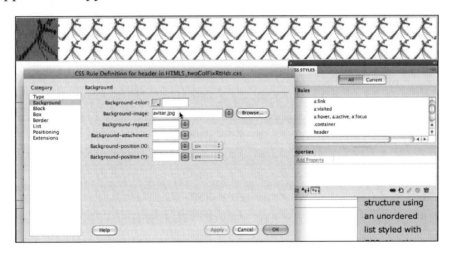

# Defining size, margins, and padding

If you think about translating a design to a webpage, the heart of the process is to create some kind of positioning containers to hold the content. Those containers are defined essentially by their size and location.

However, here things get complicated. First, positioning on the Web is positioning for a moving target. A layout element that is inviting and accessible on a laptop may be hidden and uninviting on an iPhone. We will address that challenge in *Chapter 5, Defining and Implementing Multiscreen Previews and Media Queries*.

Typically, both page size and position are defined by one, master container, often with an element name like "container." The page content is typically centered by creating a single such container whose main function is to constrain the size and positioning of all the page content. We will explore how this is done briefly here, and shortly in more detail when we dissect one of the HTML5 layouts.

# Assigning a page size

The size of a web page is defined, as alluded to earlier, by the master container that holds all the page content. In recent years, a standard page size of 960 pixels has emerged. This size fits in and works well with both laptops and popular handheld devices.

The 960 pixel wide page also has mathematical advantages. It can be divided into as many as 16 evenly sized columns. This allows web designers to collaborate easily with graphic designers who can layout pages in programs such as Adobe Illustrator, Adobe Flash Catalyst, or even programs designed for other purposes such as Adobe Photoshop with which some designers might be more comfortable. As long as everyone in the workflow is using a 960 pixel wide grid, designs can be translated from wireframes and design files to HTML5 page layouts.

The following screenshot shows a container `<div>` generated by a Dreamweaver HTML5 layout with a defined width of 960 pixels:

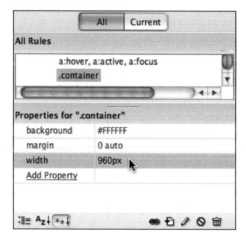

Margins and padding are also part of positioning elements on the page and we will explore that next.

# Margins versus padding

Margins define the space between any layout element and other content that element abuts. So, for example, if a vertical margin of 10 pixels is defined for a `<header>` element, then a space of 10 pixels high will be generated under the header, before any content that follows it.

Padding defines a space within an element, between the edges of an element, and the content within it.

Sometimes, either a margin or padding produces the same effect. At other times, the effect is more subtle. For example, using a margin combined with a border to separate content from other content will place space outside the border, while using padding to create space within the same element and border would create space between element content and the border.

Margins play a particular role in centering page content. Assigning a margin of `auto` to an HTML element used as a page container, as shown in the previous screenshot, is the standard technique for centering page content within a browser window.

## Element padding versus content margins

One specific area where two approaches to spacing can be used is in creating space between the content of a layout element and the border of the element (or the outer edges of the element, whether or not a visible border is displayed).

As noted earlier, this spacing can be created with padding between the content (such as text) and the edge of the element. The same spacing can be created, alternatively, by assigning margins to the content itself. Therefore, for example, a 10-pixel margin applied to a text within an element creates more or less the same result as 10 pixels of padding applied to the element itself.

When to use which? This is often a decision involving more art, convention, and custom than anything else.

## Positioning with float

As noted earlier, the page content is macro-positioned by defining the margin of the container holding all page content. Within that container, the content is often best positioned by using the `float` attribute.

In the following screenshot, for example, the `.sidebar1` element used in the Dreamweaver HTML5 layouts includes float settings that align it on the left-hand side of the page (in the 3-column layout) or the right-hand side (in the 2-column layout):

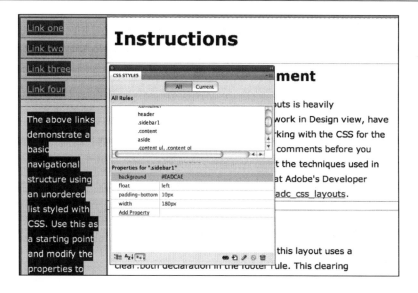

# Customizing HTML5 elements

As a final referential segue before diving into the HTML5 elements used in the Dreamweaver layouts, it will be helpful to identify particular design and formatting issues specific to the `<header>`, `<section>`, `<footer>`, `<aside>`, `<nav>`, and `<article>` elements.

For the `<header>` and `<footer>`, it will often be the case that you want to define a customized background, along with tweaked padding.

The formatting for `<section>` and `<article>` elements is often inherited from parent elements, that is, the global HTML tags such as the `<body>` tag, or enclosing tags such as a container tag, discussed earlier. However, within that, `<section>` and `<article>` elements might well have unique margin or padding, and specific formatting applied to text only within those elements.

The `<nav>` element, containing links, might well have a specific link formatting (colors, underlining, and so on). The `<aside>` element will have either a float attribute assigned to it or will inherit a float (right or left) from an enclosing `<div>` tag.

# Back to the future: ID and class styles

Up to this point, we have alluded to two possible, different approaches to page design with HTML5 elements. The first is to assign actual layout attributes (size, position, float, and so on) to HTML5 elements. This is a basic, simple, intuitive, and potentially very powerful way to use HTML5 elements to design pages.

When we build HTML5 pages from scratch in the next chapter, we will use that approach. Moreover, as we will see then, such an approach has specific applicability for HTML5-friendly environments such as iPhones, iPod Touchs, and iPads.

However, that is not the approach taken in the Dreamweaver layouts, and for arguably valid reasons. In those layouts, much (not all) of formatting and positioning is defined by old-fashioned `<div>` tags that envelope (surround, and supply inherited formatting and positioning to) the HTML5 elements.

There are three basic advantages to this approach:

1. They solve compatibility issues by rendering HTML5 elements supplemental to page design.
2. They allow designers who have not yet acclimated to HTML5 elements to work with familiar techniques.
3. They "plan ahead" for dimensions of HTML5 elements that are works in progress, including the use of HTML5 elements in indexing the page content for search engines.

So, prepare yourself to find this approach applied as we examine the HTML5 layouts. We will look more specifically at the ubiquitous `<div>` tags, both with class and ID styles applied.

# Layout with class styles

Class styles are the wildcard of web design. They can be used multiple times within a single document. Moreover, multiple class styles can be applied to a single element.

Let's walk through both these dimensions of class styles. As they can be used multiple times on a page, class styles have traditionally been used for layout elements such as boxes for pictures and captions, sidebar text boxes, boxes for media, and so on (elements that are often used more than once on a page).

Moreover, because multiple class styles can be applied to a single element and used repeatedly on a page, they are often used to "batch" formatting attributes that are then applied to more than one element.

# The role of ID styles

ID styles are applied only once on a page, to a single element. They can and often are used to define `<div>` tags used for page layout, like a container `<div>`.

The big advantage of using ID styles instead of class styles for formatting is that the DIV tags with ID styles are programmable. Other books I have written on web and interactive design with Adobe Creative Suite explore programming interactive elements (elements that respond to visitor actions) in detail by generating JavaScript. That won't be a focus of this book, but you should be aware that this is a consideration in choosing which type of `<div>` tags to use in formatting.

# Recipe: Customizing the HTML5 page layout

In the course of customizing the HTML5 layout elements that are generated with Dreamweaver, we learned to control foundational components of modern web page design.

In this recipe, we will focus on formatting HTML5 layout elements generated with the 2-column HTML 5 layout. Therefore, we will work with the generic content supplied with the layouts (for a systematic recipe for customizing the content, see the previous chapter).

Our recipe here, as promised, is somewhat extensive and is divided into two parts. The first part focuses on defining the position and size of the `<header>`, `<footer>`, `<nav>`, and `<aside>` elements. The second deals with changing the way links are displayed in the `<nav>` element.

In order to complete this recipe, you will need to have a few things in place. One is a defined Dreamweaver site. This is necessary and if you are not positive that you have defined and are working within a Dreamweaver site, please review the discussion of that in *Chapter 1*.

# Recipe: Customizing the size and position for header, footer, nav, and aside

With a site defined, and open, the following steps walk through the process of inspecting and customizing the key layout elements in the HTML5 2-column layout:

1. Generate a page by choosing **File | New**. In the **New Document** dialog, choose the **Blank Page** category. Select the **HTML5: 2 column fixed, right sidebar, header and footer** layout. Note that the **DocType** is HTML5 by default and the **Layout CSS** is set to **Create New File**. Click on the **Create** button.

2. The **Save Style Sheet File As** dialog opens. Change the name of the saved CSS file to **2col.css**, as shown in the following screenshot, and click on **Save**:

3. Save the file as 2col.html, and add a title, "2 column layout."

4. Examine the <body> tag definition in the CSS Styles panel (as shown in the following screenshot). While the <body> tag is not an HTML5 layout element, HTML5 elements will inherit attributes assigned to this tag unless the HTML5 elements, or CSS styles attached to them, overwrite those attributes. So, note that the background color, font (including 1.4 line spacing, which creates 40% extra vertical spacing between lines of type), font color, padding, and margins are defined by the <body> tag:

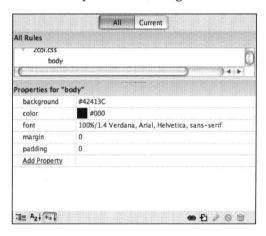

5. The second global defining element is the .container style. Examine it in the Global to note the background color (#FFF=gray), the margin (the operative attribute being auto (for left and right), which centers the container), and the 960 pixel width, which adheres to current design standards.

6.  Now we will change the alignment of the `<nav>` and `<aside>` elements from the right-hand side of the page to the left. As discussed in the chapter, the attributes for these elements are defined in an enclosing class style, not the elements themselves. Click anywhere within either the layout links or the sidebar content below them. In the tag bar at the bottom of the **Document** window, click on the **div.sidebar1** tag in the tag bar to see elements defined by that style highlighted in the Design view of the **Document** window, as shown in the following screenshot:

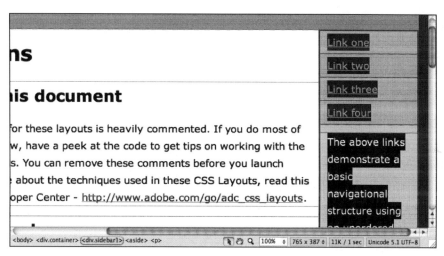

7.  In the CSS Styles panel, change the Float for the `.sidebar1` style from right to left, as shown in the following screenshot:

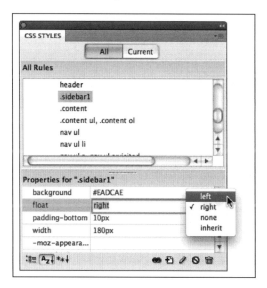

8.  Next, we will change the size and background of the page header by editing the <header> element. First, click on the **Insert_logo (180 x 90)** box and press your *Delete* key. Customized sites created in Dreamweaver should have customized header content not generically sized and placed logos that stamp a page as being constructed using out-of-the-box templates from a blogging app like WordPress. Without the placeholder image to expand the height of the header, we will define our own header height. In the CSS styles panel, click on the **Add Property** link and enter height in the first column and a value of 100 px, as shown in the following screenshot:

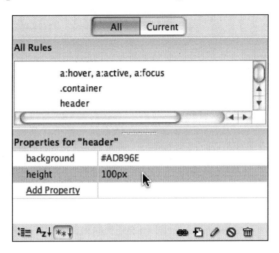

9.  Examine the style attributes for the <footer> element. The height of the footer is undefined—the footer expands (or contracts) to accommodate the content placed within it. Defining a fixed height for the footer can be done in the same way we just defined a height for the header. No width definition is necessary, as the footer expands to fill the space available. The position: relative attribute backs up the clear:both code for Internet Explorer 6. While the position attribute is only necessary to present the page correctly in IE6, the clear attribute is essential in any environment—it keeps the page from collapsing—by "turning off" any float attributes that are inherited from other page elements. In order to see for yourself how this works, click to the left of the clear attribute for the footer style in the CSS Styles panel to disable it (as shown in the following screenshot) and examine the disastrous result this has on how the different page elements fit together. Then, of course, click again to enable the clear attributes and restore the page.

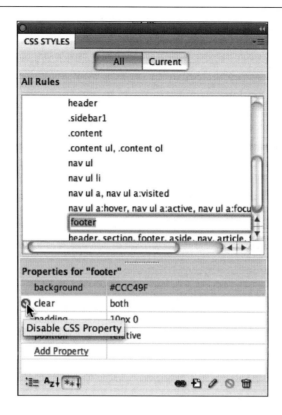

# Customizing links in the nav element

In examining and changing the appearance of content in the nav element, we will have a chance to dig rather deeply into how CSS styles are applied to specific tags within an element. In this case, we are going to solve the challenge of turning off the default underlining that appears in the <nav> element for unvisited links. The documentation that comes with the layout justifies this underlining as necessary to make it clear these are links. For the purposes of posing an instructive resolution to that, we will maintain underlining for links elsewhere on the page, but redefine links within the <nav> element.

1. As defined by the HTML5 layout, unvisited links throughout the page are displayed with underlining, while visited links, hovered links, active links (that display while a link is being selected), and focused links (links clicked in devices where hovering is inoperative, such as mobile devices) display with no underlining. There are several ways to test this, but the most effective way is to view the Style Rendering toolbar (**View** | **Toolbars** | **Style Rendering**). Use the link, visited (shown in the following screenshot), hover, active, and focus buttons to see how links display in each of these modes. Note that in the visited mode, links display with underlining outside the <nav> element, but without underlining within the <nav> element. Our mission in this second recipe is to identify why that is, and change the formatting, so that unvisited links inside the <nav> element also display without underlining, while allowing links outside the <nav> element to continue to display with underlining:

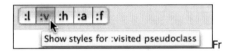

2. There are almost countless approaches we could take to identifying why, within the <nav> element, unvisited links are underlined, while visited links are not. However, often a good place to start on detective work such as this is the **Current** tab of the CSS Styles panel. With one of the links selected in the <nav> element and the link selected in the Style Rendering toolbar, note that the underlining style for links is defined in the style attached to a:link, as shown in the following screenshot:

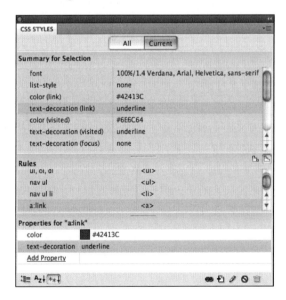

3. Now, let's compare the style rules in effect for unvisited links within the
   `<nav>` element, to the rules in effect for visited links. Select the **:v** (visited)
   button in the Style Rendering toolbar and note that here, a different, specific
   rule is in effect defining `text-decoration:none` for visited links (see the
   following screenshot). This rule has been defined to apply to visited links
   (`a:visited`) within an unordered list (`ul`) within a `<nav>` element:

> **Unordered lists:** We will explore the generalized
> implementation of unordered lists (aka bullet lists) in
> defining and styling menus in `<nav>` elements in the
> next chapter of this book, when we build pages from
> scratch relying on HTML5 layout elements.

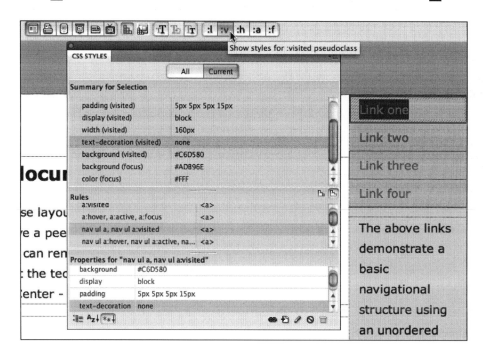

4. To sum up what we have learned from this investigation so far: the style sheet provided with the HTML5 layout includes specific styles that turn off underlining within the unordered list in the <nav> element for visited links. If we did further, similar investigation, we would learn as well that underlining is turned off for other link states (hovered, active, and focused) throughout the page. Therefore, our mission is to duplicate the CSS rule that turns off underlining for visited links in the <nav> element, but tweak the duplicate, so that it applies to unvisited links as well. There are many ways to do that; for example, we could go into the code for the CSS file and copy, paste, and edit. Alternatively, we could start from scratch and create a new CSS rule, jumping back and forth to remember what attributes we want to steal from the rule for visited links in the <nav> element. The first option is too code-centric, the second too tedious. So instead, we can switch to the **All** tab in the panel and select the rule nav ul a, nav ul a:visited. With that rule selected, right-click (Windows) or Control-click (Mac), and choose **Duplicate** from the context menu, as shown in the following screenshot:

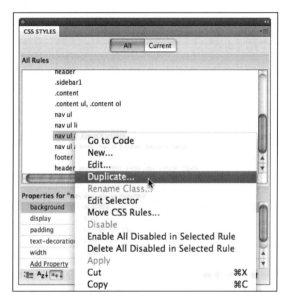

5. Selecting **Duplicate** opened the **Duplicate CSS Rule** dialog. Edit the selector name to **nav ul a, nav ul a:link** as shown in the following screenshot. By doing this, the new (duplicate) rule will apply to links within the same parameters as the original (links in the nav element, in unordered lists):

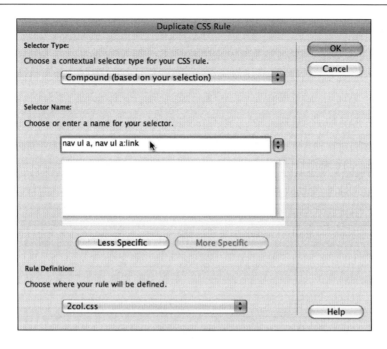

6. Verify the results of this recipe by examining the new style in the CSS Styles panel: nav ul a, nav ul a:link. With a regular link selected in the Style Rendering toolbar, note that unvisited links in the <nav> element no longer display with underlining, while unvisited links elsewhere (such as the link to adobe in the sample text) do display with underlining, as shown in the following screenshot:

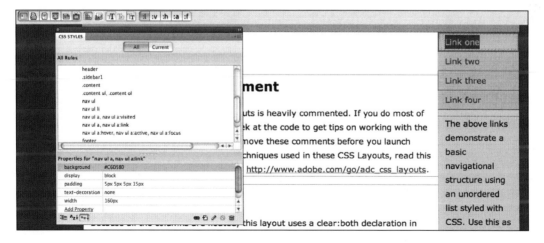

Tracking down the source of the CSS definitions for a link displayed within the <nav> element was a good experience. We actually solved what I consider one of the most difficult problems to solve in changing Dreamweaver HTML5 layouts. Moreover, beyond that, we explored how formatting can be applied within an HTML5 element through multiple layers of CSS styles.

# Summary

In the course of dissecting and customizing the size, position, background, and other attributes of HTML5 layout elements generated with the HTML5 Pack, we learned to format the key design components of these foundational elements of a modern web page design.

In addition, we prepared ourselves to construct web pages from scratch using HTML5 elements using truly next generation design techniques. We will do that in the next chapter.

# 4
# Building HTML5 Pages from Scratch

In the previous chapter, we completed our journey through the HTML5 layouts generated by Dreamweaver CS5. In the process, we learned to customize both the look and content of these layouts, and accomplished two things: we can build attractive, flexible pages; and we got an insight into real world application of HTML5 layout elements in combination with older HTML tags and older DIV tags.

In this chapter, we will learn to build web pages in Dreamweaver relying entirely on HTML5 layout tags. There are four things we will accomplish by learning to do that:

- Building page layouts relying exclusively on HTML5 layouts will hone our skills at using these new tools for page design, and introduce HTML5 Code Hints in Dreamweaver

- Relying on standardized, defined HTML5 layout elements (as opposed to custom-defined, irregularly implemented Div tags) streamlines page design

- There are actual, significant real-world scenarios where building pages relying exclusively on HTML5 layout elements is the best way to design them (for example, when designing pages for iPhones or iPads)

- There are functional advantages beyond design considerations for organizing page content in HTML5 layout elements. We will examine those advantages as we build HTML5 pages

In the course of building pages using just HTML5 layout elements, in this chapter, we will explore all four advantages of relying on HTML5 as listed above.

# Dreamweaver CS5 and HTML5

Before diving in to create HTML5 pages from scratch, let's survey how we are going to get our money's worth out of Dreamweaver in the process.

All recent versions of Dreamweaver (CS3, CS4, and CS5) with the HTML5 Pack installed can assist our work in creating HTML5 pages from scratch in three ways.

First, with the HTML5 Pack installed, code hints that automatically prompts us in completing HTML5 coding are updated in Code view for HTML5 elements. Those code hints will help us avoid mistakes in spelling elements or constructing the (minimalist) coding syntax that we will need to place HTML5 elements.

Second, we will avail ourselves of Split view, so that we will see our layout congealing in Design view as we sketch out what code we need to create in Split view.

Third, we will take advantage of what is arguably the single most valuable panel in Dreamweaver—the CSS Styles panel. We will be defining CSS Style rules to associate with each of the HTML5 layout elements we use. Without styles, HTML5 layout elements are nothing, so the interplay between the HTML5 elements we create and formatting we do with the CSS Styles panel will drive our page design process.

Moreover, here it is important to review, or at least reinforce two foundational techniques in building any professional-quality website in Dreamweaver:

- Do nothing without first defining a Dreamweaver site. Review *Chapter 1* of this book if you are not currently working within a defined site.
- Secondly, and not quite so essential but still pretty foundational, we always work with external style sheets. This allows the styles we define to be applied globally, across an entire website, and makes updating sites possible. As we begin to coordinate styling in the CSS Styles panel and constructing pages with HTML5 elements, I will be reminding you and when necessary walking you through the steps required to make sure all styles are saved to an external style sheet.

With this as a preview, and cautionary reminder, let's dive in to creating pages with HTML5 layout elements.

# Building an HTML5 page from the top

If you have been working through this book sequentially (which is not a requirement), you have assimilated the basic concept behind building pages with HTML5 layout elements. As opposed to laying out pages with tables (grids of rows and columns), or non-standardized Div tags (layout blocks you name and define yourself), we will use HTML5's new, standardized layout elements.

The most basic of these are self-explanatory `<header>`, `<nav>`, `<article>` and `<section>`, `<aside>`, and `<footer>` tags.

In addition, as alluded to in the introduction to this chapter, we will use additional elements to help make content more accessible to search engines. For example, within articles, we will use new HTML5 elements that make it easy for people looking for online content (or those making such online content accessible through various forms of search engines) to find things such as the publication date of content, or the date of an upcoming event.

# HTML5 structural elements

In order to alert browsers that we are presenting HTML5 content, we need to indicate at the top of our HTML5 code that this is an HTML5 page. As for those browsers that respond, "huh, what's that?", we will address that challenge shortly. However, first use the following steps to create a new HTML5 page from scratch:

1. With your Dreamweaver site defined, choose **File | New**. In the **New Document** dialog, choose **Blank Page** from the category list on the left of the dialog. Choose **HTML** in the **Page Type** column. Choose **None** in the **Layout** column.

2. In the **Layout CSS** popup if you already have a CSS file you use with HTML layouts, you can choose **Link to Existing File**, and select your existing HTML5-related CSS file as the styles file for your page.

3. From the **DocType** popup choose **HTML5** as shown in the following screenshot:

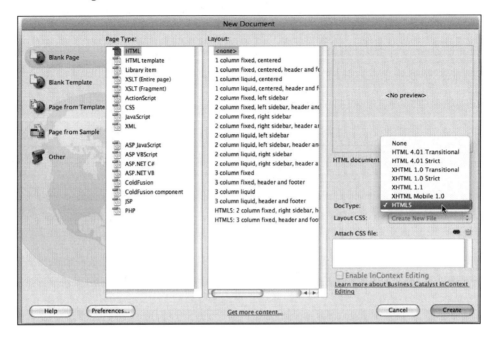

4. Click on **Create** to generate the blank page.

A blank page appears in Design view of the Document window. In Split view, we can see some basic code has been generated:

```
<!DOCTYPE HTML>
<html>
  <head>
    <meta http-equiv="Content-Type" content="text/html;
      charset=UTF-8">
    <title>Untitled Document</title>
  </head>
  <body>
  </body>
</html>
```

Let's briefly walk through this to situate ourselves. The `<!DOCTYPE HTML>` and `<html>` tags are sort of evolutionary holdovers from previous versions of HTML, and not actually required for HTML5 browsers. This code though, might be useful when taking into account non-HTML5 browsers, as we will examine shortly.

The `<head>` and `</head>` tags demarcate head content that is not displayed on the page, but serves as instructions to browsers.

In this case, the content inside identifies that the current, most widely applicable character set, UTF-8, is implemented. This character set allows the display of characters from a wide range of languages.

All the content we create for the page will be placed within the <body> and </body> tags. For this reason, our first step in creating our CSS styles for this page, will be to define a couple of basic attributes for the </body> tag.

Finally, save this page as an HTML file. Choose **File | Save**. In the **Save As** dialog, make sure the folder selected in the **Where** popup is your Dreamweaver site folder (or a subfolder within that). Give the file a name, like html5_test, and click on **Save**.

While we are at it, enter a descriptive title in the **Title** box of the Document toolbar. Resave periodically.

# Creating a CSS file

Hand-in-hand with our HTML5 file, we will create and use a CSS file to organize and manage all the styling in the page. Therefore, let's create that CSS file now, and as we do, add a line that will make our HTML5 page compatible with all current browsers, and most older ones.

To do that, follow these steps:

1. Choose **File | New**, and in the **New Document** dialog, choose the **Blank Page** category on the left, and **CSS** from the **Page Type** category. Click on **Create** to generate, and open a new CSS file.

2. The file opens in Code view. We will be editing it in the CSS Styles panel, so except as a learning experience we won't need to view this page again. However, we do need to save it. Choose **File | Save**, and give the file a name like **html5_layout.css**. Make sure the site folder is selected in the **Where** pop up, and click on **Save** as shown in the following screenshot:

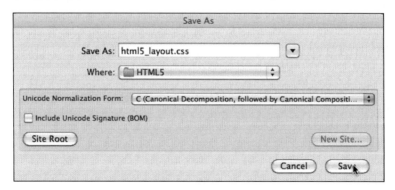

3. In the tab bar at the top of the document window, toggle back to the HTML file you created, as shown in the following screenshot:

4. View the **CSS STYLES** panel if it is not visible (choose **Window | CSS Styles**), and click on the **Attach Style Sheet** icon as shown in the following screenshot:

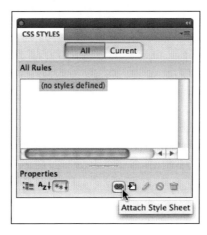

5. The **Attach External Style Sheet** dialog appears. Use the **Browse** button to navigate to the CSS file you just created, and click on **OK** to attach the style sheet. The CSS file appears in the **CSS Files** panel (use the **All** tab in the CSS Styles panel as the norm, unless you are doing particular styles detective work that requires the **Current** tab). You will also see the link to the CSS file in Code view if you look.

Next, we will add a single attribute that enables most browsers to interpret the HTML5 elements, even if they are not HTML5 compliant. Here, we will be revisiting the technique we noted in the previous chapter, when we saw how Dreamweaver CS5's HTML5 layouts use the `display:block` CSS attribute to keep HTML5 layouts from collapsing in non-HTML5 browsers.

To do that, follow these steps:

1. Click on the **New CSS Rule** icon at the bottom of the **CSS Styles** panel, it is just to the right of the **Attach Style Sheet** icon identified in the preceding screenshot. The **New CSS Rule** dialog opens.

2. In the **New CSS Rule** dialog, choose **Compound** from the first popup. We are creating a rule that will apply to more than one HTML5 layout element. These are HTML5 tags that we want to prevent from collapsing when viewed in non-HTML5 browsers.

3. In the **Choose** or **Enter a Name for Your Selector** field, enter header. We actually want to apply the rule we are working on to additional HTML5 elements, but we will add those shortly. In the **Rule Definition** section of the dialog, make sure your attached CSS file is selected (it will be by default). Click on **OK**.

4. In the **CSS Rule Definition for header** dialog, select the **Block** category, and choose **block** from the display popup as shown in the following screenshot, then click on **OK**.

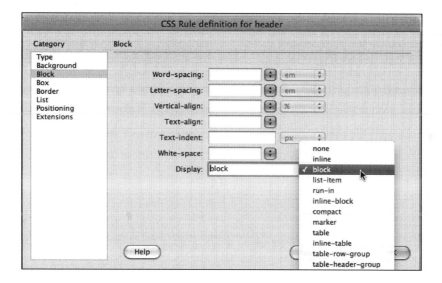

5. The Header style appears in the CSS Styles panel when you expand the CSS Styles file linked to the page. You can see that the display property for the header style has a block attribute associated with it in the CSS styles panel.

6. We want to expand the list of HTML5 elements to which this `display:block` attribute is assigned. The long, slow way to do that is to duplicate steps we have traversed so far for each additional element. To do that the quick, easy way, click once in the header row, in the top half of the CSS Styles panel, and edit the list of elements `to include address, article, footer, nav, section`. Use commas (",") to separate the additional elements as you type them in. These are HTML5 tags that we want to prevent from collapsing when viewed in non-HTML5 browsers. The CSS Styles panel should now look like the following screenshot:

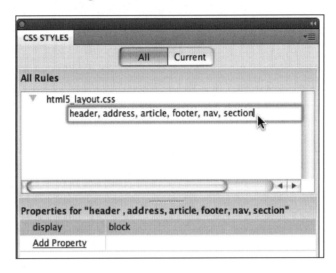

With the preceding set of steps, we have told most non-HTML5 browsers to keep our basic HTML5 building-block elements on their own distinct horizontal row, so they don't smush into each other.

Our basic model and scenario here is creating pages that are intended only for HTML5 browsers (like iPhones or iPads). In *Chapter 5, Defining and Implementing Multiscreen Previews and Media Queries*, we will learn to apply other style sheets when visitors come to our page content with non-HTML5 browsers. However, as a backup, we have also made one quick change to our CSS code that will make our HTML5 elements work in all current generation browsers.

# Using HTML5 to make content accessible

Having set up our HTML5 document with basic web page coding, we are now ready to create and format the HTML5 layout elements that will define how the page looks.

But wait... as the TV pitchmen say... there's more! Before diving into the page design dimension of HTML layout elements, it will be helpful to quickly survey another reason to use HTML layout elements to organize content: accessibility.

As alluded to in the introduction to this chapter, there are advantages beyond design considerations for relying on HTML5 layout elements to organize page content. These advantages revolve around the way HTML5 layout elements package content for metadata compilers (such as search engines). This emerging connection can make content organized into HTML5 layout elements more searchable, easier to organize and access. Moreover, this will be even more the case in the future as search engines and other web content organizing tools integrate HTML5 layout elements.

We will take a rather simple, but interesting example of how this works right now. If you have ever copied and pasted the content between apps on an iPhone (for example, the address of a web page into an app that helps you find public transportation options or content from an article or posting that you read online in an e-mail), then you maybe familiar with the routine where you hold your finger down on the screen and are prompted with a Copy prompt. The next step is to use the somewhat awkward process of using one's fingers to define the content to copy to the clipboard, as shown in the following screenshot:

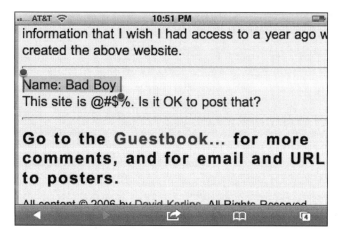

On the other hand, when content is organized into articles (or sections), a touch on the iPhone screen instantly selects an article or article section for copying, as shown in the following screenshot:

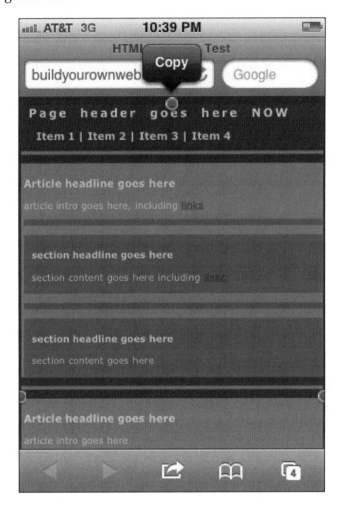

Now, in terms of added value to a website, the convenience associated with iPhone users easily selecting articles or article sections probably isn't going to turn the world upside down, although visitors are likely to note positively the convenience they experience selecting articles from your page to share. However, the fact that the iPhone browser recognizes sections (and articles, and other HTML5 layout elements) also gives a sense of the potential for the associations between content and HTML5 layout elements to make content more accessible. We can expect, for example, that in the not-so-far-off-future, people will be able to tune their search engine queries for "articles" about this or that topic.

**HTML5 layout and search engines**: By relying on HTML5 layout elements to organize page content, you are building (in advance) support for search tools and other ways that HTML5 will facilitate finding content.

# HTML5 layout strategy

Having surveyed the emerging value of organizing content into HTML5 layout elements, we turn to the more dramatically impactful aspect of using HTML5 layout elements: design. However, keep in mind; design and content are linked in HTML5. Unlike previous generations of web page markup language, HTML5 organizes content both to facilitate displaying that content, and to facilitate accessing that content.

A basic HTML5 page layout is illustrated in the following screenshot, with self-explanatory placeholder text:

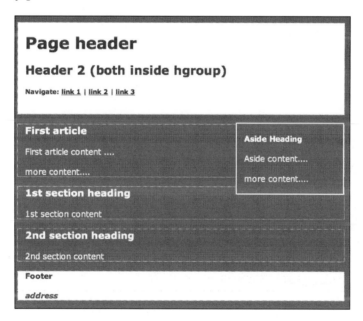

The visible borders in the preceding screenshot, by the way, are a product of Dreamweaver CS5's CSS Layout Outlines (if they are not functioning, choose **View | Visual Aids | CSS Layout Outlines**).

Again, before diving into an exploration of the specific elements in HTML5 layouts, and how they are implemented, keep in mind they both define design components of the page, and organize content.

# Using code hints

Dreamweaver, with the HTML5 Pack, is HTML5-friendly, but not exactly HTML5-compatible. By this, I mean that it is necessary to resort to Code view to apply HTML5 elements. However, within that, you get help.

As noted earlier, Dreamweaver CS5 helps create the coding for HTML5 code hints. As you begin typing HTML5 elements in Code view, beginning with "<", Dreamweaver prompts you with a set of tags that begin with the letter you type. So, for example, typing **<he** produces the following code hints, from which you can click on **<>header** and press *Enter* (Windows) or *Return* (Mac) to place the code.

>  You can use control spacebar on Mac or PC to bring up the full code hinting list.

```
<he|
    <> head
    <> header
    <> thead
```

To close (define the end of) an HTML5 layout element, simply type **</**. When you do that, Dreamweaver auto-enters the close coding for the open element, as shown in the following screenshot:

```
<header>
Header content goes here
</header>|
```

As we walk through the coding involved in defining different HTML5 layout elements in the remainder of this chapter, you can enter the necessary code in Split view, utilizing code hints, and seeing the results in the Design half of Split view.

# Adding header, header nav, and hgroup

The `<header>` element is used to organize all the content that goes at the top of a page. As you saw in the preceding screenshot, this includes a main heading, a subheading (where that is used), and the navigation structure.

## Navigation within a header

So, the `<nav>` content—the links at the top of a page—are included in the `<header>` element when they are placed at the top of a page. Navigation elements placed in sidebars are also enclosed within the `<nav>` element, but as—in this case—they are not part of the header, they are not enclosed in the `<header>` element.

Within a `<header>` element, CSS styles associated with tags (such as `<h1>`, `<h2>`, and so on), or with class Div tags can be used to supply additional formatting rules for how content will be displayed.

## Organizing header content with hgroups

With the aim of making content within a header more easily categorized, HTML5 includes the hgroup element. The formal requirements for hgroup content is that it be content with heading tags applied (`<h1>`, `<h2>`, `<h3>`, `<h4>`, `<h5>`, or `<h6>`).

The concept is that heading content such as subheadings, alternative titles, or taglines all be grouped, within a header, for easy access. So, for example, in the following screenshot, the two heading lines have been wrapped in an `<hgroup>` element. However, the navigation content, although part of the header, is not included in the `<hgroup>` element.

In the following code, an `<h1>` heading and an `<h2>` heading, along with a `<nav>` element, with its own `<h5>` heading (and three placeholder links) are all part of a `<header>` element.

```
<header>
  <hgroup>
    <h1>Page header</h1>
    <h2>Header 2 </h2>
  </hgroup>
  <nav>
    <h5>Navigate: <a href="#">link 1</a> | <a href="#">link 2</a> |
      <a href="#">link 3</a></h5>
  </nav>
</header>
```

The following screenshot illustrates how this looks in Split view in Dreamweaver (with Live view on in the Design view side of Split view).

```
11   <header>
12 ▼ <hgroup>
13   <h1>Page header</h1>
14   <h2>Header 2 </h2>
15 ▲ </hgroup>
16   <nav>
17   <h5>Navigate: <a href="#">link 1</a> | <a href="#">
     link 2</a> | <a href="#">link 3</a></h5>
18   </nav>
19   </header>
```

**Page header**

**Header 2**

Navigate: <u>link 1</u> | <u>link 2</u> | <u>link 3</u>

# Creating articles and sections

If you write for a living, as I do, you learn to organize content into chunks, and sub-chunks, concepts and sub-concepts, ideas and more detailed ideas, and so on. The basic rule for organizing content in this way is that if you create a sub-section, you have to create two sub-sections. Otherwise, there is no point in creating a sub-section.

In line with our recurring theme of the unity between content and design in HTML5 layout, content in HTML5 pages (where it has to be broken down) is broken down into **articles**. Moreover, where there is a need for distinct sub-sections within an article, those sub-sections are **sections**.

As you create a CSS file to match your HTML layout elements, you might well assign specific formatting to articles, and to sections. For example, you might choose to indent section content, or place a unique background behind it. In the following example, article content is set off with a unique background and text color, and within articles, sections are indented.

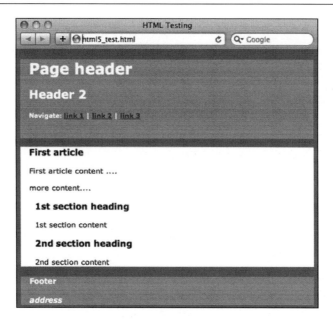

The code for the `<article>` and `<section>` elements in the preceding illustration, including placeholder text and headings is:

```
<article>
  <h3>First article</h3>
  <p>First article content ....</p>
  <p>more content....</p>
  <section>
    <h3>1st section heading</h3>
    <p>1st section content</p>
  </section>
  <section>
    <h3>2nd section heading</h3>
    <p>2nd section content</p>
  </section>
</article>
```

Or… you might not apply specific CSS rules to articles and sections, and simply wrap content in the `<article>` and `<section>` elements for content organizing purposes, while relying on the `<body>` tag, the `<p>` (paragraph) tag, or custom class styles that you define in Dreamweaver for formatting article and section content.

# Adding aside content

Aside content is reserved for sidebar content that is dependent on content in an article or section of an article. The `<aside>` element is not intended, for example, to serve as a container for navigation content (navigation content is supposed to be identified by, and wrapped in the `<nav>` element discussed earlier).

Given that aside content is generally formatted as a sidebar, there is a particular style generally associated with the use of `<aside>` elements: **Float**.

The CSS Float attribute moves a container to the left (`Float:left`) or right (`Float: right`) of other content, and flows other content around the container.

**Defining CSS Attributes**: In *Chapter 3* of this book, we explored the routine for defining CSS styles that apply to HTML5 elements and other tags in some depth. Therefore, in this chapter, we will simply note CSS attributes that are assigned to HTML5 elements without walking through the steps to implement those attributes. The short version, however, is to create a new CSS Rule for each HTML5 element, and define those rules, all using the New CSS Rule in the CSS Styles panel. For another angle on defining and applying CSS Styles to HTML5 elements, see the Recipe at the end of this chapter where we will walk through that process step-by-step.

The following screenshot shows an `<aside>` element defined at 33% of the page width, and floated left.

# Creating a footer

The final piece of an HTML5 page layout is usually a `<footer>` element. Early in this chapter, when we walked through standard HTML5 page coding, we noted the `<footer>` element (along with `<header>` elements and others have the `display:` `block` attribute assigned to them). That attribute, which prevents other content from "sharing" the horizontal row on which the footer content is displayed, is pretty much the main, and only essential formatting element required for footer.

Beyond that, you can apply features such as height, background color, and so on by defining a CSS Style rule for the `<footer>` element. Do that by clicking on the **New CSS Rule** icon at the bottom of the **CSS Styles Panel**. Choose **Tag** from the **Selector Type** popup, choose **Footer** in the **Selector Name** popup, in the **Rule Definition** popup, choose the external style sheet file to which you are saving your CSS rules, as shown in the following screenshot, and then click on **OK** to define rules for the `<footer>` element.

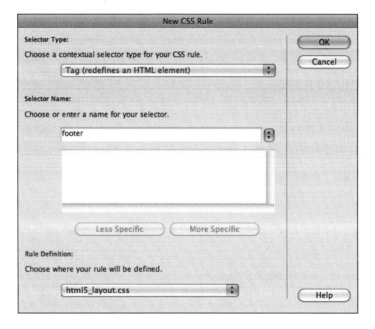

As with all HTML5 layout elements, `<footer>` elements have content assignments. Footers usually include content site author information, legal notices (such as copyright information), and so on. While it is technically allowable to have more than one footer on a page, it is difficult to envision a situation where more than one footer would be appropriate—the point of the element to organize all the information that should be available at the bottom of a page.

# Adding metadata

The HTML5 layout elements that we have explored thus far have—as we have seen—a dual function: they serve as stylable elements that can control how content is displayed, and they organize content for accessibility.

Both the style and content dimensions of HTML5 layout elements are evolving, but they already serve as tools for designing pages, and for delivering content. The example we explored earlier of selecting an article, or an article section easily for copying in an iPhone gives a taste of how this is likely to evolve in the near future.

In addition to the key layout elements explored so far, it is worth briefly noting a few HTML5 elements whose main role is to index content (even as they can be used to apply styles as well).

# Defining an address

Often, one of the first things a visitor to a site is seeking is contact information—an URL if the page is not a site home page, an e-mail address, a physical address, if he or she is looking to locate the hottest underground club or nearest highly rated shish-kabob stand.

A `<footer>` element can be associated with (placed within) an `<article>` element if it is providing contact information for the author of (or topic of) the article. Alternatively, an `<address>` element can be associated with (placed within) a `<footer>` element if it is providing contact information for the entire page. The following shows an `<address>` element embedded in a footer along with the associated HTML5 code, in Dreamweaver's Split view.

# Figures and captions

The `<figure>` and `<figcaption>` elements identify (intuitively enough) a figure and an associated caption. Again, assigning these elements to content helps content aggregators and indexing programs (such as search engines) interpret your page content, and make it more accessible. Moreover, you can use these elements to style figures and/or captions as well.

The following screenshot, for example, has a `<figure>` element wrapped around both an image, and the caption (`<figcaption>`). Moreover, as is illustrated in the CSS Styles panel (as shown in the following screenshot), some basic styling has been applied to the `<figure>` element, including `float: right` (which right aligns the `<figure>` element and everything within it), a width, a background color, and margins and padding. Note the coding in the Code side of Split view.

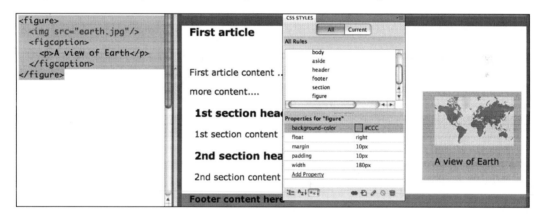

# Indicating date and time

Speaking of using HTML5 elements to convey content, there are different HTML5 elements associated with different kinds of time and date information.

The `<time>` element is used to mark off times and dates for upcoming events, along with other date-specific content. It is not intended to define every reference to a date and time. For example, you would not, use the `<time>` element when writing a historical article citing dates for different historical events.

The `<time>` element can be used to set off a specific time, as in the following HTML5 code:

```
The show starts at <time>12:00 midnight</time>.
```

Alternatively, date and time information can be encoded within text using the datetime parameter, as shown in the following example:

```
<time datetime="2012-01-01">all night jam session!</time>
```

The format for time and date is: YYYY-MM-DDThh:mm:ssTZD, where TZD is the time zone.

You are unlikely to use the `<time>` element as a styling tool. Instead, it is best used to demarcate dates and times of upcoming events.

# Recipe Part 1: Build a style sheet for an HTML5 page layout

In this two-part recipe, we will first define a CSS style sheet that will supply formatting for the HTML5 elements we need for our page, and then we will build a page, applying those CSS styles as we associate HTML5 elements with page content.

At this stage of our journey, we can rather quickly walk through the process for creating a CSS file, and defining CSS rules for HTML5 elements. We can focus more on which parameters we are applying in this recipe, and why.

As always, before embarking on this recipe, be sure you have a Dreamweaver site defined. If you are not sure what that means, or whether you are working in one, review the discussion of sites in *Chapter 1*. Working within a Dreamweaver site is essential in coordinating the HTML5 page and CSS style sheet that need to work together here.

1.  To begin, choose **File | New** to open the **New Document** dialog. From the **Page Type** category, choose **CSS**, and click on **Create**. A new CSS file opens in Code view (which is the only way you can view a CSS page, as it is just code).

2.  Save the CSS file (choose **File | Save**), name it html5_layout.css. A blank CSS page appears (with the exception of two lines of code, one defining the character set and the other a comment).

3.  Let's create our first style for the `<body>` tag using the CSS Styles panel:
    -   Click on **New CSS Rule** in the **CSS Styles Panel** (if it is not open, choose **Window | CSS Styles**).

○ In the **Selector Type** popup, choose **Tag**. In the **Selector Name** popup, choose **Body**. In the **Rule Definition** popup, leave the setting at **(This Document Only)**. Click on **OK** to open the **Rule Definition** dialog.

○ In the **Type** category of the **Rule Definition** dialog, select the **Verdana** group. In the **Background** category, select a background color of medium gray (**#999**). Click on **Apply** to generate CSS code for the `<body>` tag. You can see the code in the CSS file, as shown in the following screenshot. Then click on **OK**.

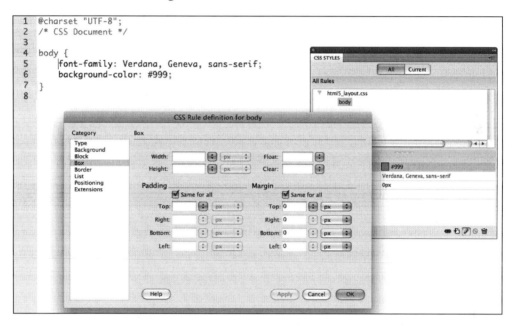

4. Having defined the `<body>` tag using the **CSS Styles Panel**, let's use a different technique to define style attributes that will apply to most of the HTML5 layout elements—`display:block` to prevent content from different elements from appearing on the same line; and padding: 10px (10 pixels) to create spacing within each of these elements. Do this by simply typing the code into the CSS page, after the "}" character that closed the definition of the `<body>` tag:

```
header, address, article, footer, nav, section{
    display: block;
    padding: 10px;
}
```

Your CSS page will look like this:

```
 1  @charset "UTF-8";
 2  /* CSS Document */
 3
 4  body {
 5      font-family: Verdana, Geneva, sans-serif;
 6      background-color: #999;
 7      margin: 0px;
 8  }
 9  }
10  header, address, article, footer, nav, section{
11      display: block;
12      padding: 10px;
13  }
```

Now that we have reviewed two ways to generate CSS code, choose one or the other to create the following additional CSS code, and save the page:

```
header {
   color: #FFF;
   background-color: #CCC;
}
footer {
   color: #000;
   background-color: #FFF;
}
article {
   color: #000;
}
aside {
   float: right;
   width: 25%;
   border: thin solid #FFF;
   background-color: #999;
   padding: 10px;
   margin: 10px;
}
figure {
   background-color: #CCC;
   margin: 10px;
   padding: 10px;
   float: right;
   width: 160px;
   height: 180px;
}
section {
   padding: 0px;
}
```

**A few notes on the CSS we created**: We are using very minimalist background and text colors (shades of gray plus white and black) both to make a minimalist aesthetic statement and to keep our project simple.

The float attribute on the <aside> element aligns the aside (sidebar) box with the right side of the page, flowing content around it to the right. The extra padding and margin enforce spacing between both the aside content and the border of the box, and between the box and content that flows around it. We will see how this works out in Part 2 of this recipe, shortly.

Similarly, the float and margin attributes assigned to the <figure> element align the box that will hold images and captions to the right side of the page.

Setting the margin to zero for the article sections keeps that content from indenting further, beyond the indent inherited from the margin assigned to the <article> and <section> elements in step 4.

# Recipe Part 2: Build an HTML5 layout from scratch

Having defined and saved CSS styles, we are ready to create a page that can serve as a customized, fully HTML5, customizable page layout of our own.

 A trick to have up your sleeve before we start: We will be working in Split view, and doing much of our work in the Code side of the split. Take advantage of code hints. Start typing a tag as indicated, and press *Enter* (Windows) or *Return* (Mac) when the code hint settles on the code you need. To close the code, simply type </, and press *Enter* (Windows) or *Return* (Mac).

With Dreamweaver's code hinting at the ready, create a new HTML5 file and connect your CSS file with placeholder text using the following steps:

1. Choose **File | New**. In the **New Document dialog,** choose **Blank** Page in the first column, **HTML** from the **Page Type** column, **<none>** from the **Layout** column, and **HTML5** in the **DocType** pop up. However, do not click on **Create** quite yet!

2.  Click on the **Attach Style Sheet** link next to the **Attach CSS File** box. Navigate and select the `html5_layout.css` file created in the first half of this recipe. Don't worry about the warning message that the file should be saved to ensure the validity of the link between the HTML file and the CSS style sheet. We will address that in the next step. Now click on **Create**.

3.  Save your new file as `html5_layout.html`.

4.  Under the first `<body>` tag, avail yourself of code hints to enter the following code that will generate a `<header>` element, an `<hgroup>` element within the header with placeholders for a heading 1 title and heading 2 subtitle, and a `<header>` element with placeholder links:

```
<header>
  <hgroup>
    <h1>Page header</h1>
    <h2>Header 2 </h2>
  </hgroup>
  <nav>
    <h5>Navigate: <a href="#">link 1</a> |
      <a href="#">link 2</a> | <a href="#">link 3</a></h5>
  </nav>
</header>
```

5.  Now comes the heart of the page layout — an article, with an aside, a figure, and two sub-sections. Any of these elements can be duplicated when the page is used as a template layout, and customized actual content pages are created. The article code is:

```
<article>
  <aside>
    <h3>sidebar content
    </h3>
    <p>placeholder text
    </p>
  </aside>
  <h1>First article headline
  </h1>
  <h3>Subhead for first article...
  </h3>
  <p>placeholder text.
    <section>
      <figure>
        <img src="" alt="fig goes here"
```

```
            name="figure_placeholder" width="160"
            height="120" style="background-color: #FFFFFF">
              <br>Caption here
                <figcaption>
                </figcaption>
        </figure>
      </section>
    </p>
    <section>
      <h3>1st section heading
      </h3>
      <p>placeholder text
      </p>
    </section>
    <section>
      <h3>2nd section heading
      </h3>
      <p>placeholder text
      </p>
    </section>
  </article>
```

 **A few notes on this code**: Within the <figure> element, we are using a placeholder to save space for a figure that will be inserted. The figure size is defined at 160 px wide, and 120 px high—a nice setting for thumbnails that will appear in our target browsing environment, an iPhone screen.

6. After closing the <figure> element, we can complete our page with coding for a footer that includes an <address> element by adding the final code:

```
<footer>
  <h4>Footer content here</h4>
  <address>
    contact this site at <a href="http://www.xyz.com">
    http://www.xyz.com</a>
  </address>
</footer>
```

After you save your page, you can view a rough preview of how the page will look in an iPhone by defining a 480 pixel wide by 320 pixel high iPhone preview screen (for an iPhone turned sideways). Do this by first choosing **Edit | Preferences** (Windows) or **Dreamweaver | Preferences** (Mac), and selecting the **Status Bar** category in the **Preferences** dialog. Create a new preview size of 480 pixels wide and 320 pixels high, as shown in the following screenshot, and then click on **OK**.

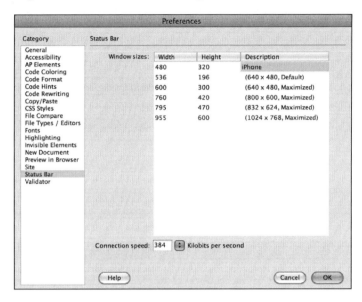

Once defined, this Status Bar setting can be used to preview your page in Dreamweaver as you experiment and tweak the layout, as shown in the following screenshot:

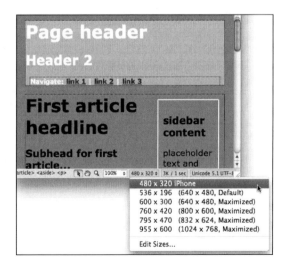

# Summary

In this chapter, we completed a survey of building HTML5 pages, using HTML5 layout elements. We saw how these elements function as both design containers, and as content identifiers. We also saw how, for some environments, an entire page could be built using only a few basic HTML tags, plus HTML layout elements.

Based on what we have covered so far, we are ready to design HTML5 pages that work, differently, in different media such as iPhones, iPads, and laptops.

# 5

# Defining and Implementing Multiscreen Previews and Media Queries

It is a multimedia world. What we mean by this is that people experience and interact with the web content with a variety of media, ranging from large-screen projections of websites to hand-held devices. This presents specific challenges for web designers.

One of those challenges revolves around designing pages that are accessible, inviting, and functional at extremely different sizes. A page with centered content (left and right side sidebars) and text flowing around images may be inviting on a laptop, but a jumbled mess on an iPhone.

With the advent of HTML5 and its companion CSS3 (the latest iteration of style sheets), it is possible to design pages that detect the size of a viewing device and to present pages customized for that device. Therefore, for example, you can create three alternative views of a page: one for cell phones, one for tablets, and one for full-sized monitors.

In this chapter, we will learn to design pages in Dreamweaver that detect media automatically by using Dreamweaver-generated Media Queries and present appropriate page designs tailored to the visitor's viewing environment.

In the course of that, we will:

- Introduce CSS3—the companion to HTML5
- Use Dreamweaver's Multiscreen Preview
- Customize Multiscreen Preview for specific devices
- Create multiple styles for different sized viewing devices with Dreamweaver's Media Queries
- Troubleshoot Media Queries for Apple's i-gadgets

# Web design for a multimedia web world

As discussed in the introduction of this chapter, recent times have seen an explosion in the variety of media through which people interact with websites, particularly the explosion of "smart phones" and tablets. Moreover, as discussed, a web page design that is appropriate, even necessary for a wide-screen experience, is often inappropriate, overly cluttered, or just plain dysfunctional in a tiny screen.

The solution to this is Media Queries, a new element of CSS introduced with CSS3. However, before we examine new media features in CSS3, it will be helpful to understand the basic evolutionary path that led to CSS3 Media Queries. That background will be useful both in getting our hands around the concepts involved, and because, in the crazy wild-west state of browsing environments these days (with emerging and yet-unresolved standards conflicts), designing for the widest range of media requires combining new CSS3 Media Queries with older CSS Media detection tools. We will see how this plays out in real life at the end of this chapter, when we examine particular challenges of creating Media Queries that can detect an Apple iPhone, for example.

Therefore, stepping back in time a bit, the current (pre-CSS3) version of CSS already can detect media and enable different style sheets depending on the media. Moreover, Dreamweaver CS5.5 (and to lesser degrees CS5, CS4 and CS3) provide very nice, intuitive support for these features.

The way this works in Dreamweaver is when you click on the **Attach Style sheet** icon at the bottom of the CSS Styles panel (with a web page open in Dreamweaver's **Document** window), the **Attach External Style sheet** dialog appears.

The Media pop up in the dialog allows you to attach a style sheet specifically designed for print, aural (to be read aloud by reader software), Braille, handheld devices, and other output options, as shown in the following screenshot:

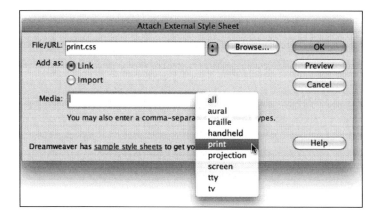

So, to summarize the evolutionary path, detecting media and providing a custom-designed style for that media is not new to HTML5, its companion CSS3, and support for those features in Dreamweaver. Detecting and synchronizing styles with defined media has been available in Dreamweaver.

However, what is new is the ability to detect and supply defined style sheets for specific screen sizes. Moreover, that new feature opens the door to new levels of customized page design for specific media.

# CSS3 and Media Queries

With CSS3, Media Queries have been expanded. Now we can define all kinds of criteria for selecting a style sheet to apply to a viewing environment This includes orientation irrespective of whether a mobile phone, tablet, and so on are held in portrait ("up and down") or in landscape ("sideways") view, or whether the device displays color, the shape of the viewing area, and—of most value—the width and height of the viewing area.

All these options present a multitude of possibilities for creating custom style sheets for different viewing environments. In fact, they open up a ridiculous array of possibilities. However, for most designers, simply creating three appropriate style sheets, one for laptop/desktop viewing, one for mobile phones, and one for tablets, is sufficient.

In order to define criteria for which style sheet will display in a set environment, CSS3 allows us to use "if-then" statements. Therefore, for example, if we are assigning a style sheet to tablets, we might specify that if the width of the viewing area is greater than that of a cell phone, but smaller than that of a laptop screen, we want the tablet style sheet to be applied.

Dreamweaver's Media Query tools generate such criteria and coding automatically! Moreover, as we will see, Dreamweaver CS5.5 and CS5 suggest appropriate criteria for different viewing environments.

# Styling for mobile devices and tablets

While a full exploration of the aesthetic dimensions of creating styles for different media is beyond the scope of our mission in this book, it is worth noting a few basic "dos and don'ts" vis-à-vis styling for mobile devices.

In a word, the challenge is: simplify.

In general, this means applying many or all of the following adjustments to your pages:

- Smaller margins
- Larger (more readable) type
- Much less complex backgrounds, no image backgrounds
- No sidebars or floated content (content around which other content wraps)
- Often no containers that define the page width

The HTML5 page layout we created in the previous chapter is a positive example of this kind of layout, and you can refer back to that, with our new understanding of the challenges of designing for mobile devices in mind.

The following screenshot, for example, shows a page in a laptop browser window that includes a number of elements, including a sidebar that should be reconfigured for display on a 320 pixel wide mobile device:

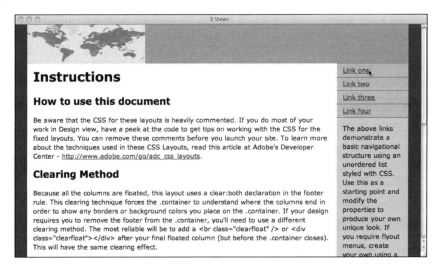

In the following screenshot, the background for the header has been removed, the navigation elements have been moved from a sidebar to the top of the page, and the color scheme has been simplified, making it easier to navigate the site with a mobile device:

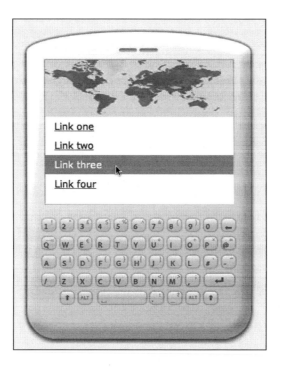

 **Design advice online**: If you search for "css for mobile devices", then you will find thousands of articles with different perspectives and advice on designing web pages that can be easily accessed with handheld devices.

# Previewing with the Multiscreen Preview

Dreamweaver's Multiscreen Preview provides an instant (if not precise) preview of how an open web page will look in three different viewing environments.

In order to view an open page in the Multiscreen Preview, either click on the **Multiscreen Preview** button in the Document toolbar (if not visible, then select **View** | **Toolbars** | **Document**), or select **Window** | **Multiscreen Preview** from the Document window menu. When you do, the **MULTISCREEN PREVIEW** window opens, with three views, as shown in the following screenshot:

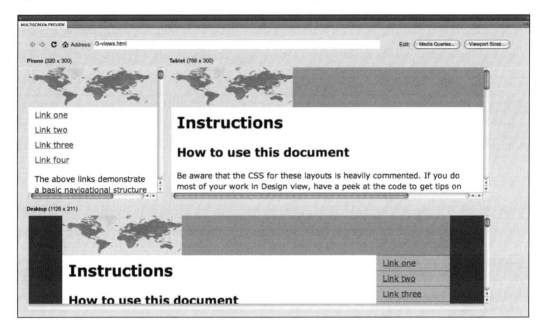

Multiscreen Preview is a form of a Live view. You cannot edit the content here you can only preview it.

You can, however—as we shall see—edit the style sheets associated with each view, and observe the effect in Multiscreen Preview.

The three preset viewport sizes in the Multiscreen Preview window provide a widely applicable set of screen sizes for previewing how an open page will look in a cell phone, a tablet, and on a desktop (or full sized laptop, with a screen width of 1024 pixels or more). In particular, the width settings are a good, general way to preview how your page will look in different media.

On the other hand, if you are designing for a specific viewing environment, you can customize these settings. In order to do that, click on the **Viewport Sizes** button in the upper right-hand corner of the Multiscreen Preview window. That opens the **Viewport Sizes** dialog. You can change the width and (in the case of phones and tables) the height of any of the three available views by changing the values in the **Width** or **Height** boxes, and then clicking on **OK**.

The most useful adjustment you make in **Viewport Sizes** might actually be the height of the **Phone** preview. By making that value a bit larger, you can get more of a sense of how pages will look in smartphones with longer viewing screens.

In the following screenshot, the height of the **Phone** preview window is being changed to **400** pixels:

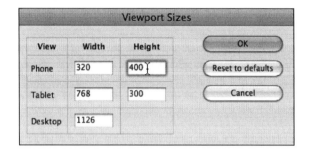

Most likely, when you first preview a page, you won't like the way it looks in the phone and tablet preview windows. At that point, you can do one of the following two things:

1. Elect not to worry about how the page looks and works in mobile devices under the assumption that this mobile device thing is a passing fad that will soon go away.

2. You can use Dreamweaver to generate a Media Query to present more inviting, accessible content in mobile devices.

Assuming that you chose the second option, let's move on to explore how to create style sheets for phone and tablet display and to apply these style sheets in appropriate environments.

# Generating a Media Query in Dreamweaver

There are a number of valid approaches and possible protocols, which you can use to generate sets of styles for a Media Query in Dreamweaver CS5.5 and CS5. Before walking through one that works well, let's survey what it is we are trying to accomplish.

Essentially, we need three sets of style sheets: one for phones, one for tablets, and one for full-sized monitors. Both because full-sized monitors are still, at this point, a "standard" in terms of how the web content is viewed, and because the phone and tablet styles will likely have less complex styles, it makes sense to start by creating a style sheet for a full-sized page.

In other words, the first step is to create a basic CSS Style sheet that works well with the page when it is opened in a full-sized desktop or laptop monitor. Then, variations on that page can be generated with simplified layouts that work on phones and tablets.

# Building alternative style sheets

As noted, from a style and accessibility perspective, it makes sense to start with a "full-sized" web page style and then build permutations of that style that work with phones, and on tablets.

There is also a technical reason to use that workflow. Keep in mind that all three CSS Style sheet files will be providing styling rules for the same page. This means that all three alternative CSS files have to provide rules for the same set of HTML elements and tags.

For example, if a `<div>` tag defines a main container on a page, then the style sheets for all three media (phone, tablet, and desktop) have to define how that `<div>` tag should appear. The rules for the phone CSS might include a narrower width, a simpler background color, and other attributes. However, the point is, all three style sheets will have rules for this main container `div`. Moreover, that must be the case for all the layout elements, whether HTML5 layout elements, `<div>` tags, or some combination of the two.

# A 3-step protocol for preparing to generate a Media Query

One effective protocol for preparing to generate a Media Query is to have three CSS files ready to assign to different media.

A simple protocol for doing that is as follows:

1. Create a basic CSS file for your page that works for desktop/laptop-sized monitors. If you are generating pages from Dreamweaver's HTML5 layouts, then you can use the CSS file that comes with the respective layout as this "main" layout.

2. Save the "main" CSS file with a file name `query_fullsize.css` and then resave it twice, with two different file names (such as `query_phone.css` and `query_tablet.css`), creating three identical style sheets.

3. With the three alternative style sheets saved, you can customize them right in the Multiscreen Preview menu.

With three alternative CSS files available for assignment and editing, you are now ready to define Media Queries. We will walk through that process next.

# Assigning styles to different media

The best way to avail ourselves of Dreamweaver's new HTML5/CSS3 tools for building Media Queries is work in Multiscreen Preview mode. Remember, this means we will not be editing content as we adjust styles. However, that constraint is something we can definitely live with, and in fact, as a general approach, adjusting the content and style should be thought of and approached as distinct processes.

Therefore, our scenario is that we have opened Multiscreen Preview for an opened web page. Moreover, we have the three different CSS files ready—the ones discussed in the "3-step" protocol identified just a bit earlier in this chapter.

With the three CSS files saved as part of your Dreamweaver site and with a web page open in Multiscreen Preview, carry out the following steps to define custom styles for each view:

1. Click on the **Media Queries** button to open the **Media Queries** dialog.

We will start with the "Desktop" view, which will function for us as a desktop/laptop view aimed both at desktops and full sized laptops, but also those tiny Netbook computers, since their normal 1024 pixel wide screens fall within the scope of "full sized" screens for most design purposes.

2. Select **Use Existing CSS File** from the pop up, in the **Large (Desktop)** row. Click on the folder icon as shown in the following screenshot:

3. The **Select File** dialog opens. Navigate to the CSS file you prepared to display the full-sized version of your web page. Navigate to and choose the CSS file you prepared for full-sized devices.

> **A couple of notes here**: First, just to be clear, we are operating on the assumption that you have prepared three CSS files to apply to the full sized, phone, and tablet versions of your site. In order to review the point of that and the way to do this, you can jump back to the "3-step protocol" discussion a bit earlier in this chapter. The other point to emphasize is that at this point in the process, we are not at all worried about how each version of our site will look. All we want to do at this stage of the game is assign separate CSS files to each of the three target screen sizes. We will format these styles shortly.

4. Similarly, attach the CSS files you prepared for tablets and phones in the **Media Queries** dialog. Your completed screen will look something like the one shown in the following screenshot (with your own file names of course):

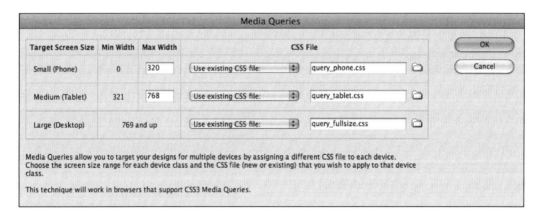

**One more option**: If, for some reason, you want to tweak the target screen sizes for the phone and tablet styles, then you can do at this point. If you do so, however, Dreamweaver will make sure that you do not leave any "gaps" in the sizing. So, for example, if you up the Phone Max Width value to 480, Dreamweaver will change the Tablet Minimum Width to 481.

5.  At this point, you have completed the first part of defining a Media Query for your page. You have identified the CSS files to link to the page. Click on **OK**. Dreamweaver will generate the HTML code that diverts different browser sizes to different CSS files. You can examine that code in the **Split** or **Code** view in the **Document** window. The generated code will be something similar to the following:

```
<link href="query_phone.css" rel="stylesheet" type="text/css"
  media="only screen and (min-width: 0px) and
    (max-width: 320px)" >
<link href="query_tablet.css" rel="stylesheet" type="text/css"
  media="only screen and (min-width: 321px) and
    (max-width: 768px)" >
<link href="query_fullsize.css" rel="stylesheet" type="text/css"
  media="only screen and (min-width: 769px)" >
```

In the preceding example code, the three CSS styles are query_phone.css, query_tablet.css, and query_fullsize.css.

With the criteria for each style sheet defined and the links created, we can now edit each of the three CSS files.

# Formatting CSS files for Media Queries

With a Media Query defined for a web page, we can now interactively create and adjust the styles for each targeted browsing environment. In order to do this we will re-open the Multiscreen Preview for the page.

Wait! You might exclaim, how can we edit the page in Multiscreen Preview, when that window functions like the **Live** view in the **Document** window — locking out any content editing. A thoughtful concern, but here we will be only editing the CSS styles, not the page content. Moreover, we can do in Multiscreen Preview.

In order to edit styles in Multiscreen Preview, view the CSS Styles panel (**Window | CSS Styles**). The three attached styles, along with parenthetical notes helping us remember which style is which, appear in the top half of the CSS Styles panel. You can expand any of those three styles by clicking on the triangle next to the style name in the top half of the CSS Styles panel. In the following screenshot, **the query_phone. css style** is expanded. Moreover, clicking on a style rule within the style (in this case the body tag style) reveals the parameters for that style in the bottom half of the CSS Styles panel:

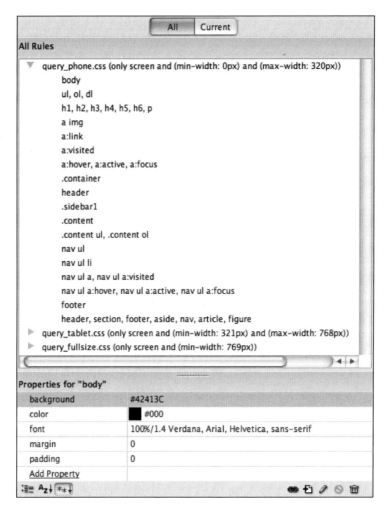

# Caution: Don't delete style rules

You can edit the parameters for different rules within each style sheet. In order to take one very simple example that helps illustrate how this works (in the following screenshot) a different background color has been applied to the <body> tag for each style sheet: white for the phone, gray for the tablet, and black for full-sized browsers:

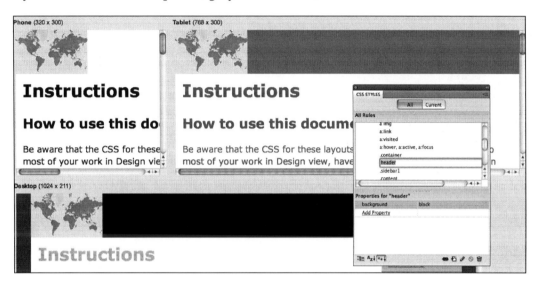

As pointed earlier, the art of designing styles for mobile devices is an art. In addition, as suggested earlier, there are tons of online resources opining and advising on what to include in phone and tablet styles. However, before highlighting a few widely agreed on elements of mobile device styling, it is important to issue a warning: Don't delete style rules from any of your style sheet files.

Our protocol for creating the three alternative style sheets for a Media Query started with one style sheet from which we created two copies. Those style sheets "came into the world" with identical sets of style rules.

# Styling for mobile devices

It is fine and necessary to change the parameters of those style rules. You can have different formatting for containers, text, backgrounds, and so on in your phone style than you have in your tablet style. No problem, but keep in mind that all three of your styles have to mesh with the same HTML file, with the same CSS style names used to define formatting and layout tags and elements.

As for styling mobile devices, the following techniques are widely applicable:

- Keep the type size large
- Keep links easy to find. Underlined links are passé in full-sized web pages, but helpful on cell phones
- Use nice large margins and/or padding in containers to make it easier for big stubby fingers to select tiny content on cell phone screens
- Avoid sidebars (don't use the `float` attribute)
- Use visibility: none to hide non-essential elements in phone styles. In the following screenshot, the visibility has been set to hidden for the header in the phone style and the height of the header reduced to 1 pixel so as to not occupy precious space on a cell phone screen.

The following screenshot shows three style sheets applied to the same page in Multiscreen Preview. The tablet view only required a few adjustments: reducing the widths of the layout elements (the main container, the sidebar, and the header). The phone style sheet took more trial-and-error experimentation, including removing all `float` attributes and reducing the width of different elements. Different color schemes were applied to each style sheet as well, with a very basic color scheme (black and white) applied to the cell phone style.

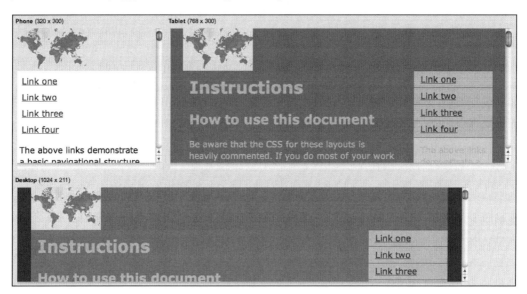

As they say in the commercials for weight-loss products, "your results may vary." Here, this means that tweaking a style sheet for a phone does require some trial and error. Again, the basic rule is simpler. Eliminating floats (so no content appears in a second column) is usually the first step.

# Troubleshooting for Apple i-Gadgets

Every element of web design, including working with HTML5 and CSS3 has its bugs, exceptions, and things that just don't work right. Our aim here is to provide tools, approaches, and techniques so that you can dissect and solve as many of those issues as possible, without addressing every likely hurdle specifically.

However, Apple's iPhone is both the dominant and defining player in the smartphone realm and as you might have guessed, the resolution-based media query technique that we have explored here (that is supposedly "standardized" in CSS3) does not work on iPhones.

The reason is, put somewhat over-simply, that Apple has decreed that the tiny screen on an iPhone is actually a full-sized screen. Here is the math behind that assertion: A typical laptop computer might display something like 130 pixels per inch (ppi). Resolutions vary significantly, but that 130 pixels per inch standard is a useful mean for understanding the iPhone challenge. Calculated by the screen resolution in this range, the 320 pixel wide cutoff point that Dreamweaver defines as the default width of a phone screen is pretty reasonable, about a quarter the width of a laptop screen.

However, small devices, such as iPhones, have smaller pixels. According to Apple, the resolution of the screen on an iPhone 4 is 326 ppi and so, the entire screen width figures out to be the same—measured in pixels—as a regular laptop screen.

The problem, of course, is that those tiny pixels on the iPhone screen are tiny. Thus, even if an entire web page designed for a full-sized monitor fits on an iPhone screen, the content is still likely to be too small to be accessible, much less inviting.

In short, in designing for iPhones, we face this problem: Media Queries based on monitor width in pixels will interpret an iPhone screen as a full-sized screen and display the content with style sheets designed for full-sized monitors. However, the content designed for a cell phone will be more accessible and definitely more inviting for iPhone browsers.

In various niches of cyberspace, innovative designers are debating on how to handle this challenge. One emerging solution is to go back, before CSS3 Media Queries and create Media Queries based not on screen width in pixels, but on the type of media.

iPhones and iPads use weird ways of counting screen resolution to show full-sized screens, so you have to detect them specifically. Here is how:

Within the `<head>` and `</head>` tags (and typically after the `<title>` and `</title>` tags), enter the following code:

```
<link href="full.css" rel="stylesheet" type="text/css">
<link media="only screen and (max-device-width: 960px)" href="ipad.
css" type="text/css" rel="stylesheet" />
<link media="only screen and (max-device-width: 480px)" href="iphone.
css" type="text/css" rel="stylesheet"/>
```

This code displays an attached style sheet (`full.css`) unless either a smaller viewport is detected, or an iPhone is detected.

> **Ever changing challenges**: There are varieties of this code online and as Apple upgrades its phones, you will find new solutions by searching for "media query iPhone 4" (or "media query iPhone 5" when that comes out, and so on).

By the way, when you "code your own" media queries, the display in the Multiscreen Preview window will be unreliable and editing Media Queries with the Media Queries button in Multiscreen Preview will be disabled. In the following screenshot, you can see that (for the code we just noted) the tablet style sheet (white type on the black background) is supported in Multiscreen Preview. So is the tablet style sheet (the black type on a gray background). The hand-coded iPhone Media Query, however, is not supported in Multiscreen Preview and the **Media Queries** button is blocked:

# Exercise: Defining a Media Query for a cell phone

In this recipe, we will take our old friend, the flexible and highly useful 2-column HTML5 layout, and create a Media Query to display this two-column content in a layout more appropriate for cell phones—without columns or sidebars.

As always, the starting assumption is that you are working in a Dreamweaver site (refer back to *Chapter 1* if that does not register). With a site defined, the following steps will produce a nice, appropriately minimalist layout for your page in a cell phone:

1.  Select **File | New**. In the **New Document** dialog, select the **Blank Page** category. Select **HTML** from the **Page Type** column; and choose the first HTML5 layout, the 2-column fixed... layout from the **Layout** column. In the **New Document** dialog, leave the **Layout CSS** pop up selection at **Create New File**. Make sure that there are no files selected in the **Attach CSS file** box (if there are, use the **Trashcan** icon to delete them). With these settings in place, click on **Create**.

2.  The **Save Style sheet File As** dialog opens. Change the saved style sheet name to `fullsize.css` and click on **Save** to save the style sheet to your site folder.

3.  The web page opens in the Dreamweaver Document window. We will make one edit to the content. Delete the rather long link `http://www.adobe.com/go/adc_css_layouts`. This link is inappropriately long, particularly for a cell phone. If (in real life) we wanted to link to a site with a long URL, then we could assign the link to much shorter text using the **Insert | Hyperlink** menu option.

**Customizing the content for layouts**: For an in-depth exploration of customizing the content in a Dreamweaver-generated layout, see *Chapter 2, Customizing HTML5 Layout — Content and Look.*

4.  Select **File | Save** to save the edited HTML page as `2_views.html`.

5.  Next, we will create an empty CSS file to build from to display the content in a mobile device. Select **File | New**. In the **New Document** dialog, select **CSS** from the **Page Type** list, and click on the **Create** button. Select **File | Save** and save the new blank CSS file as `mobile.css`.

6.  Return to the `2_views.html` page in the **Document** window. You can do that either by clicking on the file in the files tab bar at the top of the **Document** window, or by using the **Window** menu.

7.  Click on the **Multiscreen** button in the **Document** window. Click on the **Media Queries** button in **Multiscreen Preview** to open the **Media Queries** dialog.

8.  In the **Small (phone)** row of the **Media Queries** dialog, select **Use Existing CSS file** in folder from the pop up. Use the folder icon in the first row to navigate to and select the **mobile.css** file.

9.  For tablets and full-sized computers, for the sake of this recipe, we will simply display the already attached CSS file (`fullsize.css`), so use the same routine you used in the previous step to assign the `fullsize.css` file to both of these viewports. Then, click on **OK** to see the results in **Multiscreen Preview**.

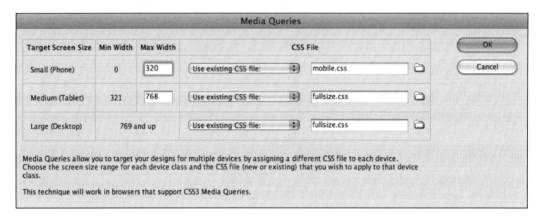

10. Viewing our page layouts in Multiscreen Preview, the layout for the phone viewport is not bad. It is clean and simple, but probably a bit too simple. We can do a bit of editing to make it more inviting. View the CSS Styles panel right in Multiscreen Preview by selecting **Window | CSS Styles**. Select **mobile.css** in the **CSS Styles** panel, and click on the **New CSS Rule** icon in the toolbar at the bottom of the panel. In the **New CSS Rule** dialog, select **Tag** for the **Selector Type**, **Body** (already selected) as the **Selector Name**, and leave the **Rule Definition** pop up set to **mobile.css**. Click on **OK** to open the **CSS Rule Definition** for **Body** in **Mobile.css** dialog. Select **Verdana** from the **Font-Family** pop up and in the **Font-size** pop up, select **Large** (for easier viewing on cell phones). Click on **OK** to survey the results, which will look something similar to the following screen:

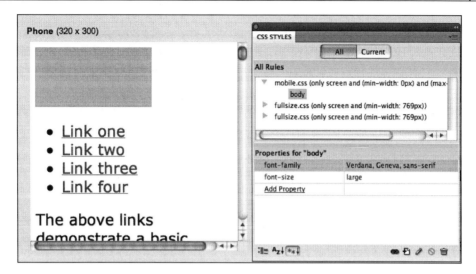

11. We are close! Add the following tags to the `mobile.css` style sheet, with the following parameters:

    ◦ h1, with font-size: smaller

    ◦ ul, with **list-style-type**: none; and **margin-left**: **-40px**

The preceding setting is depicted in the following screenshot:

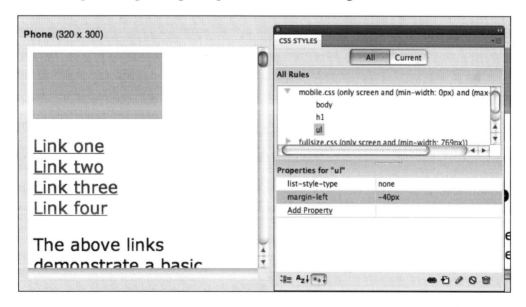

The smaller font size for Heading 1 reduces the size of headings in the page, solving the problem of the horizontal scrollbar that appeared. Removing a list style from the unordered list tag removes the bullet point symbols and the negative left margin undoes the indenting that comes with the list.

12. That is it! There is more tweaking we could do, but remember, in designing for mobile devices, less really is more. Exit the Multiscreen Preview by selecting **Window** | **Multiscreen Preview** to deselect this view. Save your page with changes to the CSS.

# Summary

Older versions of HTML and CSS allowed Media Queries to identify output devices including printers, Braille readers, and audio reader devices. New additions in HTML5 and CSS3 allow Media Queries to detect screen size (in pixels), as well as other more esoteric properties of a browsing environment.

Dreamweaver's Multiscreen Preview and Media Queries dialogs work together to preview and edit how the same HTML page content will display differently in a smartphone, a tablet, and a full-sized monitor.

In the next chapter, we will explore new tools in Dreamweaver, which provide for applying CSS3 effects such as rounded rectangles, drop shadows, and rotated, scaled, and skewed boxes.

# 6

# Applying CSS3 Effects and Transforms

CSS3—the current version of style sheets—provides easy access to *effects* such as drop-shadows, rounded box corners, and opacity (transparency). In addition, CSS3 introduces *transforms* that change the shape, location, rotation, and size of objects. Together, CSS3 effects and transforms open the door to making web pages more dynamic, more inviting, less "boxy", and more interactive.

Effects and transforms can be made interactive by changing the appearance of objects as he/she hovers over them with a mouse. Together, effects and transforms, with or without animation, make it much easier than previous tools to add accessible, inviting design elements, and dynamism to web pages.

CSS3 effects and transforms are defined through *style sheets* and thus we can take advantage of Dreamweaver's CSS Styles panel to avoid much recourse to hand coding to create them, if any.

In this chapter, we will explore:

- Defining and applying CSS3 transforms: translate, scale, rotate, and skew

- Defining and applying CSS3 effects: border radius, shadows, opacity

- Combining multiple transforms and effects

- Making CSS3 transforms and effects interactive with hover pseudo-classes

# New in CSS3: Effects and transforms

CSS3 effects such as shadows, rounded corners, and opacity can make web pages more stylish, less harsh, and more welcoming. Used with discretion (that is, not overused), they give web pages that nice *je ne sais quoi* that visitors can't exactly put their finger on, but that make their experience at a web page more intriguing and positive.

Effects and transforms can be, and often should be combined to produce eye-catching elements. For example, the following text, has both a skew transform and a shadow (box-shadow) effect applied.

Transitions, such as skewing, rotation, scaling, and translation (moving) objects are particularly engaging when combined with interactivity. For example, a visitor to a website who hovers over an object experiences a subtle but inviting change in it.

In the pre-CSS3 era, these kinds of effects or transitions required some combination coding, and embedding Flash objects, relied on (and programming with) JavaScript, substituting images with Photoshop effects for features such as shadows or outlining. The other tools that there were (are!) expensive and/or have a high learning curve.

In the course of this chapter, we will explore several new effects, and all the new 2D (two-dimensional) transforms in CSS3. Beyond the scope of our survey are the 3D transforms that are much less widely supported in browsing environments, and that—in general—require additional scripting (usually JavaScript) to make them effective.

The bulk of this chapter will consist of walking through how to create particular CSS3 effects and transforms.

# Compatibility challenges

Within parameters, we will now introduce and explore in more detail the compatibility challenges in the course of this chapter. CSS3 effects and transitions are widely supported without the need for plugins (such as JavaScript or Flash).

On the other hand, it is important to emphasize that HTML5 and CSS3 feature all this as work in progress. In searching for a formulation to describe the state of support for CSS3 in browsers, I bumped into the formulation: irregular standardization. I realized that's an oxymoron, but what I mean is that the CSS3 effects and transforms we are creating in this chapter *are*—generally speaking—supported in current versions of all major browsers (and yes, that generally includes Internet Explorer 9, along with Safari for mobile and desktop; Firefox, and Opera).

However, Safari, Firefox, and Opera all require unique code prefixes. For example, the CSS3 code to apply rounded corners to a 150 pixel square box with a thick red border might look like the following:

```
#box {
    height: 150px;

    width: 150px;
    border: thick solid #F00;

    -webkit-border-radius: 10px;

    -moz-border-radius: 10px;

    -o-border-radius: 10px

    border-radius: 10px;
}
```

The -webkit-border-radius code applies to Safari and other browsers that adhere to the webkit standard (which includes, by the way, Dreamweaver's Live View). The -moz-border-radius code applies to Mozilla Firefox. The -o-border-radius code applies to the Opera browser. Moreover, the generic border-radius code applies to "everyone else" including Internet Explorer 9, which does not require a browser prefix to interpret these (or other) effects. These standards are, as noted, work in progress, and by the time you read this book, they will have evolved in one form or another. However, at this stage of the game, we need to provide alternative code for different browsers.

The lack of standardized coding is not as big a problem as it might seem. It just requires a bit of redundancy as we define and apply effects and transforms.

What about browsing environments, like older versions of Internet Explorer, that do not support CSS3 effects and transforms at all? There is an easy and a hard answer to that challenge. The hard solution is to patch together JavaScript and other coding solutions that can be found online or concocted to simulate the effects and transforms that were not supported in CSS3. This means, you can revert to tools and techniques such as JavaScript and Flash that were required to produce these effects before the advent of CSS3.

The easier and probably more sensible solution in most cases it to employ transforms and effects in ways that do not *require* a browser to support the effect in order for a visitor to absorb page content. For example, look at the rounded rectangle in the following screenshot that is created using the border-radius effect.

In the preceding example, if someone visits this page in an older version of Internet Explorer like IE6 he/she will forgo the experience of seeing the type in a circle (defined by the border-radius effect). Not quite as inviting an experience, but they will still be able to read the text, as shown in the following screenshot:

Lorem ipsum dolor sit amet, consectetur adipiscing elit. Phasellus nec lacus tellus. Aenean ac euismod lectus. Aliquam ac tristique est. Etiam mattis pretium libero eget tristique. Phasellus convallis dignissim tellus, nec consectetur dui molestie ornare. Nam neque justo, mollis quis suscipit vitae, consectetur nec lacus.

Aenean commodo, nunc vitae pretium dictum, nulla augue dictum lorem, in scelerisque sapien neque ut felis. Sed sit amet dui eget libero consequat aliquet. Proin libero leo, adipiscing eget adipiscing ut, pretium sit amet dolor. Vestibulum ultricies feugiat hendrerit. Mauris varius tincidunt tellus, a euismod mi vehicula lobortis. Aenean ante libero, aliquam vitae ultrices eget, venenatis sit amet nibh. In hac habitasse platea dictumst. Mauris auctor, ante ac gravida interdum, dui arcu malesuada ligula, sit amet congue elit arcu at ante. Fusce convallis egestas adipiscing. Donec ullamcorper adipiscing convallis. Aenean eget blandit libero. Nulla a odio sed nibh luctus tincidunt. Etiam tempor enim in ligula pellentesque congue.

**Cutting edge... but accessible**: Here we should emphasize a theme that has been alluded to throughout this book. Design sites and pages so that they take advantage of new HTML5 and CSS3 tools to provide an inviting, modern experience for visitors using browsers up to current standards, while making sure content is still accessible for visitors with out-of-date browsers.

Before diving into *how* to apply transforms and effects, let's reflect for a moment on the advantages involved in using these CSS3 features to format the examples we have previewed so far:

- No Flash or JavaScript was created, injured, mistreated, or worse in creating these effects. All that was required was a few lines of CSS that we will generate in Dreamweaver's CSS Styles panel.

- It was not necessary to use "image text", type saved as an image, to create these effects. The page can load almost instantly, without waiting for an image to download.

- In the absence of plugins or images, the shaping and formatting downloads more or less instantly, without browsers having to mess with plugins or downloaded images.

- Finally, the text is still selectable. Meaning that text to which transforms or effects have been applied can still be copied and pasted into a map program, a calendar event, or selected as a text link as shown in the following screenshot:

# CSS3 styles in Dreamweaver's HTML5 Pack

Having surveyed the advantages of using CSS3 styles, let's explore the best way to generate them in Dreamweaver.

Dreamweaver's HTML5 Pack provides some features for defining and applying CSS3 effects. While not the most powerful tools in Dreamweaver, they do make it possible to create and apply new CSS3 techniques without resorting to coding, or where coding is essential Dreamweaver with the HTML5 Pack helps out with code hints.

Dreamweaver CS5.5 introduces interactive dialogs in the CSS Styles panel for defining border radius and box shadow parameters, and we will explore how those work.

There are essentially two options for getting our money's worth out of Dreamweaver as we generate CSS3 transforms and effects. If we enter CSS code in Code view, Dreamweaver (with the HTML5 Pack) will help with the coding by supplying code hints.

For example, the following screenshot shows a code hint being offered after
-moz-bor has been entered in Code view, code hints for the style sheet provide
easy access to the border-radius attribute.

```
}
.box {
    margin:
    padding:
    float: 1
    height:
    width: 1
    -webkit-
    -moz-bor
    background-color: #000;
    text-align: center;
    border: thick;
    color: yellow;
}
```

- border-bottom-colors
- border-left-colors
- border-right-colors
- border-top-colors
- border-end
- border-end-color
- border-end-style
- border-end-width
- border-image
- border-radius

**Redundant CSS code**: The preceding screenshot shows what is a big
part of an ongoing dimension of defining and applying CSS3 transforms
and effects. You have to create four versions of the code, one for Webkit
(Safari), one for Mozilla (Firefox), and one for Opera (a browser with a
large user base in Europe), and a generic version (with no browser prefix)
that is recognized by Internet Explorer 9. We will return to this challenge
shortly in this chapter.

The other option is to generate CSS3 effects and transforms in the CSS Styles panel.
The downside to this is that these new CSS3 style rules do not show up in the CSS
Rule Definition dialog, normally the most user-friendly and intuitive environment
for defining CSS Styles in Dreamweaver.

You *can* however, enter CSS3 effects and transforms through the **Add Property** link at the bottom of the CSS Styles panel. Moreover, Dreamweaver CS5 (or older versions with the HTML5 Pack installed) *will* generate CSS code based on the style rules and parameters you enter in the CSS Styles panel. With this option, Dreamweaver *will* at least "bust" you if you attempt to enter an invalid CSS3 rule as shown here (in the following example, I *should* be entering `-moz-transform` and then defining the skew transform in the right column in the CSS Styles panel).

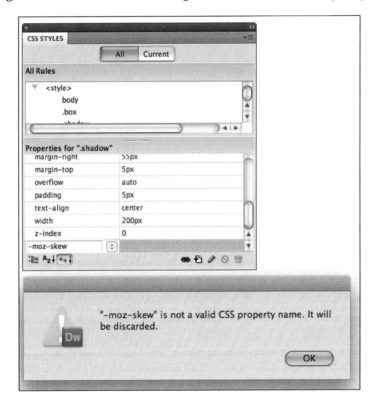

Beyond these tools, Dreamweaver CS5.5 has added intuitive features for defining CSS3 effects, which we will look at shortly.

# CSS3 effects

As noted already, support for CSS3 effects and transforms is irregular, and a work in progress. Within that framework, the four available transforms (`scale`, `translate`, `rotate`, and `skew`) are relatively stable and widely supported. Effects, on the other hand, are even less consistently supported, and less finite in the sense of there being a "list" of available effects that are supported (albeit with unique coding prefixes) across browsing environments.

Part of the reason for this is that a number of effects are very flexible. For example, the `text-shadow` effect can be tweaked to produce outlined type, as shown in the following screenshot:

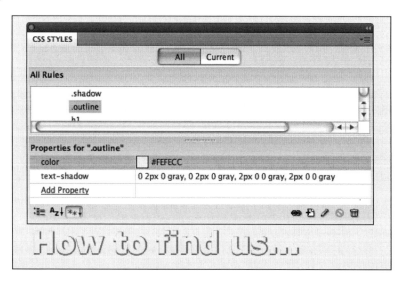

With what has been discussed so far about the flexible and open-ended nature of CSS3 effects, let's examine three of the most useful effects: opacity, border radius, and shadow (for both boxes and text).

# Opacity

The opacity effect in CSS3 allows you to apply varying degrees of opacity / transparency to objects. Full opacity (a value of 1) is normal; the object to which opacity is applied covers over everything else. Full transparency (a value of 0) makes an object invisible. An opacity value of .6 makes an object 60% opaque, and so on.

In spite of all the preceding warnings that CSS3 effects have to be defined specifically for different browsers, the opacity effect is one that does *not* require a prefix for identifying target browsers.

> **Simple… or Complicated**: With CSS3, implementing opacity (transparency) is quite simple…. or, rather hopelessly complex, depending on what one is aiming for. If you are trying to use the opacity effect to create a complex set of layered objects, with various elements having their own assigned opacity, then that requires coding that is complex, and not supported with any uniformity at all among browsers.

Opacity can be applied to a tag (conceivably, for example, the img tag that defines how images appear). Of more efficacy is the technique of defining a class style that applies opacity. You can do that with the following steps:

1. In the **CSS Styles** panel, click on the **New CSS Rule** icon at the bottom of the panel to launch the **New CSS Rule** dialog. Choose **Class** from the **Selector Type** popup; enter a name (no spaces or special characters – **semi_opaque** would work) and select your external style sheet from the **Rule Definition** popup. Click on **OK**.

2. The **CSS Rule Definition** dialog opens. Sadly, as discussed earlier, CSS3 effects cannot be defined in the CSS Rule Definition dialog. So, simply click on **OK** to create a new CSS rule with no properties at this point. However, the new rule *will* appear in the CSS Styles panel and here we will define opacity settings.

3. With your newly created class style selected in the CSS Styles panel, click on the **Add Property** link in the bottom half of the CSS Styles panel. In the first column, type **opacity** and press the *Tab* key to move to the second column. In the second column, type a value between 0 (for complete transparency) and 1 (for full opacity). The value .5, for example, as shown here, defines 50% transparency.

With the class style defined, you can apply it to selected objects (like an image) by choosing the class style from the **Properties** inspector, as shown in the following screenshot:

You can test opacity effects in different browsers. While opacity is not supported in all browsers, particularly older versions of browsers, usually its application is such that if it works, it can enhance a page, but if it doesn't work, no essential content is lost. The following screenshot shows an image with full opacity, and again (on the left) with .5 opacity applied, viewed in Firefox. The image with the .5 opacity setting allows visitors to see some page background behind the semi-opaque second version of the graphical text.

# Border radius

The CSS3 `border-radius` effect is used to define rounded corners. At the time of this writing, it *was* necessary to use browser-specific prefixes when defining a border radius.

Dreamweaver CS5.5 provides new interface tools for defining a `border-radius` effect interactively, using a simple popup dialog. If you are working in an older version of Dreamweaver, you will type the parameters directly into the CSS Styles panel. Let's dive right into an example and examine both options.

In this case, we will create and apply a class style that applies 12 pixel radius rounded corners to a 150 pixel square box with a yellow background, and a thick, solid red line around it. In the previous discussion of creating a class style to apply opacity effects, we used the technique of building the class style in the CSS Styles panel. That worked well because opacity effects are pretty simple. Here, let's build the style in a CSS style sheet. Assuming you have an external style sheet linked to an open web page in Dreamweaver, you can add this code to the CSS file to define a `border-radius` class style:

```
.box {
    background-color: yellow;
    height: 150px;
    width: 150px;
```

```
    border-radius: 12px;
    border: thick solid red;
    -webkit-border-radius: 12px;
    -moz-borer-radius: 12px;
}
```

The following screenshot shows this class style applied to selected text in Dreamweaver:

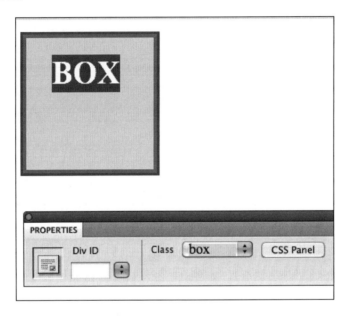

In a browser, the preceding screenshot looks like the following screenshot:

In Dreamweaver CS5.5, border-radius parameters can be defined with a popup in the CSS Styles panel that appears when you click on the arrow in the right-side column in the bottom half of the panel. The coolest thing about this is that you can adjust the parameters of an external CSS file (style sheet) in the CSS Styles panel, and examine the effect on the page in Live view, as shown in the following screenshot:

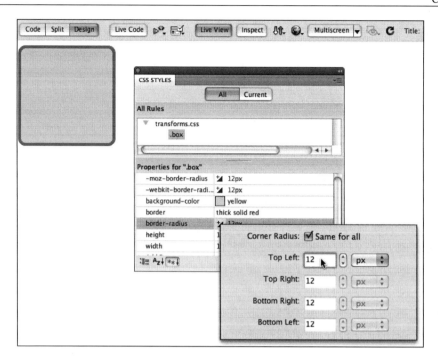

One fun technique to try is to create a circle effect by making the rounded-radius value equal to half the height (and width) of a square box. The following example shows the effect, with the values adjusted from the earlier example so that the rounded-radius is 75 pixels, half the 150 pixels that define the dimensions of the original square.

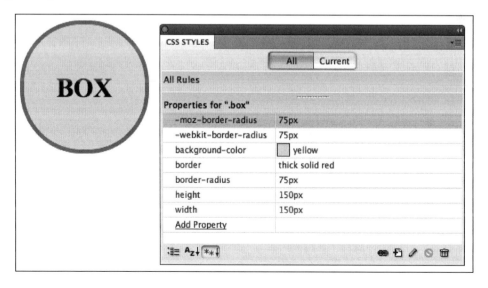

# Shadows

Drop-shadows may well be the most widely applied effect in graphic design. Don't quote me on that, but certainly shadows are a ubiquitous element in many designs, and now they are easy to apply to selected objects using CSS3.

There are two different shadow effects: box-shadow, and text-shadow. The application of them is pretty self-explanatory, box shadows apply to boxes, and text shadows to text.

Both `box-shadow` and `text-shadow` effects are defined with a minimum of two parameters: x-offset (vertical distance), and y-offset (horizontal distance). In addition, they usually include a blur parameter (the thickness of the blur gradient) and a color (if no color is specified, a browser default color appears).

The x and y offset values can be positive or negative. Positive values generate a shadow to the right of the text, while negative values generate a shadow to the left of the text. For the offset-y values, positive values generate a shadow below the text, while negative values create a shadow above the text. Values are normally defined in pixels.

Before examining how this works for boxes, text, and outlines, it is useful to note that *multiple* shadow definitions can be combined. So, for example, if you wish to generate a shadow under *and* over text (and you will want to do this when you define an outline style), you can combine two, or even three shadow definitions, and they stack on top of each other.

# Box shadow

As noted, `box-shadow` effects, are usually defined with four parameters: offset-x (horizontal distance), offset-y (vertical distance), blur (width in pixels), and the color of the shadow.

The following code, for example, defines a box shadow with 5 pixels of horizontal and vertical offset, a blur length of 5 pixels, and a gray shadow — and does so for four different browsers, Safari, Firefox, (using the un-prefixed code) Internet Explorer 9, and Opera.

```
.shadow {
    box-shadow: 5px 5px 5px gray;
    -webkit-box-shadow: 5px 5px 5px gray;
    -moz-box-shadow: 5px 5px 5px gray;
}
```

Opera and Internet Explorer 9 support the box-shadow effect with no prefix.

Dreamweaver CS5.5 has added an interactive popup for defining parameters for the box-shadow effect. Here's how that looks in the CSS Styles panel (and you could define the class style in the CSS Styles panel).

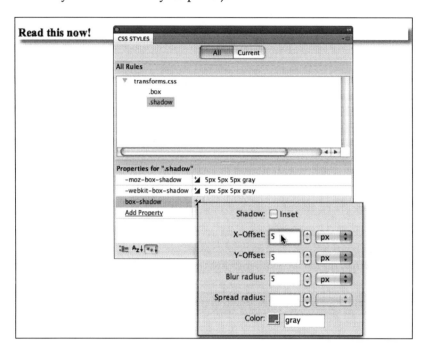

# Text shadow

The text-shadow effect is very similar to the box-shadow effect except that it is applied to text, not boxes. Moreover, for whatever reason, unlike the box-shadow effect, which requires a special prefix for Firefox, the text-shadow effect does not require vendor-prefixes.

The parameters for the text-shadow effect are the same as those of box shadows: you define four values: x-offset, y-offset, blur distance, and color. Without the hassle of creating three versions of the effect, the following CSS code can be used to define a text shadow with 5 pixels of horizontal and vertical offset, a blur value of 5, and a gray color.

```
.text_shadow {

    text-shadow: 5px 5px 5px gray;
}
```

The `text-shadow` effect settings in the preceding example produce an effect as shown in the following screenshot:

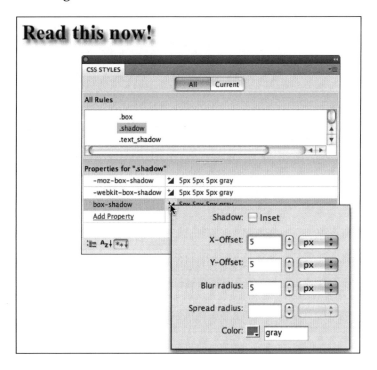

## Text outline

As alluded to earlier in this chapter, there is no such thing as a "text outline" effect. However, there *is* a way to apply text outlines using the `text-shadow` effect. In general, this involves matching the text color of the "outlined" type with the page background, and then defining a particularly thin, black "shadow" with no blur at all that looks like an outline.

Creating effective outline effects requires stacking additional defining parameters, in order to stack up very thin "shadows" both above and below, and to the right, and left of text to which the style is applied. For example, applied to text that sits on a white page background, the following class style combines (stacks) three different sets of parameters to create an outline effect.

```
.outline {
    text-shadow: 0 1px 0 black, 0 -1px 0 black, 1px 0 0 black,
      -1px 0 0 black;
    color: white;
}
```

This level of detail is not supported by the new popup feature in the CSS Styles panel of Dreamweaver CS5.5. Therefore, we have to enter the parameters by hand in the right column in the bottom half of the CSS Styles panel. Here's how that looks in a browser, and in the CSS Styles panel.

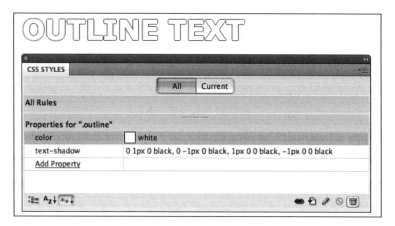

Essentially the preceding code generates a thin (1 pixel) "shadow" below the text, another one below the text, and a third 1 pixel thick "shadow" above the text. For a thicker outline, you could increase the pixel values uniformly to two pixels.

# CSS3 transforms

The four CSS3 *transitions* `resize`, `translate` (move), `rotate`, and `skew` are applied to selected content as *effects*. That is to say, they change the *display* or *appearance* of objects, but not their underlying properties.

These transformations make it possible to present distortions of text or images that, before the advent of CSS3, normally was done through images using an image of text to present that text skewed, rotated, or scaled.

Rather than pushing my written communication skills beyond their limits, let's take advantage of the following screenshot to illustrate these four transitions:

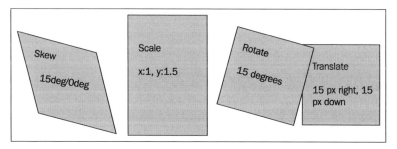

# When to use transforms

The skew and rotate transforms can be used to present text or images in an intriguing and unique way, while maintaining the user's ability to select (and copy, paste, click on, and so on) *text*. The translate transform can be used to place one block of content over another (as in the illustration above). The scale transform can be used to stretch, or resize type or images.

[ **When images overlap**: When two div tags overlap, the one that appears in front will be the one with the highest z-index value. You can set z-index in the CSS Styles Panel. ]

In many instances, these effects work well as interactive animation, where a visitor triggers the transform by hovering over an object with his or her mouse. We will explore that technique as the final element of this chapter.

As with the CSS3 effects explored earlier in this chapter, transitions can be applied to tags such as a heading (h1, h2, and so on) and images (using the img tag). Alternatively, more typically, class styles are defined to apply these transitions.

# How to generate transition coding in Dreamweaver

Before examining the relatively basic syntax necessary for defining a transform, a bit of disappointing news to Dreamweaver CS5.5 users, those cool pop ups that helped define at least some effect parameters in the CSS Styles panel for CSS3 transitions are not available for transforms. That means we'll be entering those parameters from our keyboards.

You *cannot* define transforms in the CSS Rule Definition dialog. You can apply CSS2 (earlier) styles that way, rules such as background color, font definition, and so on. However, we would search in vain though the categories in Dreamweaver's CSS Rule Definition dialog for skew, scale, transform, or rotate. Therefore, our two choices remain a) type CSS code in Split or Code view, directly into the CSS file; or b) use the limited resources of the CSS Styles panel to define transforms.

I will let you jump back and review the more detailed discussion earlier in the chapter for a more step-by-step walk-through of how to either enter code in the CSS file you are working with, or define styles using the CSS Styles panel. But there is one, new factor to examine here, you get a bit more help in the CSS Styles panel defining transform parameters than you do for the effects (such as shadows) explored earlier in this chapter.

Here's how that additional help works. In the course of adding a rule to a style in the CSS Styles panel, if you enter one of the transform options (`-webkit-transform`, `--moz-transform`, or `- transform`) in the bottom of the CSS Styles panel, Dreamweaver supplies a popup in the second column of the panel with various transform options, as shown in the following screenshot:

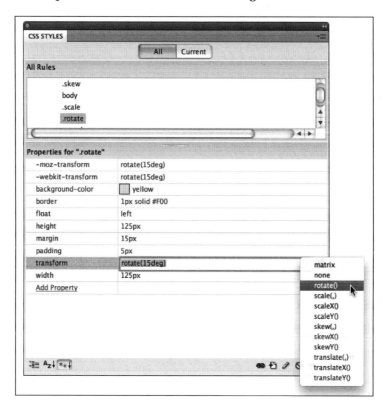

Bottom line is you have to decide which environment is more comfortable for you in generating the CSS3 code for transforms. In the exploration of the specific transforms in the remainder of this chapter, I will give away my own choice (just typing coding in Code view). However, when you are becoming familiar with the CSS3 code for transforms, you might find the popup help in the CSS Styles panel helpful.

# Resizing with scale

Scaling is defined by two parameters, x, and y. The x value defines how much to increase or (with a value less than one) decrease width, and the y value applies to height. Values are normally multipliers, so that a value of 2 = 200%, or doubling the size, and a value of .5 = 50% or reducing the size to half of the original value.

The following lines of code apply a scale transform that leaves the width of the object unchanged, but increases the height by 50%:

```
transform: scale(1,1.5);
-webkit-transform: scale(1,1.5);
-moz-transform: scale(1,1.5);
-o-transform: scale(1,1.5);
```

Here's a sample of a class style (called .scale) that incorporates the preceding code, and defines a class style that generates a 125 pixel square (before rescaling) box with scaling:

```
.scale {
    height: 125px;
    width: 125px;
    background-color: yellow;
    transform: scale(1,1.5);
    -webkit-transform: scale(1,1.5);
    -moz-transform: scale(1,1.5);
    -o-transform: scale(1,1.5);
    float: left;
    margin: 15px;
    padding:5px;
    border:1px solid #F00
}
```

 **Floating the box**: In the preceding example, the float attribute allows us to arrange a bunch of these, or similar boxes, in a single row.

# Moving with translate

The translate transform moves objects relative to the position they are inserted in a web page. As noted earlier, this can be an effective technique for having boxes, including boxes of selectable text, overlapped on a page.

The syntax for the translate transform is similar to that for the scale transform except that the first parameter, the x value, defines how far to the right (left, if you use a negative value); the y value defines how far down (up if you use a negative value) the object will move. Values are normally defined in pixels.

Here's the same class style we used as an example for the `scale` transform in the preceding section, but with the `translate` transform set to move the object 35 pixels to the left, and 15 pixels down:

```
.translate {
    height: 125px;
    width: 125px;
    background-color: yellow;
    transform: translate(-35px,15px);
    -webkit-transform: translate(-35px,15px);
    -moz-transform: translate(-35px,15px);
    -o-transform: translate(-35px,15px);
    float: left;
    margin: 15px;
    padding:5px;
    border:1px solid #F00
}
```

# Applying rotation

The `rotate` transform is perhaps the simplest to define, as there is only one parameter, rotation angle. That angle can be positive (rotates clockwise) or negative (rotates counter-clockwise).

Here's an example of code that rotates an object 15 degrees clockwise:

```
transform: rotate(15deg);
-webkit-transform:rotate(15deg);
-moz-transform:rotate(15deg);
-o-transform:rotate(15deg);
```

Moreover, the following code is an example of a class style that rotates an object 15 degrees, with the same size and other attributes of the examples we have used previously:

```
.rotate {
    height: 125px;
    width: 125px;
    background-color: yellow;
    transform: rotate(15deg);
    -webkit-transform:rotate(15deg);
    -moz-transform:rotate(15deg);
    -o-transform:rotate(15deg);
    float: left;
```

```
        margin: 15px;
        padding:5px;
        border:1px solid #F00
    }
```

 **Caution – Leave space for rotate (and skew)**: When you rotate an object (or, as we will see, if you skew it), the object will overlap with nearby objects. Typically (unless such overlap is part of the design), this is addressed by adding margin values to the object style large enough to prevent overlap.

# Creating a skew transition

The skew transform is defined by two parameters, separated by a comma. The first defines the x-axis (horizontal) transform in degrees; the second value defines vertical distortion. If you use zero as a value for one of the two axes, the result is a parallelogram, as shown in the following screenshot:

Here's an example of code for a class tag that applies the yellow background, red border, and other attributes of our preceding examples, that skews an object 15 degrees on box axes:

```
    transform: skew(15deg);
    -webkit-transform:skew(15deg);
    -moz-transform:skew(15deg);
    -o-transform:skew(15deg);
```

In addition, the following code is an example of a class style that rotates, skews an object 15 degrees, with the same size and other attributes of the examples we have used previously:

```
    .skew {
        height: 125px;
        width: 125px;
```

```
    background-color: yellow;
    transform: skew(15deg,15deg);
    -webkit-transform: skew(15deg,15deg);
    -moz-transform: skew(15deg,15deg);
    -o-transform: skew(15deg,15deg);
    float: left;
    margin: 25px;
    padding:5px;
    border:1px solid #F00
}
```

# Other CS3 transform effects

In addition to the two dimensional (2D) transform effects of CSS3 that we have explored in this chapter, there are other three-dimensional (3D) transforms in emerging states of support. They are, in general, not supported by any browsers except the webkit set (Safari and Chrome), and from what I have been able to understand, at this point they are not that applicable without additional JavaScript that animates them.

That said; stay tuned. The world of CSS3 transforms is one of constant motion and development, and 3D transforms may gain broader support and become more accessible to developers.

# Compound transforms

You can combine as many as all four transforms into a single transform rule. For example, to create a transform that applies skew (5 degrees on both the x and y axes), scale (1.5 multiple on both the x and y axes), and rotate (45 degrees), with a prefix that works with webkit browsers, you would use this code:

```
  -webkit-transform: skew(5deg,5deg) scale(1.5, 1.5) rotate(45deg);
```

As transforms tend to apply rather radical changes to objects, and given that skew and rotate create similar effects, the aesthetic and accessibility that warrant combining multiple transforms in a single object are limited; however, available.

# Interactive effects and transforms

Having surveyed and walked through the process of creating and applying CSS3 effects and transforms, we now turn to one of the most exciting, dynamic aspects of these new style features: interactivity.

By interactivity, we mean that an object or elements of a page react to a visitor's action with their own action. A visitor hovers over an object, and that object moves, resizes, rotates, skews, develops a shadow, becomes semi-transparent, or some undergo some other change.

There are two basic techniques for combining interactivity with effects and transforms. One of these techniques is to use JavaScript along with transforms and effects to create interactivity.

The other, more accessible technique is to avail ourselves of the widely supported, and easy to use :hover pseudo-class. If you are familiar with defining a "hover" state for a link, where a link takes on a unique appearance when hovered over, you have a basic idea of how this is going to work. Moreover, we will walk through that in more detail in the following section.

# Effects and JavaScript

There are several definite limitations to creating interactive effects and transforms with JavaScript that place it beyond the scope of what we can address in this book. The first is that in order to implement this approach, one needs to know JavaScript, and while that knowledge is available in thick books, massive online resources, and pay-to-use tools that generate JavaScript, it is well beyond what I could cover in this chapter, let alone this book. Further, JavaScript is not universally supported

in browsing environments, and much of the appeal of HTML5 and CSS3 is that, with proper accounting for non-HTML5 environments, nearly everything we are exploring in this book will work, or at least not cause harm in any browsing environment.

Dreamweaver's under-rated but also under-supported tool for generating JavaScript, the Behaviors panel, does not support CSS3 effects and transforms, and thus is, yet, impotent when it comes to combining JavaScript and effects and transforms.

We have enumerated the drawbacks (and plusses) for combining JavaScript with CSS3 effects and transforms in part because you are likely to encounter examples, models, and much discussion on the Web among developers exploring the cutting edge of CSS3, and combining their work with JavaScript.

# Interactivity with the :hover pseudo-class

There is, however, a much more accessible tool for applying interactive effects and transforms: the :hover pseudo-class.

Pseudo-classes are CSS modifiers that define the appearance of a web page object depending on the state of an object. They are best known for—and most widely applied as— modifiers on links.

By default, for example, unvisited links on a web page are displayed as underlined blue, visited links as underlined purple, and active links as underlined red. These parameters are easily changed in Dreamweaver's CSS Styles panel. *Moreover,* they are supported in every modern and even older browser.

But in addition to the `:visited`, and `:active` pseudo-class styles (pseudo-classes), there is another, more dynamic state, `:hover`. This definable state applies to anything on a page that a visitor hovers his or her mouse over.

By applying effects and transforms to the hover state of an object, you can make it interact in a defined way with a visitor's mouse actions.

# Animating CSS3 transforms in Dreamweaver

Let's now walk through exactly how CSS transforms and effects work with `:hover` pseudo-class.

The basic concept is that you define a `:hover` pseudo-class for the object you wish to transform when hovered over. That object can be an HTML tag (like `img`) or, a div tag (either a class or ID div).

In the case of the `img` tag, for instance, this line of code in the CSS file would define a scale transform increasing height and width by 10% when the image is hovered over:

```
img:hover  {
    -webkit-transform: scale(1.1,1.1);
}
```

Alternatively, to take another example, a div tag, the following code would cause a class style container named .box to rotate 45 degrees when hovered over:

```
.box:hover {
    -webkit-transform:rotate(45deg)
}
```

It will produce an effect as shown in the following screenshot:

# Recipe: Create an animated effect and transform

This recipe creates a class style box that can be reused repeatedly on a page that displays with a CSS3 effect, and a CSS3 transform when hovered over. As such, it is an easily adaptable recipe, you can use the information in this chapter to substitute different effects and transforms that we will use in the recipe.

In our particular scenario, we will apply rounded corners and slightly enlarge the box when it is hovered over.

## Putting the pieces in place

Here's what you need to have in place before diving into this recipe: You need to have defined a Dreamweaver *site*. Jump back to *Chapter 1*, and review the discussion and steps there for creating a Dreamweaver site.

With your site defined you are ready! Everything we need is right in Dreamweaver CS5. Let's first set up the files we need:

1.  Choose **File | New** to open the **New Document** dialog. Choose **Blank Page** in the **Category** column, **HTML** in the **Page Type** column, and **<none>** in the **Layout** column. From the **DocType** popup, choose **HTML5**. The **Attach CSS File** box should be blank at this point. With the new file defined, click on **Create** to create a new, blank Dreamweaver page.

2.  Enter **Hover** in the title area of the Document toolbar. Choose **File | Save** and assign a filename. Let's use `hover.html`.

3.  Next, we will create the CSS file that will hold our styles, particularly the CSS3 effect and transform styles we will be using. Choose **File | New**. The **New Document** dialog opens.

4.  Select **CSS** in the **Page Type** category and click on the **Create** button. Save the CSS file, use the filename `hover.css`. A blank CSS page opens.

5.  Select the HTML file. You can do this from the files tabs at the top of the Dreamweaver Document window, or to avoid any possible confusion (given we have two similarly named files open), click on the **Window** menu and click on the `hover.html` file.

6.  In the HTML page (you can be in any of the three views, but Design view works fine), choose **Window | CSS Styles** to display the CSS Styles panel (if that panel is not visible).

7. Click the **Attach Style Sheet** link icon at the bottom of the CSS Styles panel, and navigate to and link the `hover.css` style sheet file. The (empty) style sheet file appears in the CSS Styles panel. You can see all the elements we have defined so far, and your screen should look at this point like the one shown in the following screenshot:

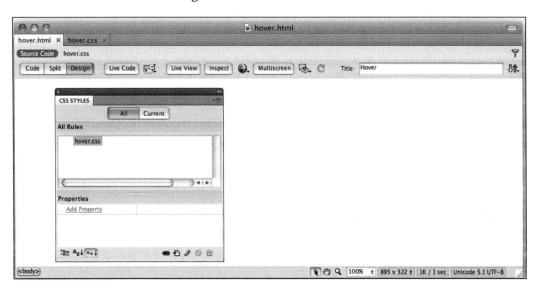

 **Setup**: With our HTML page and CSS style sheet file defined, saved, and linked, it's showtime! We will define two elements to make our hoverable box operative: the box itself, and a hover pseudo-class that activates the scale transform and the rounded corners effect. We will do that next…

8. Click the **New CSS Rule** icon at the bottom of the **CSS Styles** panel to open the **New CSS Rule** dialog. From the **Selector Type** pop-up, choose **class** in the **Selector Name** box, type **box**. In the **Rule Definition** area (if `hover.css` is not already selected) choose it from the **Rule Definition** pop up). Click on **OK** to open the **CSS Rule Definition** dialog for `.box` in `hover.css`.

9.  In the **Background** category of the **CSS Rule Definition** dialog, choose a light colored background color (such as yellow). In the **Box** category, apply the following rules as illustrated below. Don't click on **OK** yet! We will define a border next.

    ◦ **Width**: **200 px**

    ◦ **Height**: **200 px**

    ◦ **Float**: **left**

    ◦ **Padding**: **25** (for all)

    ◦ **Margin**: **50** (for all)

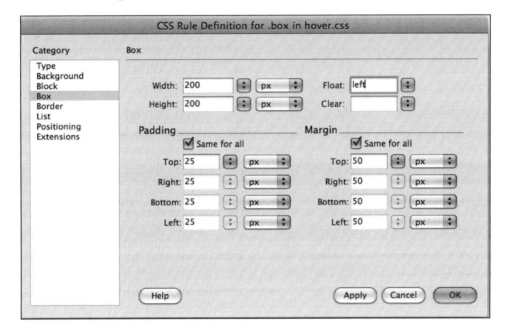

A note on the settings: We are creating a 200 pixel square box, which is a nice size to hold a sidebar message or picture and caption. We floated it left so other content can wrap around the box on the right. The large margin and padding provides plenty of flexibility for effects that might expand box, or impinge on the space of nearby elements.

10. Next, let's create kind of a fun border. In the **Border** category of the **CSS Rule Definition** dialog, define the border as dashed, thick, and red as shown in the following screenshot. Then click on **OK** to create the style rule.

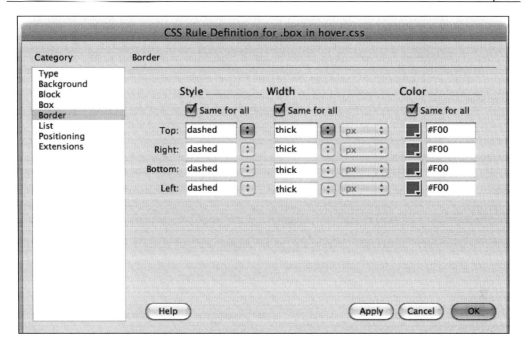

11. Let's now place one (or your option, more than one) instance of this class style on the page. Choose **Insert | Layout Objects** to open the **Insert Div Tag** dialog. Choose **box** from the **Class** popup and click on **OK**. Note that you can do this repeatedly if you wish to use this box as a page design element, as shown in the following screenshot. You can also use this figure to double-check the rules for the .box class style in the CSS Styles panel.

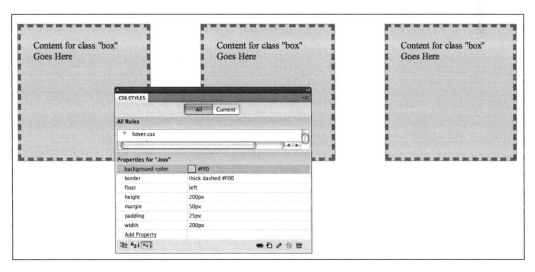

**Final steps**: We can now define the hover pseudo-class style to animate this box with scaling and rounded corners. We were able to create a sized, floated box with a defined border using Dreamweaver CS5's CSS Styles panel and dialogs. For the CSS3 styles required in the next step we won't be quite so lucky. We will define a style using the CSS Styles panel. However, we will have to enter the CSS3 style code ourselves using just Dreamweaver CS5's code hints.

12. Click on the **New CSS Rule** icon at the bottom of the **CSS Styles** panel to open the **New CSS Rule** dialog. From the **Selector Type** popup, choose **Compound;** in the **Selector Name** box, type **.box:hover**. In the **Rule Definition** area, if hover.css is not already selected, choose it from the **Rule Definition** pop up). Click on **OK** to open the **CSS Rule Definition** dialog for .box:hover in hover.css.

13. As the rules we need are not available in the **CSS Rule Definition** dialog, click on **OK** to save the style **.box:hover** with no rules as yet.

14. Choose **Window |** hover.css to open the CSS styles file in Dreamweaver's code view.  Refer to the figure below for coding to define a scale transition that bumps the size of the box up a noticeable but not obnoxious 2%, and applies subtle rounded corners. The code makes this effect accessible for Safari (-webkit); IE9 (generic); Opera (-o); and Firefox (-moz) users.

```
hover.html ×   hover.css ×
Source Code   hover.css

Code  Split  Design    Live Code      Live View  Inspect   Multiscreen

 1    @charset "UTF-8";
 2    /* CSS Document */
 3
 4    .box {
 5        background-color: #FF0;
 6        margin: 50px;
 7        padding: 25px;
 8        float: left;
 9        height: 200px;
10        width: 200px;
11        border: thick dashed #F00;
12    }
13    .box:hover {
14        -webkit-transform:scale(1.02);
15        -webkit-border-radius: 10px;
16        -transform:scale(1.02);
17        -border-radius: 10px;
18        -o-transform:scale(1.02);
19        -o-border-radius: 10px;
20        -moz-transform:scale(1.02);
21        -moz-border-radius: 10px;
22        }
23    |
```

The code here specifically for the `.box:hover` style is:

```
.box:hover {
        -webkit-transform:scale(1.02);
        -webkit-border-radius: 10px;
        -o-transform:scale(1.02);
        -o-border-radius: 10px;
        -moz-transform:scale(1.02);
        -moz-border-radius: 10px;
        transform:scale(1.02);
        border-radius: 10px;
        }
```

15. Save the CSS file (choose **File | Save**). Use the **Window** menu to return to the `hover.html` page. Test the effect and transform in Live view, as well as other browsers using the **File | Preview** in browser. The following screenshot shows the effect in Firefox, the middle box displays slightly larger with rounded corners.

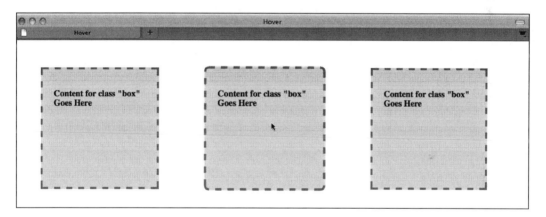

Once again, this is a highly adaptable recipe and can be the basis for creating page layout elements that interact with visitors hovering over them. You could, for example, replace scale with rotate, skew, or even translate to alter the transform. Moreover, you could replace the border-radius effect with shadows or opacity changes.

# Summary

In this chapter, we covered a wide range of effects and transforms available with the emergence of the CSS3 standards for style sheets. Those "standards" are inconsistent, thus a need to provide alternate (prefixed) rules for different browsers.

These transforms and effects are useful as design tools in their own right. And they are even more dynamic design factors when made interactive by defining :hover pseudo-class elements that cause them to appear when (and only when) an object is hovered over.

It cannot be said that at this point Dreamweaver CS5 with the HTML5 Pack fully supports these innovative design techniques. However, we explored how the Dreamweaver framework provides a solid structural backdrop for defining and applying CSS3 transforms and effects. Moreover, we examined Dreamweaver's limited CSS3 tools like the ability to use code hints in Code view, and useful prompts for transforms in the CSS Styles panel.

In the next chapter, we will venture into the world of HTML5 audio, how to create it and how to embed it so that it plays with native (browser-defined) players.

# 7
# Embedding HTML5 Audio in Dreamweaver

In this chapter, we will learn how to add audio to web pages using HTML5. The advantage to embedding audio using HTML5 in Dreamweaver CS5 is that it does not require any external player to work. For browsers that support the HTML5 Audio element, it is the most elegant way to present an audio online.

The Dreamweaver CS5 HTML5 Pack makes adding HTML5 audio painless, without having extensive knowledge of or worrying about HTML coding.

We will learn how to use the HTML5 audio element through several steps:

1.  We will make sure that we are prepared to add HTML5 audio files using Dreamweaver CS5.
2.  We will prepare HTML5-ready digital audio files.
3.  We will embed audio elements in web pages with Dreamweaver CS5.
4.  We will provide alternative audio for non-HTML5 compatible browsers.
5.  We will define additional audio parameters.

We need to perform each of these steps to make sure that the HTML5 audio that we include in our site will work for every visitor.

# Audio and compatibility

Before launching our journey to embedding audio with HTML5, we will step back for just a moment to survey the terrain. Students of the Web ecosystem, including me, have extensive online collections of commentary on the weird state of online audio and video, and you can look that up if you wish. Here, I will provide the most compressed overview of online audio and the framework from which HTML5 audio emerged.

Until HTML5, if you wanted to listen to audio from a website, you had to do so through the agency of a browser plugin of one kind or another. That plugin might have been QuickTime Player (typically on a Mac), Windows Media Player (typically on a Windows computer), Real Media Player, a plugin supplied by your hardware manufacturer, or some other program. This meant that the visual dimension, at least, of experiencing the web audio was almost completely out of the control of the web designer. HTML5 provides what is called native audio (as well as native video, as we will see in the next chapter). Native video does not require a plugin. The player and controls still vary depending on the browsing environment, but with HTML5, the audio player is relatively standardized.

There are two compatibility issues in presenting HTML5 audio, which are as follows:

1. A visitor's browser must be HTML5-complaint.
2. A visitor's browser must support the particular audio format to which the audio is saved.

Therefore, in walking through the process of presenting HTML5 audio, we will explore how to handle both of these compatibility issues.

To elaborate a bit more on compatibility issues: embedding the audio is complicated because of several factors:

- There are competing methods of presenting media online, such as HTML5 versus Flash
- As we saw in *Chapter 4, Building HTML5 Pages from Scratch*, there are different browser standards which support different elements of HTML5
- There are a wide variety of audio formats — WAV, MP3, AIFF, Ogg Vorbis (or OGG) being the main ones

Fortunately, these issues are solvable. So let's get started.

# Laying the groundwork: HTML5 and page-building

Support for HTML5 audio in Dreamweaver—of any version to date—is primitive. Essentially, the help you get, whether you are working in Dreamweaver CS3 or CS4 with the HTML5 Pack, or versions 5 or 5.5, is code hinting in the Code View.

Let me quickly review the essential things you need to work with HTML5 audio in Dreamweaver:

- Make sure that you have the HTML5 Pack installed and loaded.
- If you have not yet, make sure that you have a Dreamweaver site defined. This is an essential first step. In order to learn how to define a site, you can take a look at *Chapter 1* of this book to find out how to do so.
- Make sure that you have a blank Dreamweaver site to use during the tutorial. Learn more about setting up a blank HTML5 site in *Chapter 4*.
- Collect MP3, OGG, and WebM format audio files. Keep in mind that many sites have free MP3 and OGG files which you can use as samples, such as the "Free Music from Artists on the Rise" on Amazon. Put the MP3 and OGG files in your site folder.
- View Dreamweaver CS5's **Document** window in Split mode. We will need to be able to see the code because you cannot use the Design view menu to insert HTML5 Audio into your page.

## Making audio HTML5-ready

The first thing we need to do, before we can put them on our website, is make our audio files HTML-5 ready.

Before sifting through various audio formats to figure out which one goes with which browser, let me provide a very basic overview of audio compression.

## Audio compression

You probably are familiar with at least some of the popular audio formats such as MP3, WAV, AIFF, and so on.

Raw, uncompressed audio files, in the WAV (for Windows) and AIFF (for Macs) formats, provide the highest available online audio sound quality. However, these files are very large, and download too slowly for most users. MP3 audio files, on the other hand, are substantially smaller in file size. A compression algorithm is used to squeeze extra data out of files as they are converted to MP3. Moreover, for most listeners, and most audio files, MP3 quality is sufficient. Thus, when we talk about making audio files available online, we are often talking about compressed audio files in formats such as MP3. Another compressed file format is the OGG format.

# Browser support for audio files

What audio format works in all browsers? Unfortunately, and oddly enough, no one format can be used to embed HTML5 audio for every browser. The four popular browsers Firefox, Chrome, Safari, and Opera all support HTML5 audio, but the different browsers support different formats.

Which audio formats are supported by which browsers changes over time, but as this book goes to press, the breakdown was:

- Firefox 3.6+, Safari 5+, and Opera 10.5+ support WAV format
- Safari 5+ and Chrome 6 support MP3 format
- Firefox 3.6+, Chrome 6, and Opera 10.5+ support the open source, but less common OGG format
- Google (and Google's Chrome browser) are promoting the WebM format

Internet Explorer 9 supports MP3 and WAV through HTML5.

So which format should we use? There is not really a "right" answer to this question, and you can decide for yourself, but if I have to choose just one format, I tend to choose MP3. When you embed HTML5 audio into a page, you are mostly targeting users of Apple products such as the iPhone that uses Apple's own browser, Safari. Moreover, Safari supports the MP3 audio. You could also use WAV, which Safari also supports, as Firefox (a very popular browser) supports WAV as well, but this leads to a problem with the file size. As WAV files are not compressed the way MP3 files are, they take much longer to load. In the meantime, the average visitor will give up, especially if it is a large audio file.

You can choose another file type if you prefer, but be aware that any file type will only work for some browsers. MP3 files are just one solution, and they will also work using alternative audio options.

The most reliable and "standards compliant" solution to presenting HTML5 audio is to provide the option of all three HTML5 supported audio formats, MP3, OGG, and WebM.

# Embedding an HTML5 audio element in a Dreamweaver CS5 web page

Once we have laid the groundwork, we are ready to get started. Carry out the following steps to embed an audio element into your open Dreamweaver CS5 HTML5 page:

1. In the Code part of the Split View, place your cursor right after the `<body>` tag and hit *Enter* on a PC or *Return* on a Mac to create a new line of code.

2. Start typing `<au` and press *Tab* and the HTML5 pack will auto-complete that into the beginning of the `<audio>` tag, as shown in the following screenshot:

```
1    <!DOCTYPE HTML>
2    <html>
3    <head>
4    <meta http-equiv="Content-Type" content="text/html; charset=UTF-8">
5    <title>Untitled Document</title>
6    <link href="styles/html5_layout.css" rel="stylesheet" type="text/css">
7    </head>
8
9    <body>
10   <au
11   </b<> audio
12   </h
13
```

3. Placing your cursor right after the word audio, press the spacebar and a pop-up menu will appear again. Type the letter "s" and then double-click on `src` in the list. This is the code for "source" as in, where the file will come from.

4.  When you select src A **Browse** link will appear. Double-click on the **Browse** link to open the **Select File** dialog, as shown in the following screenshot:

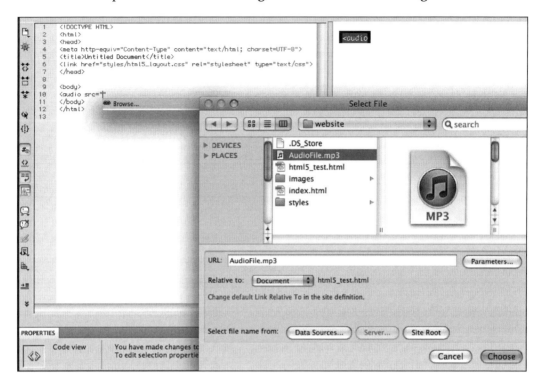

5.  Find the audio file you copied before, in our case an MP3 file (but it could be WAV or OGG). Select that file by double-clicking on it.

6.  You want to have a controller, or player, for this audio, so we will set a parameter to display one. Press the spacebar key again and this time, type "*c*," which in this case will be for controls. Double-click on controls and when a pop-up box appears, double click on controls again as shown in the following screenshot:

```
1    <!DOCTYPE HTML>
2    <html>
3    <head>
4    <meta http-equiv="Content-Type" content="text/html; charset=UTF-8">
5    <title>Untitled Document</title>
6    <link href="styles/html5_layout.css" rel="stylesheet" type="text/css">
7    </head>
8
9    <body>
10   <audio src="AudioFile.mp3" controls="">
11   </body>                                          controls
12   </html>
13
```

7.   Finally, type "</" and it will auto-complete to </audio> which will close the code.

Now we want to preview the file, which we can only do in Safari or Opera, assuming that you chose an MP3. In order to preview in Safari, select **File | Preview in Browser | Safari**. It should look similar to one shown in the following screenshot:

If we had used a WAV or OGG file, then we could perform the same steps, but preview in Firefox instead.

# Alternative media options

So now, you have audio on your page. However, three things are missing:

*   First, your audio player does not have many special features
*   Second, not everyone who visits the site will be able to access the audio file
*   Finally, you could provide different HTML5 supported audio formats as options for different browsing environments, as we have identified earlier, not all HTML5-friendly browsers support the same audio file formats

# Providing alternative HTML5 audio formats

Let's start with providing alternate audio file formats. As we have noted, some HTML5-complaint browsing environments support the MP3 file format, others support the OGG format, and others support WebM.

Therefore, we can make our audio more accessible by providing multiple source files. That way, an HTML5-compliant browser can find and play the file format that meshes with those browsers.

In order to do this, we will vary the HTML we created earlier to separate the player control code from the audio source code. Here is how that code looks:

```
<audio controls="controls">
  <source src="audio.ogg" type="audio/ogg" />
  <source src="audio.mp3" type="audio/mpeg" />
</audio>
```

In the preceding code, you replace audio.ogg or audio.mp3 with your own audio file names.

# Audio for non-HTML5 browsers

For those users whose browsers don't interpret HTML5, such as users using older versions of Internet Explorer or users using other older browsers, we will want to provide an alternative method of accessing the audio. In order to do this, we can create a link to our audio file. If we do this, when the link is clicked, the audio file will open in its own browser. The browser will then use a plugin player such as QuickTime, Flash, or Windows Media to play the audio file. It is not the most elegant solution, but it will work.

In order to do this, we can add a line of code to the HTML we just explored. This line of code creates a text that will appear in browsers that do not interpret (support) the HTML5 <audio> tag and can link to a page that presents an audio in a legacy format such as QuickTime, Windows Media, or Flash Video (FLV).

Here is how that code looks:

```
<audio controls="controls">
   <source src="sound.ogg" type="audio/ogg" />
   <source src="sound.mp3" type="audio/mpeg" />
   Your browser does not support the HTML5 audio element but you
      can hear the audio file <a href="sound.html">here</a>.
</audio>
```

This last line of code, that begins "Your browser...," links to an HTML page (sound.html) that can be used to present the legacy audio format that will play in plugin software on older browsers.

# Adding play parameters

Now that (almost) everyone can access our audio, let's look at what other parameters we can use to add features to our audio element.

When we added the code controls="controls" in defining our source file, we added a control parameter. If you played with the controller in Safari when you tested it out, you have already discovered that this controller will let you play, pause, mute, and restart your MP3. We can also use the bar, or scrubber, to move around in the audio track, rewind, or fast-forward.

There are four significant HTML5 audio parameters we might want to use. To enable each of these parameters, we will want to use the HTML5 code hints the same way we did to enable controls:

1. Controls, which we already discussed.

2. Loop plays the audio file repeatedly, or in a loop. In order to enable this looping, place your cursor after the code controls="controls" and press the spacebar key to activate the code hints. Type "l" and then double-click on loop to add the code loop.

3. Autoplay starts the audio file immediately when someone opens the page, as opposed to the viewer having to press play the way we did with the controller. You can have both loop and autoplay enabled at the same time. In order to make the audio play automatically, place your cursor after the code controls="controls" and press the spacebar key to activate the code hints. Double-click on autoplay to add the code autoplay ="". For auto playing, you don't need to put anything between the quotation marks in the code, the way we did with controls and loop. Just adding the code enables it, as shown below.

**A note on autoplay**: Mobile devices (including iOS Apple devices) and some versions of Android mobile operating system do not support autoplay, which argues for including controls.

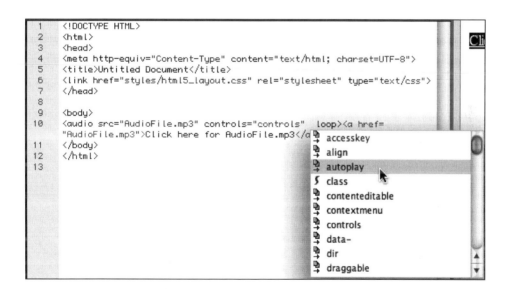

```
1   <!DOCTYPE HTML>
2   <html>
3   <head>
4   <meta http-equiv="Content-Type" content="text/html; charset=UTF-8">
5   <title>Untitled Document</title>
6   <link href="styles/html5_layout.css" rel="stylesheet" type="text/css">
7   </head>
8
9   <body>
10  <audio src="AudioFile.mp3" controls="controls"  loop><a href=
    "AudioFile.mp3">Click here for AudioFile.mp3</a
11  </body>
12  </html>
13
```

accesskey
align
autoplay
class
contenteditable
contextmenu
controls
data-
dir
draggable

4.  `Preload` starts downloading the audio file when the page is opened, before **Play** is clicked. This is not relevant if we are using `autoplay`, as it will load immediately either way, but when we are not using `autoplay`, it allows the audio file to launch quicker when a visitor clicks **Play**. If you want to preload the track, then simply place your cursor after the code `controls="controls"` once again and press the spacebar key to activate the code hints. Type "p" and then double-click on `preload`, and then double-click on `auto` to add the code `preload="auto"`.

You can enable multiple parameters at the same time. Just press space after the code `controls="controls"` each time to activate HTML5 code hints, and then repeat for whatever other code you want. Therefore, you can have a track that both autoplays and loops, for example.

Remember to about what will make the most sense for the audio you have and the preferences of visitors to your site. Keep in mind that many visitors will not appreciate sound automatically playing when they enter the main page of your site. They may be at work, or just not want the sound on. Unless it is a linked page, they expect sound on (it is more considerate to your visitors to have audio be something they can choose to turn on) rather than something they must choose to turn off.

# Recipe: Embedding HTML5 audio

In the following recipe, we will embed an MP3 audio file using the HTML5 audio element and provide an option for visitors whose browsers do not support HTML5. I will assume that you are working in a Dreamweaver site and that you have a file open, saved as an HTML5 web page (saving the file first is important to ensure the integrity of the link to the audio file). Moreover, it is assumed that you have an MP3 audio file ready to embed.

With those pieces in place, carry out the following steps:

1.  In the Dreamweaver **Document** window, jump into the Split view and in the Code side of the Split view; click where you wish to create a new line of code. This can be anywhere in between the `<body>` and `</body>` tags.

2.  Start typing `<audio>` element. A couple of letters into the process, you can press the *Tab* key to complete the beginning of the element. Then press the spacebar key.

3.  Double-click on **src** in the pop-up list, as shown in the following screenshot. A **Browse** link appears:

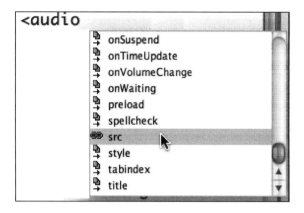

4. Double-click on the **Browse** link to open the **Select file** dialog, navigate and select the MP3 audio file.

5. Press the spacebar key once again, and double-click on **controls** in the code hints that appear. Double-click on **controls** again in the next code hint, so that your line of code looks similar to one shown in the following screenshot, except that you'll have your own audio file selected:

```
<audio src=
"01_KR-test.mp3"
```

6. Type `</` and the HTML5 Pack will complete the closing element `</audio>`.

7. Now, to support non-HTML browsers, add a line of text in your web page with a link to the audio file you just embedded with the HTML5 `<audio>` tag. In order to do that, locate an insertion point (click with the mouse in the Code side of the Split view) just before `</audio>` that closes the audio element. Type a closing angle bracket (**>**) to complete the element. Then, type "Listen to the audio file" – as regular HTML text, and use the Property inspector to attach a link to the audio file for the text you embedded with the HTML5 `<audio>` tag.

This code provides seamless HTML5 audio for HTML5-enabled browsers that can handle MP3 files and a link to the MP3 file for everyone else.

# Summary

In this chapter, we saw how to embed an audio file directly into a web page to play in the browser window, rather than using a new window and a browser plugin. We also saw how to have a link to a browser window that will use a media-playing plugin for those browsers not compatible with HTML5. We covered adding more properties to an embedded audio file. Finally, we saw how to use the HTML5 Pack in Dreamweaver CS5's pop-up hints to help us with all the code and make it easier.

Based on what we have covered so far, we are ready to explore other dimensions of HTML5, including how it works with its companion, CSS3, to create effects and provide access to graphics and video in new and exciting ways.

# 8

# Embedding HTML5 Video in Dreamweaver

In this chapter, we will learn how to add different kinds of video to web pages using HTML5 and Dreamweaver CS5.5.

Online video is undergoing a radical evolution. Those changes can be very briefly summed up as the following: You don't need a plugin player anymore. Dreamweaver CS5.5 provides limited but valuable support for embedding this native video (so-called because it plays in the native browser environment without plugins).

We will learn how to use the HTML5 video element through several steps:

- Understanding the concept of native video and the way it relates to early evolutionary steps in the development of web video and also, which video formats work in which browsers
- Creating HTML5-ready digital video files
- Using the <video> tag to embed a video with Dreamweaver CS5
- Providing alternative options for non-HTML5 compatible browsers
- Defining additional video display parameters

We need to perform each of the preceding steps to make sure that the HTML5 video we include in our site will work in every browsing environment.

## HTML5 video and Dreamweaver CS5.5

In order to understand the challenges of presenting an online video today, it is illuminating to frame things in the evolution of web video to this point. For one thing, older web video is still an issue, as are older browsers. We have to address the challenge of presenting a video in both new browsers that support current standards and older browsers that do not.

Moreover, the current rather crazy state of competing online video formats won't make much sense without being anchored in an understanding of how this current state of things emerged.

In order to sort all this out, it is useful to divide the emergent online video into three phases.

# Early formats

The first stage of the online video was characterized by a diffusion of different, non-compatible video formats and players. Apple's QuickTime video played in QuickTime player, which came with Apple's Safari browser. Microsoft's Internet Explorer played various Microsoft video formats such as AVI or WMF. Typically, web designers included QuickTime video in a site with the expectation that only users on Macs would be able to see the video, or included Windows Media Formats such as WMV or AVI, with the expectation that only users with Windows Media Player (appropriately updated) could handle the video. During this phase, other formats, such as Real Media's video and player gained traction for a time.

In this early phase, the lack of a single online video format was one marginalizing factor affecting web video. In addition, the absence of a critical mass of users with high-speed connections made online video less attractive. Low quality video and audio display in laptops and digital devices was another factor that kept web video from being the integral component of websites that it is today and a corresponding lack of quality online video content made web video something of a marginal element in web design.

Culturally and technically, web video was, at this point, something of an "outsider" in web browsing experience, requiring long waits for downloads, and explanation to users on how to watch video, as illustrated in the following screenshot that I created for the Himalayan Fair in 2002:

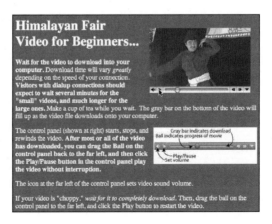

In terms of HTML and Dreamweaver technique, the `<embed>` tag was used to place a video on a page. This tag allowed some designer control over player controls and other parameters (such as autoplay) but how (and if) the video played was mainly defined by a user's browser, and the plugins he/she had installed in that browser.

# Flash Video (FLV)

Phase two in the evolution of online video, as we are delineating things here, marked the integration of video into every realm of every kind of website.

One critical factor in the move of video into the mainstream on the web was the emergence of **Adobe's Flash Video (FLV)** format and the widespread acceptance of the Flash Player. FLV presents video in a highly compressed form—radically reducing the file size (often by half compared to QuickTime) while maintaining good video and audio quality.

Flash Video (FLV) files required the Flash Player, but during this phase of the Web, installation of the Flash Player was almost universal. Dreamweaver, particularly in CS4 and CS5, included nice, customizable menu-driven Flash Player design tools. Dreamweaver designers could choose from a variety of Flash Player skins as they embedded Flash Video. The following screenshot shows a minimalist player skin:

Intersecting with the rise of FLV and near-universal support for the Flash Player was the availability of high-speed Internet connections and the proliferation of the video content. The instant popularity of YouTube, which featured FLV videos, was an expression of and an engine of these phenomena. These developments—which still are a major element of web video—transformed the web video from marginal to mainstream.

In terms of HTML and Dreamweaver, Flash Video (FLV) would be embedded in pages using the <object> tag. However, the appearance of the video player and the properties of parameters, such as autoplay or looping, are defined in the Properties panel in Dreamweaver's **Document** window for a selected FLV video, as shown in the following screenshot:

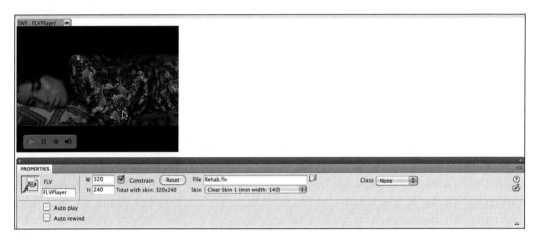

The main disadvantage of using FLV video is that it is not supported on the iPhone, iPod Touch, or iPad (or iPods). I will explain how that situation developed next, along with the implications for web designers using video.

## Apple devices and the web video

The parameters of an online video—with Flash Video as the cohering element—seemed defined, relatively stable, and globally accepted. Until…

Steve Jobs published "Thoughts on Flash" in April, 2010. The essence of that letter was stating and making permanent Apple's position that it would never support the Flash Player on its i-gadgets: "The mobile era is about low power devices, touch interfaces and open web standards – all areas where Flash falls short. The avalanche of media outlets offering their content for Apple's mobile devices demonstrates that Flash is no longer necessary to watch video or consume any kind of web content."

This decision came at a time when, despite Jobs' pronouncement, the bulk of online videos, at sites such as Hulu and YouTube for example, was in Flash Video. Moreover, people who tried to watch videos from these sites typically got and still do get messages like the one shown in the following screenshot:

Apple threw its considerable weight behind the h.264 format for packaging compressed videos. This format essentially uses the same compression technology as Flash Video, but comes in a package that adapts the player display and controls from a browser, not from a plugin player.

Setting aside the power politics and economic dimensions of this decision, the essential technical and design issues were that Apple did not want to expand limited energy resources in their digital devices on the Flash Player. Apple argued that video players should be "native" to viewing environments, rather than global cross-platform interfaces like those in the Flash Player (that look essentially the same on every operating system and browser).

Within a year of Apple's announcement, the critical mass in providing online videos had begun to tip towards native videos. However, Flash Video (FLV) remains widely distributed online. Thus, web designers using Dreamweaver CS5.5 face the challenge of embedding native videos.

# The wild world of native videos

A native video is presented in HTML5 with the `<video>` element (tag). Accomplishing that is our mission in this chapter, and shortly, we will explore tools available in Dreamweaver CS5.5 for embedding video using this tag.

Before we do that, let's identify the two big challenges to developers in providing native videos. One is that there is not one but three native video formats. The second challenge is that the older versions of Internet Explorer (8 and earlier) do not support the HTML5 `<video>` element.

## Native video formats

The three widely supported native video formats are: MP4 (h.264), supported by Safari; Theora OGG, an open source video format supported by Mozilla Firefox; and WebM, supported by Google Chrome, Opera, and reportedly soon in Firefox.

Here is a more detailed breakdown of which browsers currently support which video formats:

- Ogg: Firefox, Chrome, Opera 10.5+
- h.264 (MP4): Internet Explorer 9+, Safari, Older versions of Chrome, Apple's mobile devices, Android devices
- Web M: Chrome 6+, Opera 10.6+

However, keep in mind, all this is a moving target.

As you can see, there is no video format supported by all major browsers. In particular, Firefox and Chrome (with a combined substantial share of the browser market) do not support h.264 video.

We will solve this challenge by providing alternate videos, all with the same parameters (location, player control display, and so on).

## Browsers that do NOT support HTML5

Providing alternate video formats will solve the problem of making our native video display in all HTML5 browsers. However, older visions of Internet explorer (pre-IE 9) do not support HTML5!

In the course of walking through the nits and grits of embedding native video, we will build in backup support for browsers that do not support the HTML5 `<video>` tag. We will do this by making a version of our video available in the FLV format.

# Preparing an HTML5 video for every scenario

If you choose to provide only one of the available popular video formats for the Web, then you are going to exclude a large chunk of people from seeing your video. For example, if you elect to use the h.264 format supported on Apple mobile devices, that video cannot be viewed by the 30% or so of all users who are navigating the Web with Firefox. Conversely, if you provide Flash Video (FLV), then your video can be watched in Firefox, but not by the highly valued 5% of web browsers browsing on their *i*-devices.

Our challenge, then, is to supply a fast-downloading, compressed web video that is supported in every browser (or at least every significant browsing environment).

No problem, by the end of this chapter, you will be able to do that in Dreamweaver CS5.5.

# Compressing videos for the Web

Let's go back to our earlier discussion of the evolution of the video for the Web. A key link in the chain was the development of powerful, effective compression for web video. It might be helpful to explain very briefly how this works.

Video animation—whether digital or old school analog (like films)—is presented in frames. The more frames displayed per second, the smoother the animation.

Video compression reduces the size of a digital video not by reducing the number of frames, but by rationalizing the way frame data is saved. Say, for example, that you have a video of a person speaking against a background. It might well be the case that the background does not change throughout the video. Video compression software compresses the digital data necessary to present that video by organizing the data used to depict the background in such a way that it does not have to be repeated for each frame of the video.

I am using a very simple example here to help make a point, but the point is more broadly applicable, even to video with more complex backgrounds. Moreover, as a general rule of thumb, compression reduces file size by about a half, while maintaining the original quality.

In a typical workflow, you might start with video files in QuickTime's MOV format (or Microsoft's AVI format). These videos, straight from a video camera, or from video editing software, are not compressed. They could be presented directly online except that:

- ◦ They are unnecessarily large and double the download time
- ◦ They are not all supported by browsers unless those browsers have plugins added, and we are trying to get away from that

Therefore, after you or someone else has created the video in an uncompressed format, a key step in the process of preparing that video for the Web is to compress it.

# Video compression—open source and proprietary

The four popular compressed digital video formats used on the Web roughly divide into two groups: open source and proprietary.

WebM and Theora OGG are free, open source video formats. In order to create them, you can use a variety of free encoding programs.

Flash Video (FLV) and h.264 are not open source but proprietary. In order to generate them, we can use Adobe Media Encoder CS5.5.

While creating four additional (compressed) versions of an original uncompressed video (from a QuickTime or Windows Media format) is a bit of a hassle, it is doable.

# Converting a video to web formats with open source tools

There are a number of free downloadable applications that convert your (raw) QuickTime or Windows Media files to compressed Theora OGG or WebM.

I am currently using one named **Miro Video Converter**, a nice, free downloadable application available at the following URL:

www.mirovideoconverter.com

Whichever free video compression application you end up using, the process involves two steps: Adding your video to the cache to be converted and choosing an output format (like h.264), as shown in the following screenshot (in this case with Micro Video Converter):

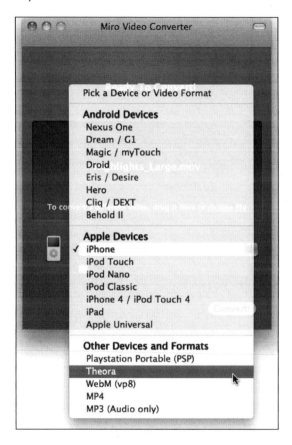

Of course, those two general steps will be performed differently depending on which open source video conversion program you end up using. In general, these free video compression applications are pretty no-frills. They don't provide options for editing, resizing, or tweaking the quality of compressed video. Thus, I advise using them to convert the open source versions of your web video (Theora OGG and WebM), but not the Flash Video (FLV) and h.264 (MP4) version of your video.

For that, I suggest taking advantage of Adobe Media Encoder CS5.5 that ships with nearly every version of the Creative Suite.

# Creating an HTML5 video in Adobe Media Encoder CS5. 5

The h.264 (MP4) is the most dynamic HTML5-compatible video format. It is the exclusive compressed video format used in Apple's i-devices, and is or will be supported by other browsing environments. Further, as h.264 is a proprietary (not open source) format, it is difficult (if not impossible) to create free open source applications that generate h.264 video.

Thus, it is appropriate and valuable that Adobe Media Encoder CS5.5 generates h.264 video. Moreover, it generates Adobe's own FLV video.

As noted, most packages of Creative Suite 5.5 ship with Media Encoder 5.5. Moreover, Media Encoder, while far from a full-featured video editing program, does provide a substantial set of features for adjusting the audio and video of a compressed video.

The following steps convert a video from other formats to FLV or H.264:

1.  Launch Adobe Media Encoder CS5.5. Before you do anything else, disable the almost dangerously irresponsible default setting that launches the compression process before you are finished defining output settings. Select **Edit | Preferences (Windows)** or **Adobe Media Encoder CS5.5 | Preferences (Mac)** and deselect the **Start queue automatically when idle for** checkbox, as shown in the following screenshot:

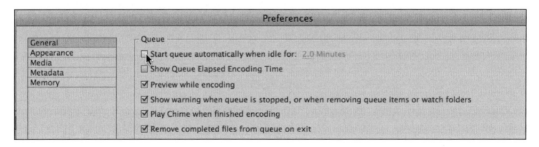

2.  This is the only essential preference setting that needs to be adjusted before you use Media Encoder 5.5. Once you have made this change, click on **OK** on the **Preferences** dialog to return to Media Encoder CS5.5's uber-minimalist "interface."

3.  Click on the **Add** button. In the Open dialog that appears, navigate to and double-click on a video from another format (such as QuickTime MOV, Flash FLV, or Microsoft AVI) to add it to the Media Encoder queue.

4. In the Format column, choose **H.264** or **FLV** as the export format. There are other export options, but they are for audio files (MP3), less supported and non-essential newer versions of FLV (FV4), or versions of h.264 for non-web use.

5. The **Preset** pop up provides a wide range of preset sizes and compression quality options that are basically self-explanatory. For example, if your target audience is most likely to be watching the video on an Apple iPad, turned landscape, with a very fast Internet connection (for example, a super-agent reviewing your video clip in his or her office), you would choose the 640x480 pixel display with the fastest download speed available, as shown in the following screenshot:

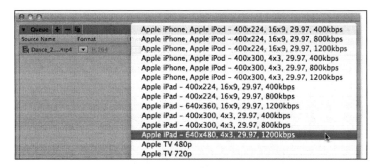

6. Click on the link in the **Output File** column. The **Save As** dialog opens. Navigate to the folder you defined earlier as the local site folder for your Dreamweaver website, and click on **Save** to designate this folder as the target for your video output.

7. If you are making more than one version of your compressed video (something you might well want to do, for example to create both an FLV and h.264 version of the video), then use the **Duplicate** button to create a second version of your video, as shown in the following screenshot. Define different compression settings for that video:

8. Click on the **Start Queue** button ( as shown in the following screenshot) to convert the entire queue of videos to the compression options you defined. The compressing video is very demanding on your computer's resources and this process will take some time. When it is complete, you are ready to embed the h.264 video in a web page using HTML5:

# Dreamweaver site management for an HTML5 video

Having now explored the process of preparing a video for HTML5, let's briefly examine how to prepare to take maximum advantage of Dreamweaver CS5.5 in this process.

There are two ways Dreamweaver CS5.5 will assist in embedding the HTML5 video. One way, which we will get to shortly, is that Dreamweaver will provide helpful code hints that facilitate creating the HTML5 code we need.

However, the other value of Dreamweaver in this process is that the **Site management** tools will keep track of all the files we need, and most importantly, maintain the integrity of links we create between the embedded video and the other files (CSS, possible JavaScript, embedded images, and so on) needed to make our page work properly in browsers.

So, as a critical next step, make sure that you are working in a Dreamweaver CS5.5 website. As we have addressed this in previous chapters, I will just review the bare bones basics involved in doing that here in three easy steps:

1. If you are not working in a defined Dreamweaver site, select **Site | New Site**. In the **Site Setup** dialog, give your new site a name and define a local site folder. Doing this defines a Dreamweaver site. Defining the Servers element of a site is not essential to embedding HTML5 video in Dreamweaver web pages, but defining the local site is.

2. Now create a new file, and save it within your defined site. To do that, choose **File | New** to open the **New Document** dialog. Select **Blank Page** in the **Category** column, **HTML** in the **Page Type** column, and **<none>** in the **Layout** column. Select **HTML5** from the **DocType** pop up. Click on **Create** to create a new, blank Dreamweaver page.

3. For good housekeeping purposes to avoid the "Untitled" page title, enter a title in the **Title** area of the **Document** window (this can be any descriptive text).

4. Select **File | Save** and assign a filename.

By saving a file, we will be able to link a video using relative paths.

# Defining the HTML5 <video> element

Once you have prepared a Dreamweaver site and created H.264, OGG, WebM, and Flash Video (FLV) versions of your video, you have all the elements you need to embed native HTML5 video, and provide an alternative for browsers without support for HTML5.

In the following steps, you will complete the process of placing a video in an HTML5 web page.

We cannot, regrettably, do this in the Design view. Dreamweaver CS5.5 does not have Design view menu options for embedding HTML5 native video. However, we can take advantage of the two useful features in Dreamweaver's Document window: **Code hinting** and the **Split view**. Code hinting will help us generate the HTML5 code we need, whereas the Split view will allow us to preview at least some of the possible ways in which visitors will see our video as we create it.

# Prerequisites

In order to review and re-emphasize the things, you need the following in place before creating HTML5 video in Dreamweaver CS5.5:

- You should have prepared an h.264 (mp4); Theora (OGG); WebM (webm) and Flash Video (FLV) version of your video. You can elect to provide support for just one, or some of the first three HTML5-compatible formats. If you provide support for h.264 and OGG, then you will have almost all modern browsers covered.

- You must create a Dreamweaver site and have an open page in the Dreamweaver **Document** window saved as an HTML5 file within your site. View the page in the **Split** view.

- Copy all your video files into a folder within the site folder you defined. If you save your video files elsewhere, then Dreamweaver will prompt you to make copies of the videos within your site folder, but it saves a step and simplifies things to create copies of the video files in the site folder at this stage.

# Creating the <video> element

In your saved HTML5 page, place your cursor after the opening <body> tag. If you are embedding a video in a page with existing content, then place your insertion point where the video should appear.

1. Type <vi and the code hinting will then show the video tag, as shown in the following screenshot:

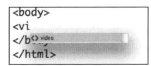

2. Press *Tab* to complete the beginning of the <video tag.
3. Use code hinting to add parameters for height, width, and controls. The height and width values can either match the original values of your video or be larger or smaller. If the values are larger than the original video, the resolution of the video will be degraded. Including the controls parameter displays player controls (for play, pause, stop, and volume). The resulting code is as follows:

```
<video width="xxxpx" height="yyypx" controls>
```

(Where, xxx is the width of the video and yyy is the height)

As we are going to support multiple video formats, we closed the video tag by typing here.

# Defining video attributes

The HTML5 video controller normally displays a play button, a pause button, and a mute button, as well as a scrubber (a horizontal bar with a movable thumb to scroll backwards or forwards within video playback).

Moreover, by default, HTML5 video controls display only when the user hovers his or her mouse pointer over the video, or when the video begins to play.

The most important video parameters are height, width, and controls.

The controls parameter displays these player controls. The height and width values are followed by units of measurement, almost always pixels.

There are other useful HTML5 Video parameters, which are as follows:

- Audio: Muted turns off volume when the video begins to play
- Autoplay: Autoplay launches the video automatically
- Loop: Loop repeats the video
- Preload: Preload loads the video when the page is opened, even before it is played
- Poster: [filename] displays artwork before the video is played

**Settings for iOS**: iPads cannot autoplay HTML5 videos, Apple does not allow it on its iOS devices, so don't rely on autoplay if your audience includes visitors on those devices. Also, preloading is appropriate for desktops and laptops, but too resource-intensive for mobile devices.

Even though preparing an HTML5 video usually means presenting multiple video source files, the other attributes can be defined for all of them all together. Moreover, normally, that is what you will want to do, as attributes such as video size, autoplay status, and so on will be the same regardless of the video file format a visitor views.

Each of these parameters is supported by code hinting, and we will explore how that works in detail in the recipe at the end of this chapter.

# Defining video source(s)

Each video source requires a separate line of HTML5 code. That code is generated in Dreamweaver (any version with the HTML5 Pack installed) with code hints.

In order to define a video source, type `<sour`, as you do, code hinting suggests the `<source` tag. Press *Tab* to complete the code. Press the *Spacebar*. Type `sr` – as you do, code hinting suggests `<src>`. Then, press the *Tab* key. A **Browse** link appears, as shown in the following screenshot:

```
<body>
<video>
<source src=""
          Browse...

</body>
</html>
```

In order to locate a source video file, double-click on the **Browse** link provided by code hinting to open the **Select File** dialog. Then, navigate to the h.264 video file you exported from Media Encoder CS5.5 into your Dreamweaver site folder. Double-click on that file to select it.

# Alternate video for non-HTML5 environments

The upcoming release of Internet Explorer 9 will include HTML5 video support. However, many folks are still watching online videos in older versions of Internet Explorer — IE 8, 7, and 6. Therefore, it is important to include alternative access to online video that does not require HTML5 support.

In order to do that, you can add a line of code that provides a link to a Flash Video (FLV) file. This line of code should be at the end of the set of parameters for the `<video>` tag, right before the `</video>` closing tag.

# Putting it all together

As discussed, we will walk through an example in the recipe at the end of this chapter that uses all the important `<video>` tag parameters, incorporates all the three HTML5 video formats, and provides accessibility for non-HTML5 browsers.

However, as a short course in that, the following lines of code display a 320 x 240 video with controls, with all the three HTML5 video formats, and an option for folks with older versions of IE to watch the video as a Flash Video (FLV) video:

```
<video width="320px" height="240px" controls>
<source src="Video/on_record.mp4">
<source src="Video/on_record.theora.ogv">
<source src="Video/on_record.webm">
<a href="Video/on_record_1.flv">Click to watch this video using
    Flash Player</a>
</video>
```

# Testing HTML5 video pages

It is more than clear, at this point in our exploration of HTML5 video, that presenting an online video in HTML5 presents major compatibility issues. Will a video really play in the whole range of browsing environments out there, ranging from an iPad to Internet Explorer 6.0 on a Windows machine?

If you supply all three HTML5 video format options and include a link to a Flash Video page for visitors without HTML5 video support, then your video should play in any environment.

# Previewing a video in the Live View

There are three options for testing your video in Dreamweaver CS5.5. One of them, **File | Preview in Browser**, simply opens your page in one of the browsers installed on your own computer. This is effective and useful for testing a video in browsers you already have installed.

A quicker way to see if your video works, at least in Safari and other browsers that follow the Webkit standard (and this includes Apple mobile devices) is to simply look at, and test the video in the **Live View**. If you are working in the **Split** view (pretty much a necessity for working with HTML5 video in Dreamweaver), then you can click on the **Live View** button, and test your video even as you see (and edit) code on the code side of Split view, as shown in the following screenshot:

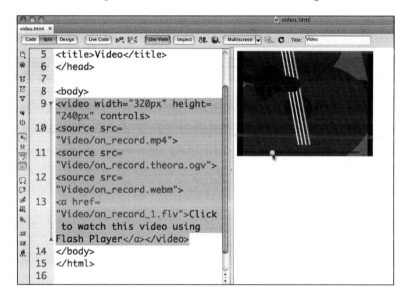

# Previewing a video in BrowserLab

It is relatively easy to test Dreamweaver-created HTML5 pages with a video on modern devices and browsers. I have been known to spend an hour in the Apple store or at a friendly Android cell phone vendor testing pages.

A bigger challenge is testing pages in older browsers. Most of us don't, for example, have Internet Explorer 6 installed on our testing computers.

However, Adobe's BrowserLab does. BrowserLab does not provide a preview for mobile devices (in some mobile devices, preview is available through Dreamweaver's **File | Preview in Browser | Device Central**). However, it is particularly useful in previewing a video in older browsers.

In order to test any web page (including those with a video) in BrowserLab, select **File | Preview in Browser| Adobe BrowserLab**. The first time you do this, you will be led through a fairly clear registration process.

If you are previewing a page that has not been uploaded to a remote server, then Dreamweaver uploads a temporary copy of your page to the BrowserLab site. There, you can select a browser and see how your page looks. Here, for example, I am previewing my page in IE 6.

# Recipe: Embedding an HTML5 video

The following recipe makes an HTML5 video available in all three available compressed video formats, along with a link to a Flash Video (FLV) page for older versions of Internet Explorer (versions 6-8).

As with all our recipes in this book, the first step is to ensure that you have defined the Dreamweaver website. With that in place, create and save a page named `video.html` in the site.

The sample code here uses real video files I uploaded to my site that you can use to experiment. Alternatively, substitute your own files in the appropriate file format.

Therefore, with your site defined, your page (`video.html`) saved — with a title — you are ready for the following steps:

1.  In the Dreamweaver Document window, jump into the Split view, and in the Code side of the Split view, click where you wish to create a new line of code. This can be anywhere in between the `<body>` and `</body>` tags. As we are working with a brand new document, place your cursor after the first `<body>` tag and press *Enter* (Windows) or *Return* (Mac) to create a new line of code.

2.  Start typing the `<video>` element. A couple of letters into the process, you can press the *Tab* key to complete the beginning of the element.

3.  Add video parameters to define the height, width, and to display controls as follows:

    ```
    width="320px" height="240px" controls
    ```

4.  Close the `<video>` tag by typing > and pressing *Return* to create a new line of code.

5.  Define the first video source with this line of code as follows:

    ```
    <source src="http://davidkarlins.com/video/on_record.mp4">
    ```

6.  At this stage, you can see (and hear!) the video in the **Live View** in the **Design** side of the **Split View**, as shown in the following screenshot:

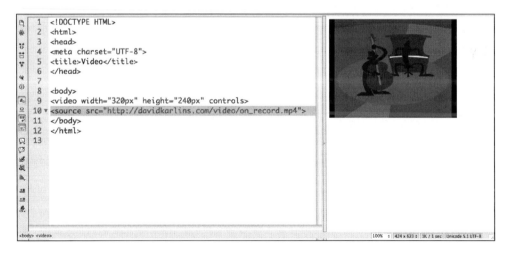

7.  In a new line of the code, enter the HTML5 code to define the Theora OGG video as a second video source as follows:

    ```
    <source src="http://davidkarlins.com/video/on_record.ogv">
    ```

8. You can test this second line of code by previewing your page in Google Chrome, if you have that browser installed. The current version of Chrome does not support h.264 video, so the .mp4 file will not be recognized, but the .ogv (OGG) file will be.

9. Add a line of code defining the third video source as follows:

```
<source src="http://davidkarlins.com/video/on_record.webm">
```

10. On a new line of code, simply type: Click here to watch the video. You can preview this by turning off the **Live View** in the **Design** side of the **Split View**. Select the text, and use the **Insert Hyperlink** dialog to define a link to http://davidkarlins.com/video/flv.html that opens in a new browser window (choose _blank from the Target pop up) as shown in the following screenshot:

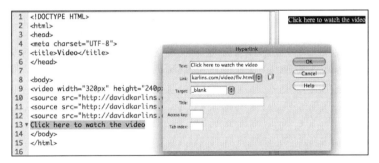

11. Feel free to touch up the page with text or styles. Or not. Save your file. If you have access to IE 6, 7, or 8, then you can test the non-HTML version, or you can test that using Adobe BrowserLab (**File** | **Preview in Browser** | **Adobe BrowserLab**).

# Summary

In this chapter, we explored the process of creating and presenting an HTML5 video. We examined the evolving, different, and competing options for compressing video supported by HTML5. Moreover, we noted the need to provide a way to present our video for non-HTML5 browsing environments by creating a Flash Video (FLV) file that will work in those pre-HTML5 browsing environments.

Then, we walked through Dreamweaver CS5.5's tools for embedding an HTML5 video. Those tools are essentially code hints, which provide help in writing HTML5 <video> tags and their properties, and the Live View which previews at least the Webkit (Safari) version of the video as we write the code.

# 9

# Creating Mobile Pages
# with jQuery

As a web design consultant, I am immersed for periods of time in studying statistical trends—who is using the Web? For what? In what environments? However, you probably don't need a summary of my research to know that both in numbers, and in impact, people using mobile devices constitute the dynamic factor in web activity. I'll share one statistic compiled from a number of surveys I have been sifting through: by 2013, about half of all visits to websites will be from mobile devices. Moreover, in categories such as entertainment and restaurants, the overwhelming amount of web browsing is already done using mobile devices.

Are they using web browsers for this? Or apps? Or both. However, from a design perspective, there is not much difference between a mobile page and an app. By the time you finish this book, you will be able to generate both apps and mobile-friendly HTML pages in Dreamweaver CS5.5. Nevertheless, at this stage of the game, focus on designing pages. The techniques we will explore in this, and the following chapter will generate mobile-friendly content that works in either environment.

This is not our first engagement with the challenges of designing for multiple media. In *Chapter 4, Building HTML5 Pages from Scratch* we began to explore pages built with basic HTML5 tags. Those simpler pages are easier for mobile devices to digest. Then, of course, in *Chapter 5, Defining and Implementing Multiscreen Previews and Media Queries*, we specifically explored designing mobile and tablet-sized pages, and added code so that browsers detect appropriate media, and present different CSS style sheet-based pages depending on the size of the viewport in the viewing media. Moreover, the preceding chapters that have explored HTML5 audio and video have prepared you to embed mobile-friendly (non-Flash) video in web pages. In short, we are approaching these last three chapters on a solid foundation. You have got tools in your skill set that will be helpful in managing web pages for mobile devices.

Here's what's new. In this chapter, create jQuery Mobile based pages—accessible, inviting, animated pages that work particularly well on mobile devices. In the next chapter, we will add additional jQuery objects such as expanding sections, layout grids, and forms. Moreover, in the final chapter in this book, you will learn to build applications—applications that run native, without a browser, in iOS (for Apple iPhones and iPads) and Android (for Google Android phones and tablets).

In this chapter we will see:

- Design for mobile – An overview
- Apps and mobile pages
- 3 components of mobile web: HTML5, CSS, and jQuery Mobile
- jQuery mobile in Dreamweaver CS5.5
- Generating mobile ready pages from starter pages
- Customizing mobile starter page content
- Adding "Pages"
- Customizing mobile page CSS
- Recipe: Build a jQuery-driven mobile page

# Mobile pages – An overview

The principles involved in designing mobile sites can boil down to one word: simple.

There is more to explore now, for sure! Mobile sites have to be simple in design as people are viewing and interacting with them on small devices, and columns, sidebars, and complex backgrounds that are not only appropriate for, but also a part of a positive experience on a laptop or desktop, make the experience uninviting and inaccessible on mobile devices.

The second dimension of "simple" when it comes to design for mobile devices is that sites cannot be loaded up with plugins (like Flash), server-side scripting (like PHP) or complicated navigation schemes. Some of these features are supported in some mobile devices (Flash is supported in new versions of the Android operating system), but most are not. Moreover, mobile devices are limited in processing power, battery time, and other constraints that take us back to the watchword: simple.

Laptops and desktops on the one hand, and mobile devices on the other, have quite different interface features. Laptops have a mouse that can hover over an object; mobile devices have touch screens that can be resized or scrolled.

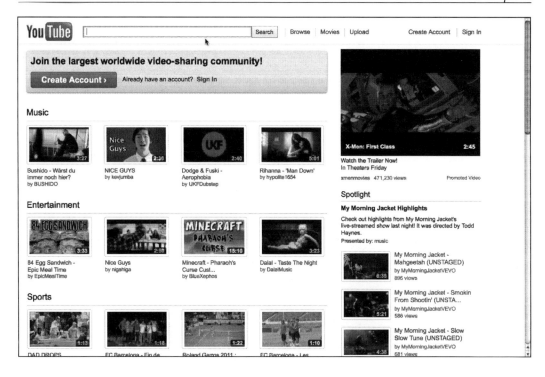

Mobile devices, by contrast, have much smaller screens, touch screens, touch scrolling and resizing, and on-screen keyboards.

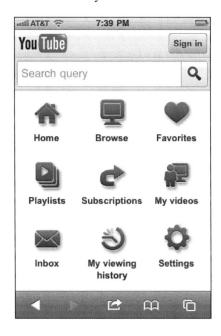

And, as noted, the rules for designing applications are pretty much the same as those for designing mobile-friendly web pages.

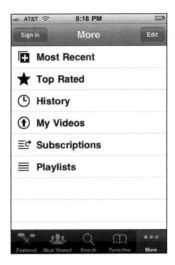

# Mobile pages, apps, and jQuery Mobile

In the introduction to this chapter I alluded to the fact that pages that are designed to be highly mobile-friendly also convert well to apps. There are three elements used to create pages that work well in any mobile operating system or device, and convert well to apps. Those three elements are HTML5 for layout, CSS3 for formatting, and... and here comes a new factor... jQuery Mobile for animation and interactivity.

jQuery Mobile tools are one of the two radically new elements of Dreamweaver CS5.5 (building apps, which we will explore in the final chapter of this book, is the second). What is jQuery Mobile? What's the big deal about it? Moreover, how does Dreamweaver CS5.5 implement it?

jQuery is a library of JavaScript objects. JavaScript has been part of Dreamweaver as long as there has been a Dreamweaver. The rather abandoned Behaviors panel generates JavaScript. Spry widgets introduced in earlier versions of Dreamweaver are JavaScript-based. Another dimension of web design that is, outside of Dreamweaver jQuery has evolved as a relatively accessible set of customizable JavaScript objects. Now, when I say relatively accessible, I mean that to implement JavaScript through the jQuery library still requires editing JavaScript code.

With the emergence of mobile devices, a distinct JavaScript library emerged—jQuery Mobile—with a set of objects particularly useful in designing for mobile devices.

# The status of jQuery Mobile

Like much of the technology used to develop mobile layouts and apps, jQuery Mobile is a work in progress. As I write this book, it is officially in the "beta" stage of development.

However, "beta" stage doesn't mean what it used to in the fast-moving world of web design technology. By the time, a technology is fully tested and mature, something else has come along to replace it. That may be a slight exaggeration, but it still pretty accurately characterizes the way things work. CSS3, for example, is still evolving out of the stage of requiring prefixes (like -moz or -webkit) before some of the effects we explored in *Chapter 6, Applying CSS3 Effects and Transforms*.

Part of what is driving this pace is rapid developments in mobile hardware and operating systems. Again, if one waits until a design tool is fully tested on a particular combination of hardware and operating system, that hardware and operating system will have changed.

In short, there is a consensus among reviewers and designers that jQuery Mobile is stable and usable. Rather than providing a list of devices and operating systems that support it —a list that would be out of date by the time you read this—I will refer you to the Mobile Graded Browser Support page that lists the current state of support for jQuery Mobile: http://jquerymobile.com/gbs.

# Using jQuery Mobile starter pages

A small but very substantial set of jQuery Mobile objects are now available, in Design view, in Dreamweaver CS5.5 without coding! The most widely used of these objects have been bundled into a very handy set of customizable starter pages. In this chapter, we will create pages using these starters, examine them, and customize the HTML and CSS that controls the content and look of these pages.

The jQuery objects that come with mobile starter pages in Dreamweaver CS5.5 are not, themselves, customizable. In this way, they differ a bit from the Spry widgets in Dreamweaver where you can often customize some of the JavaScript itself. However, as we will see, this isn't going to be much of a problem because you can do most of the customizing you can imagine doing by editing the HTML and CSS associated with jQuery Mobile objects.

How does that work? On one level, our answer here is: who cares?! Dreamweaver CS5.5 has set up tools that allow us to customize jQuery Mobile objects without worrying about what is happening under the surface. However, as a foundation, it is helpful to understand that JavaScript (and this applies to both Spry and jQuery Mobile objects) works on HTML objects (like tags, including often div tags) or on defined CSS Style properties. For example, a jQuery object might change its background color when clicked on (or tapped on a mobile device). However, the colors—both before and after—are defined in an associated CSS rule that is accessible in the CSS Styles panel. Moreover, the content (text, images, media) in that object is defined by the HTML you create in Dreamweaver's Design view.

# Creating mobile pages from Dreamweaver CS5.5 starters

Dreamweaver CS5.5 comes with three jQuery Mobile-based starter pages: jQuery Mobile (CDN), jQuery Mobile (Local), and jQuery Mobile (PhoneGap).

The content of each of the three is identical, which is reasonable since there are a few basic jQuery Mobile elements you need for mobile pages and apps, and they are included in all three.

All three jQuery Mobile Sample Pages require, and include, links to a specific CSS file that supports and integrates with the jQuery Mobile objects. As you will see when we begin working with jQuery Mobile pages, there is a very complex and essential interdependency between jQuery Mobile and the particular CSS file that enables it.

The most substantial difference between the three Sample Page options is in how the linkage is defined between the jQuery Mobile page you generate, and the required CSS file.

The jQuery Mobile (CDN) Sample Page links to a version of the CSS file at the jQuery Mobile site. Therefore, you cannot, edit this CSS file.

The jQuery Mobile (Local) Sample Page uses a version of the CSS file that is included in Dreamweaver. That CSS file is editable.

The third option, jQuery Mobile (PhoneGap) uses a local version of the CSS file, but also generates a JavaScript file required for converting your mobile page to an app. However, as you will learn in *Chapter 11*, Dreamweaver provides an easy option for adding this JavaScript file later, as you generate an app, so it really isn't necessary to choose the (PhoneGap) option unless you are certain you will be using your mobile page to generate an app.

All three starter pages are accessed by choosing **File | New** and choosing **Page from Sample** in the left column of the **New Document** dialog. Select **Mobile Starters** in the **Sample Folder** column.

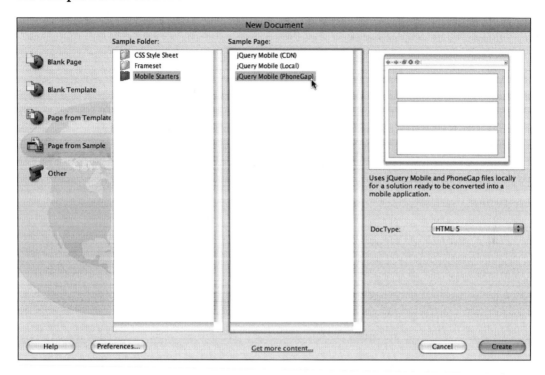

As our final objective (to be achieved in a couple more chapters of this book) is to create both a mobile web page, and an app using PhoneGap technology — the PhoneGap option works fine.

After you click on the **Create** button in the **New Document** dialog, a jQuery Mobile-based web page opens in the Dreamweaver CS5.5 document window.

# Mobile pages in Split view

You will find it most useful to examine the page in Split view for two reasons. One — and there's no new revelation here — is that in Split view you can both examine HTML code and see the page previewed as it will appear in a browser. What's new is that it's actually easier and more helpful to see a narrower preview window that will more closely simulate how your page will look in a mobile device.

It's particularly useful in designing for mobile to avail yourself of the Window size popup at the bottom of the Design half of Split view, and size the Preview window at 480 pixels wide—a dimension that corresponds to many popular mobile devices.

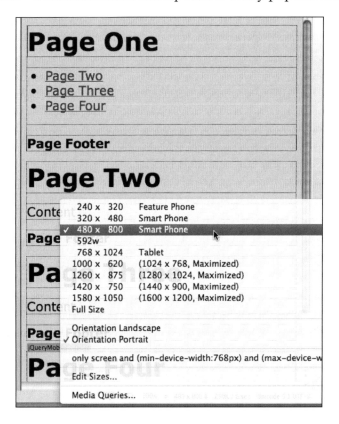

By the way, when you set a page width, you will note a **Media Queries** option at the bottom of the popup list. Defining **Media Queries** for jQuery Mobile based pages is very similar to the process we explored in depth in *Chapter 5*. We won't go back to that discussion now, but you can indeed define different jQuery Mobile based pages for different media.

I should forewarn you that as we develop jQuery Mobile content, I will be directing you to a bit more work in the code side of Split view (and Code view in general). All the jQuery Mobile objects you need to create pages are available from the regular document Window menu in Dreamweaver's Design view. But you will find that it is often much less time consuming to simply copy and paste a chunk of code to create new objects than to generate them from scratch using menu options in Design view. I will try to provide figures that show both the code and design side of Split view when I direct you to use this approach.

# Previewing jQuery Mobile pages in Live view

As you explore the template page generated by any of the jQuery Mobile starter pages, you will note one thing right away that is very different than other pages you have worked with in Dreamweaver: until you flip on Live view (click on the **Live View** button in the Document toolbar), hardly any formatting is visible. Try it toggling back and forth, turning **Live View** on and off to see what is, and is not displayed with Live View off.

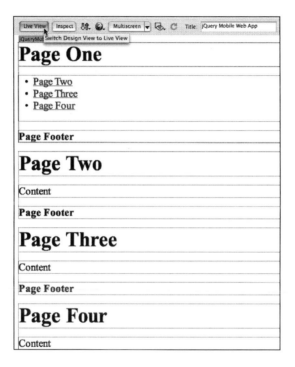

You will note right away that with **Live View** disabled, you don't see even basic CSS properties like font family, font color, and background colors. There is a CSS style sheet that is installed automatically with the jQuery Mobile pages, you can see it in the CSS Styles panel.

For example, a class style, CSS `rule` `.ui-bar-a` defines the bars at the top of each page (like the one that says **Page 1** with a dark background, and white type, but those properties aren't visible with **Live View** turned off).

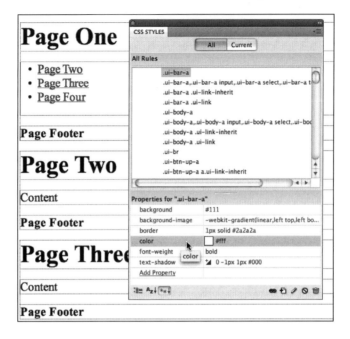

You can see the effect of the CSS styles in Live View. However, in normal web pages, basic CSS style properties are reflected without Live View enabled. So, what's up with that?

The answer is that jQuery Mobile pages depend not just on CSS, but the interaction of CSS with JavaScript to produce the look and feel of the pages. Moreover, you will see more and more as we explore how this works; you really get no idea of how jQuery Mobile pages will look until you kick into Live View.

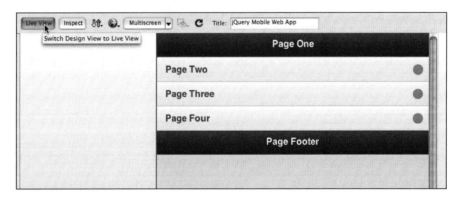

Therefore, as you can see, there is a more radical, definitive, complete separation between working with content and style in jQuery Mobile pages than in normal pages.

Later in this chapter, we will decipher and decode the complicated set of styles in the jQuery Mobile page, but for now it will be sufficient to digest the fact that in general, styles are not reflected until you turn on Live View.

# Customizing mobile page content

In a basic sense, you customize jQuery Mobile page content the same way you customize any starter page-generated content. Remember back… way back… to *Chapter 1* and *Chapter 2* of this book? Let's review the basic concept: starter pages come with template content, and you replace that with your own real content.

Isn't it simple enough? Kind of. As we have noted, there is a different order of gap between content and layout in jQuery Mobile pages. To put it another way, nothing is even close to how it appears with Live View turned off. Yet, you can't edit content in Live View. This emphasizes, again, the role of toggling back and forth between Live View off (to edit content) and on (to preview how that content will appear).

# The HTML5 data-role property

Div tags associated with jQuery Mobile script can function as different kind of elements, including ones that appear to be, and act like pages in a mobile device. This is done by implementing the data-role property in HTML5 tags, and then defining CSS (style sheet) rules to go with each data-role.

Typically, and this is the case for the starter pages in Dreamweaver CS5.5 j-Query Mobile pages are organized and laid out using four data-roles:

- Page
- Header
- Content
- Footer

# Data-role pages

It is often, even usually the case, that data-role pages play the role of basic content organizing elements in a jQuery Mobile page.

Let's distinguish a data-role page from an HTML page. Within a single HTML page, there will be several data-role pages. These data-role pages will look and feel to a user like different "pages".

If you have worked with other JavaScript elements in Dreamweaver, like Spry Tabbed Panels for example, you have seen the way JavaScript can make page elements (objects within a single HTML page) appear to be separate pages. These "pages" usually have distinct, unique headers and footers, and of course distinct and unique content.

Data-role pages, in short, look and feel like pages, but are defined within a single HTML page.

You can see how this works if you take a look at both the code, and page layout generated from a Dreamweaver CS5.5 jQuery Mobile starter.

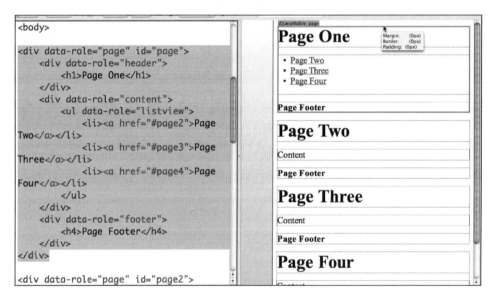

Organizing content into what are actually div tags with an HTML5 property called "data-role" allows people to navigate through what feel and act like web pages. However, these divs, acting like pages, allow visitors to hop back and forth between "pages" without having to wait for a new page to load in their browser. The use of such data-page divs is central to how the tiny space on a mobile device can be best used to present a lot of content.

People navigate between "data-role" pages in mobile devices by tapping, dragging, or otherwise navigating in a way that essentially shows, or hides different "pages". You can familiarize yourself with how this works by navigating around the "pages" in a jQuery Mobile starter page in Live View.

# Customizing page content

Now that you understand how jQuery Mobile pages are organized and function within an HTML page, customizing the content of the "pages" in the starter page will flow naturally. We are, now, back to the lessons of *Chapter 1* and *Chapter 2*, when we customized the content of HTML5 starter pages.

One way to approach this process is to ignore everything else, and simply replace the content in jQuery "pages" with your own content. Then, try the content out in Live View, see how it flows, edit, move, break up, and revise the content as necessary.

Use your own content to replace the header, content, and footer for each page. Identify this code in each generated page:

```
<div data-role="page" id="page2">

<div data-role="header">

        <h1>Page Two</h1>

</div>
<div data-role="content">

Content

</div>

<div data-role="footer">

        <h4>Page Footer</h4>

</div>

</div>
```

The highlighted code here indicates placeholder text that you customize by entering your own content. Replace the content in the highlighted lines of code with any HTML5 content (including if you wish HTML5 audio or video).

**Remember**: use only HTML5 content in your jQuery Mobile pages. Avoid plugins, like Flash Video, use the HTML5 <audio> and <video> tags instead (review *Chapter 7* and *Chapter 8* to do that).

Also, avoid server-side include content if that is something you work with. Server-side live data is not something we explore in this book, but if you are using PHP scripting, that won't fly in jQuery Mobile pages. Again, the basic rule is, stick to HTML, CSS, and JavaScript content.

Moreover, while I am an advocate for maximizing the use of Design view in Dreamweaver, in part because of the great gap between content and formatting in jQuery Mobile pages, I have to confess I generally resort to creating HTML content in the Code side of Split view, with Live View turned on in the Design side.

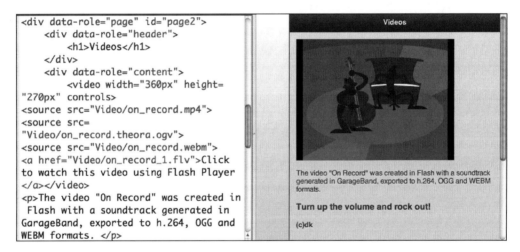

## Customizing content for different data roles

Generally speaking, the process of customizing content for "pages" will consist of going through and customizing the header, content, and footer sections of the pages.

jQuery Mobile pages also use the "listview" data role to organize sets of links. Those links are—again, generally speaking—links within the HTML page, to other data role "pages". In more conventional HTML terms, these are links to named anchors. You can see how these are set up by examining the default set of (internal) listview links that come with the starter page. As you will see, by default, they link to #page2, #page3. and #page4 and you can copy and paste these links to create more links to more "pages". Next, we will explore that process in detail.

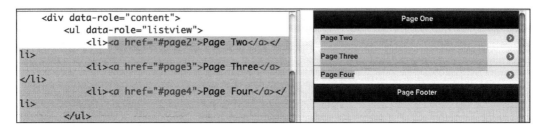

# Adding new jQuery Mobile pages and objects

The jQuery Mobile starter page comes with four pages, and links to four pages. A nice number, but what if you want to have five, six, or seven pages?

If you need to add more "pages", copy, paste, and slightly edit (change the page numbers) the fairly easily recognizable sections of HTML code that define each "page". As you customize the content, toggle Live View on and off to see how the page will look in a browser, or as an app, using the Window Size popup to define the preview environment.

## Creating new data-role pages by copying code

Here are the things you need to do to as you copy and paste to create new pages:

Copy and paste a link in the list at the top of the page, and change the link so that the link target is the new "page". So, for example, when you create a page 5, that code will be added to the list after page 4, like this:

```
<li><a href="#page4">Page Four</a></li>

    <li><a href="#page5">Page Five</a></li>
```

As you can see, there are two changes in the copied code in the list.

Then, you need to create a new page by copying and pasting the generated page 4, and changing `<div data-role="page" id="page4"` to `<div data-role="page" id="page5"`.

```
<div data-role="page" id="page4">
    <div data-role="header">
        <h1>Page Four</h1>
    </div>
    <div data-role="content">
        Content
    </div>
    <div data-role="footer">
        <h4>Page Footer</h4>
    </div>
<div data-role="page" id="page5">
    <div data-role="header">
        <h1>Page Five</h1>
    </div>
    <div data-role="content">
        Content
    </div>
    <div data-role="footer">
        <h4>Page Footer</h4>
    </div>
```

Obviously, you will want to create custom content in the header, content, and footer sections of your new page. However, in order for the link you created in the list at the top of the page to work, you also need to be sure to change the page ID to match the `href` link you defined in the list at the top of the page.

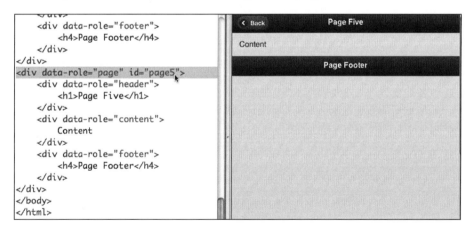

If you exhaust the potential to present content simply using "pages", as we have explored here, there are other jQuery Mobile containers you can experiment with to present content. We will walk through those options in the next chapter.

# Creating new data-role pages from the menu

Before moving on, I should note that you could have also accomplished the process of creating a new page by choosing menu options from the Dreamweaver Document Window menu.

To accomplish it locate your insertion point at the end of the last data-role page in your HTML page, and choose **Insert | jQuery Mobile | Page**. The jQuery Mobile Page dialog opens, and prompts you to define a page ID that is sequential, so if you do this after page 5, you will be prompted to make the ID of your new page page6 .

After you insert a new data-role page from the menu, you customize the content in the same way you would if you created the new data-role page by copying and pasting code.

# Customizing mobile page CSS styles

You can edit the content of jQuery Mobile pages by editing the HTML as we have just seen. However, you can customize the look of jQuery Mobile pages by changing the CSS styles associated with different jQuery Mobile objects.

This is complicated. The complications arise from the fact that there are a gazillion (roughly speaking) CSS styles that make up the jQuery Mobile style sheet.

The developers of jQuery Mobile have addressed this challenge by providing a set of themes. Themes are a formatting tool used in different kinds of auto-generated content environments. Blog generators such as WordPress or Drupal (these programs can be stretched beyond designing blogs, but that is their essential role) provide developers with a variety of themes that apply sets of colors, fonts, and background images.

As such, themes are, in general, something of an anathema to creative web page designers who want uniquely formatted pages, not paint-by-numbers pages that are clearly formatting with "out of a box" themes. Yet, themes provide an over-arching way to apply sets of formatting to pages. Therefore,, in formatting jQuery Mobile pages in Dreamweaver, we will both have to live within, and bust out beyond themes as a formatting technique.

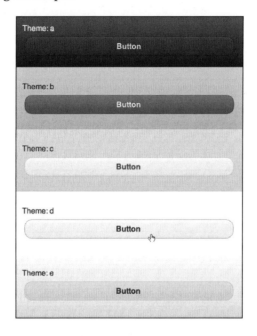

For a demonstration of all the standard jQuery Mobile themes, go to `http://jquerymobile.com/test/docs/pages/docs-pages.html#/test/docs/pages/pages-themes.html`.

Again, clearly, if you apply a jQuery Mobile theme to your page content, your mobile site won't have a unique look. There are five standard jQuery Mobile themes at the time of this writing (more are sold by vendors), and even if you mix and match different elements of the themes within a single site, your pages will have a highly recognizable cookie-cutter themed look. Not just other web designers, but savvy web surfers or app users will say, "Oh, I see someone created this site with an out-of-the-box theme... I have seen that one a million times before!"

Therefore, there are three options: One, you can live with the options available in themes, which is not an option for creative designers. Two, you can dispose of themes all together and hack your way through the massive set of CSS styles, formatting them one at a time. That might be a noble goal in theory, but far too time consuming, tedious, unmanageable and frustrating.

Or... you can apply a theme, and then customize it by defining custom CSS for the really important page elements. That will be our basic approach here.

# Default jQuery Mobile CSS

Before you start experimenting or working with the CSS file that comes with jQuery Mobile pages you might find it useful to keep the following URL handy: `http://code.jquery.com/mobile/latest/jquery.mobile.css`.

This URL leads to the jQuery Mobile CSS file. A version of the jQuery Mobile CSS file is included when Dreamweaver CS5.5 generates a jQuery Mobile starter page. If you look at the CSS file that opens when you generate a jQuery Mobile page in Dreamweaver CS5.5, you will see that it is `1.0a3/jquery.mobile-1.0a3.min.css`. Alternatively, an updated version of the CSS file that has been released since Dreamweaver CS5.5 incorporated this CSS file.

There are two good reasons to go online and grab the latest version of the jQuery Mobile CSS if that is an option. For one thing, it is periodically updated. The other is that if you corrupt the version of the CSS file that comes with Dreamweaver, something I have found quite easy to do, you can simply go to the link above, copy and paste the CSS code, and use that to create a "clean" CSS file to use when you build jQuery Mobile pages from scratch.

The CSS file you download will have a slightly different file name than the one provided with Dreamweaver, reflecting the current version. Once you download the new CSS file, you can save that CSS file with your own name to create customized CSS for your jQuery Mobile pages.

# Editing jQuery Mobile CSS

If you examine the CSS file that comes with jQuery Mobile pages, you will see that many of the class come in sets of five, indicated with "-a", "-b", "-c", "-d", or "-e" in the class style name.

You can identify these styles either in the CSS code itself, or in the friendly environment of Dreamweaver's CSS Styles panel. Many of these class styles displays in the CSS Styles panel are more or less grouped together. For example, the class styles that define the look of Theme A are listed in the beginning of the set of styles, and have "-a" at the end of, or in their style names.

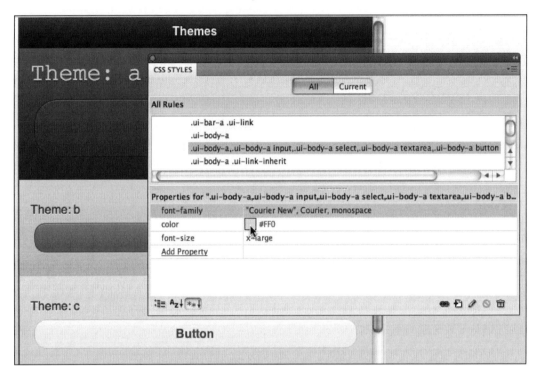

Much as it conflicts with the philosophical approach associated with Dreamweaver that is creating unique web page color schemes, font sets, and so on. If we are going to take advantage of jQuery Mobile, we have to live with jQuery Mobile themes, then, within that construct, we can stretch the envelope, distort the paradigm, bend the rules…, and so on to create fully customized pages.

# Applying and customizing themes

First, let's examine how themes are applied. You can define which jQuery Mobile theme is applied to any element by using the `data-theme` property in HTML5. For example, to apply theme "e" to a page with a div ID of "page", use this code:

```
<div data-role="page" id="page" data-theme="e">
```

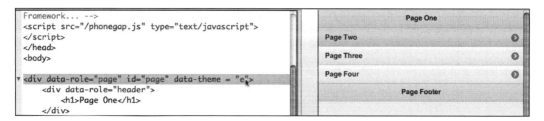

Alternatively, to take a second example, if you wish to apply theme "a" to a content element on a page, use this code:

```
<div data-role="content" data-theme="a">
```

Understanding that there are, in many cases, five different sets of class styles that define how objects are formatted in the jQuery Mobile pages demystifies the massive set of styles, and makes "trial and error" formatting less of a guessing game. Whatever approach you take towards combining formatting with jQuery Mobile themes on the one hand, and editing CSS on the other, you do need to understand which theme is in effect for your page, or element of a page.

For example, if you have applied Theme "a" to a section of a page, then any adjustments you wish to make to how that content looks will be made by editing the CSS for Theme "a" elements.

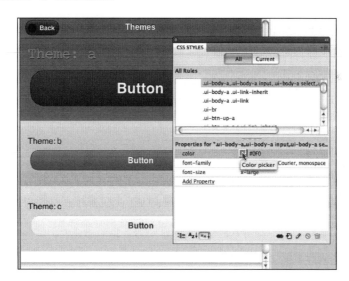

After that, again we are back to the basic lessons of *Chapter 1* and *Chapter 3* in this book: identifying CSS that is matched with page elements, and editing that CSS in the CSS Properties panel. All the CSS detective skills you picked up working through *Chapter 2* in particular will pay off now.

Without rehearsing all that, let's review a few points of approach:

- You can identify and edit div tag styles—mostly class styles—to reformat content containers and other objects

- You can identify and edit element (tag) rules in the CSS dialog. For example, you can redefine the heading and paragraph tags

- In applying both of the preceding methods, you can draw on and apply the techniques explored in *Chapter 2*, except that you have to—additionally—take into account that many objects (class styles) in the jQuery Mobile page have specific rules for each of the five themes.

With these three bits of advice, you are equipped to take the CSS style sheet provided with the jQuery Mobile page, and customize it to create a fully unique look.

# Looking ahead: Generating mobile apps

There are more jQuery objects left to explore, especially the ones that are not part of the starter page. We will examine those in the next chapter. However, we can pause and reflect here on the obvious fact that in creating customized content and styling, you have done the bulk of the work necessary to define an app!

If only Dreamweaver CS5.5 had tools to export our page to an app… Oh, right, it does! You will learn to use those in the final chapter of this book.

But the point of bringing this into the conversation now is that, as you design your mobile pages with jQuery Mobile in Dreamweaver CS5.5, be conscious of the fact that your page might well become an app. Moreover, examine your design, the navigation structure, and the accessibility of content in that light. For example, as much as possible, avoid external links that would take a visitor out of your ecosystem, and onto the Web. Such external links are more appropriate in regular websites than they are in apps. Similarly, pay more attention to consistency within your page than you might for a full-sized web page that will not become an app.

# Recipe: Build a mobile web page with jQuery Mobile objects

In this recipe, we will reload the jQuery Mobile CSS style sheet file, generate a new local jQuery Mobile page (on our own computer), and customize the content and style of the page.

As with every recipe in this book, the prerequisite is that you are working in a defined Dreamweaver site. I am calling mine jq01, but in any case if while creating a site, the essential nature of that is not clear, review *Chapter 1* and create a site.

1. In a browser, go to `http://code.jquery.com/mobile/latest/jquery.mobile.css`. This link opens the CSS file. Download the CSS file. Copy the entire content of the page, and save it as `jq.css`. One reliable technique for doing this is to choose **File | New** in Dreamweaver. When the **New Document** dialog opens, select **Blank** page in the **Category** column, **CSS** in the **Page Type** column, and click on **Create**. Delete the default code, and paste in the CSS you copied from the preceding link. Save the file in your Dreamweaver site as `jq.css`.

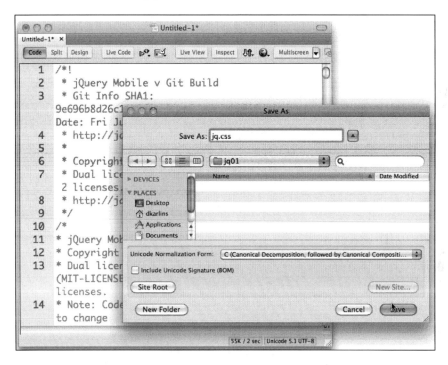

2. Create a new jQuery Mobile page by choosing **File | New**. In the **New Document** dialog, choose **Page from Sample** in the **Category** column, **Mobile Starters** from the **Sample Folder** column, and **jQuery Mobile (PhoneGap)** from the **Sample Page** column. Click on **Create**. Save the page as `index.html`, and copy files as prompted by the dialog.

3. In the CSS Styles panel, delete the default CSS file, and link `jq.css`. Resave your HTML page, and all dependant pages as prompted.

4.  Set up a convenient workspace by choosing Split view, setting the Design view Window Size to 480 pixels wide by 800 high, and viewing your CSS Styles panel.

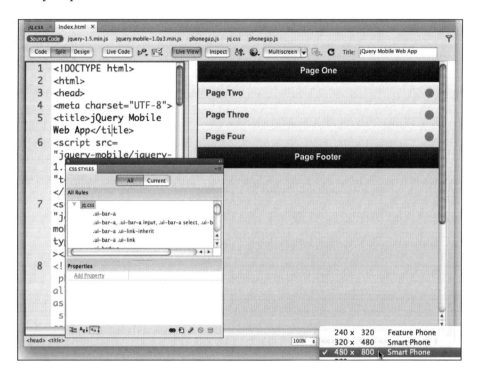

5.  Create a link to a new, fifth jQuery Mobile page by copying and pasting the following code

    ```
    <li><a href="#page4">Page Four</a></li>
    ```

    And editing the pasted new line of code to read:

    ```
    <li><a href="#page5">Page Five</a></li>
    ```

    ```
    19      <div data-role="content">
    20          <ul data-role="listview">
    21              <li><a href="#page2">Page Two</a></li>
    22              <li><a href="#page3">Page Three</a></li>
    23              <li><a href="#page4">Page Four</a></li>
    24 ▾          <li><a href="#page5">Page Five</a></li>
    25          </ul>
    26      </div>
    ```

6.  Create a new, fifth jQuery Mobile page by copying and pasting the code:

    ```
    <div data-role="page" id="page4">
        <div data-role="header">
            <h1>Page Four</h1>
    ```

```
    </div>
    <div data-role="content">
          Content
    </div>
    <div data-role="footer">
          <h4>Page Footer</h4>
    </div>
</div>
```

Edit the pasted code to read:

```
<div data-role="page" id="page5">
    <div data-role="header">
          <h1>Page Five</h1>
    </div>
    <div data-role="content">
          Content
    </div>
    <div data-role="footer">
          <h4>Page Footer</h4>
    </div>
</div>
```

```
56  <div data-role="page" id="page4">
57      <div data-role="header">
58          <h1>Page Four</h1>
59      </div>
60      <div data-role="content">
61          Content
62      </div>
63      <div data-role="footer">
64          <h4>Page Footer</h4>
65      </div>
66  </div>
67  <div data-role="page" id="page5">
68      <div data-role="header">
69          <h1>Page Five</h1>
70      </div>
71      <div data-role="content">
72          Content
73      </div>
74      <div data-role="footer">
75          <h4>Page Footer</h4>
76      </div>
77  </div>
```

7. Customize the content of the first page, and replace the placeholder header, content, and footer on each page with your own content as shown in the following screenshot:

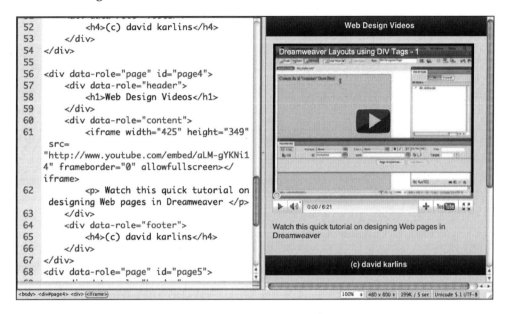

8. Apply a theme to the entire data-page by entering the code `data-theme="x"` where x is a letter from a-f. Note that Dreamweaver supplies code hints for the available data-themes. Examine the results of each theme in Live View, and select one.

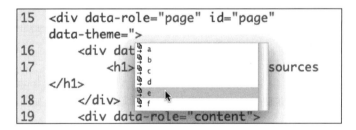

9. As you become familiar with the styles in jQuery Mobile pages, you might want to rely on the **All** tab in the CSS Styles panel. But as you familiarize yourself with these styles, experiment with using the **Current** tab in the CSS Styles panel to identify and modify styles that are applied to various elements in your page layout.

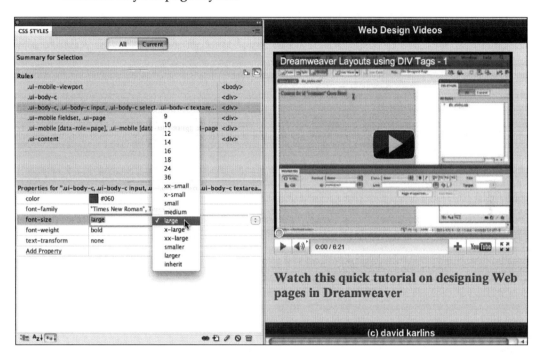

10. Continue to customize the look of your site through a combination of assigning themes to various elements using data-theme coding, and customizing CSS. Save your page.

# Summary

In this chapter, we covered the basic elements of creating complete jQuery Mobile pages in Dreamweaver CS5.5. Those "pages" are pages on two levels. On one level, they are regular HTML pages, using HTML5 (combined with CSS and JavaScript supplied via jQuery Mobile). On the other level, this HTML page has jQuery data-pages which are basically pages within a page. This technique allows us to create a mobile web page that allows visitors to navigate without having to wait for their mobile device to load additional pages.

In creating this jQuery Mobile page (with a set of data-pages), we relied on the Dreamweaver CS5.5 starter page. This page includes many of the most widely used jQuery Mobile elements. There are other useful jQuery Mobile page elements as well, and we will explore them in the next chapter.

You edit the content of jQuery Mobile pages just as you would any HTML5 page. Thus, all the blood, sweat, and tears you poured into mastering the basic techniques involved in customizing content of HTML5 pages in earlier chapters is paying off here. However, because page formatting and navigation rely so heavily on JavaScript (the jQuery Mobile library of scripts in particular), you need to rely more on Live View to see how pages will look compared to normal HTML5 pages.

Editing the CSS in jQuery Mobile pages also involves the basic skills you have learned to this point, and new challenges. Those new challenges are defined by the fact that jQuery Mobile pages involve many CSS rules, and that jQuery Mobile CSS is organized into themes. Creating truly customized pages involves some assignment of themes, along with customizing CSS associated with those themes.

In the basic jQuery Mobile page you have learned to create in this chapter, you have the foundation of mobile and tablet apps. You will learn to create those in the final chapter of this book.

# 10
# Adding jQuery Mobile Elements

In this chapter, you will learn to build jQuery Mobile-based pages from scratch. Moreover, you will learn additional techniques for designing those pages—layout grids, and collapsible blocks.

In the previous chapter, you learned to build a mobile-device-friendly page based on jQuery Mobile. That page, in turn, was organized into jQuery Mobile data-pages, which feels like distinct pages to a visitor. However, they have the advantage of actually being part of a single HTML page. This has a number of advantages, the two most important being that a) the "pages" (the data-pages) all load at once, giving a visitor a seamless, wait-less browsing experience; and b) this setup facilitates converting the entire page to a mobile device app—a process we will explore in the final chapter of this book.

One reason why it is valuable to sum up and reflect on this is that in this chapter, the two new page design techniques you will learn are alternative ways to pack content into the tiny environment of a mobile device browsing viewport. Like data-pages, these jQuery Mobile objects *also* function within a single HTML page.

In addition, we will explore some dimensions of using forms in jQuery Mobile pages, taking advantage of, and addressing unique possibilities and challenges in collecting form data in mobile pages.

The topics that we will cover in this chapter are:

- Creating a new jQuery Mobile page from scratch
- Inserting a layout grid
- Inserting collapsible blocks
- Using input forms with jQuery Mobile (Jump menu, Input form, Special Mobile form elements)
- **Recipe**: Build a page with collapsible blocks

# Creating jQuery Mobile pages from scratch

jQuery Mobile pages include HTML, JavaScript from the jQuery Mobile library, and CSS. In the previous chapter, you created jQuery Mobile pages using one of the (essentially identical) jQuery Mobile starter pages in Dreamweaver CS5.5. That page came with the three essential elements, plus template and placeholder content.

In many cases, that starter page is a good place to start in creating jQuery Mobile pages. However, there are other ways to design pages using different jQuery Mobile layout techniques, specifically layout grids and collapsible blocks. In general, given small viewport in mobile devices, you will choose *one of* these approaches to designing mobile pages. Therefore, if you are using layout elements other than data-pages, you will want to start by creating a blank jQuery Mobile page, and populating it from scratch.

# Interface options

Before embarking on the process of building jQuery Mobile pages more or less from scratch, let me introduce you to two interface options for adding jQuery Mobile objects in Dreamweaver's Design view.

The first, which I will be relying on from here on, is to insert jQuery Mobile objects from the **Document** menu. Choosing **Insert | jQuery Mobile** opens a submenu from which you can insert any of the available jQuery Mobile objects in Dreamweaver CS5.5. As noted, this is the technique we will rely on for the rest of this chapter so I won't linger on that approach here.

However, there is an alternate technique for inserting jQuery Mobile objects, and that is to use the **Insert** panel. Choosing **Window | Insert from the Document** menu opens the **Insert** panel. Moreover, choosing jQuery Mobile from the select menu in that panel provides access to jQuery Mobile insert options.

The reason I prefer to use the menu options instead of the **Insert** panel is that I do much of my work on a laptop, and thus operate with constrained workspace on my screen. I like to keep my workspace free of unnecessary panels. Moreover, even when I work in a desktop environment, I prefer an uncluttered look on my screen. But to each his or her own, and if you feel more comfortable with the **Insert** panel on your screen, feel free to insert jQuery Mobile objects from there by placing your insertion point, and clicking on an object in the **Insert** panel to insert that object.

# Step 1 – Creating an HTML5 page

jQuery Mobile pages should be HTML5 pages. Remember, any device that is new enough to support a browser is new enough to support HTML5, so support for HTML5 is not an issue when designing for mobile devices.

Once again, it is important to emphasize the critical role of working within a defined Dreamweaver *site*. Without that, the multiple HTML, JavaScript, and CSS files required for jQuery Mobile pages (not to mention the image, media, and other files needed for a *regular* web page) won't mesh properly.

So, the first step in creating a jQuery Mobile page from scratch is to choose **File | New**, and in the **New Document** dialog select **Blank Page** from the category column on the left, **HTML** from the **Page Type** column, **None** from the **Layout** column, and **HTML5** from the **DocType** popup. Then click on **Create**.

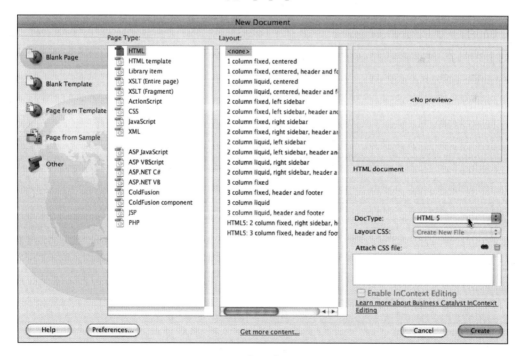

As soon as you begin to insert jQuery Mobile objects, Dreamweaver will open pages that should be linked to your page. Therefore, it is a good idea to save your page right away, before adding any jQuery Mobile objects.

Moreover, because we are working within various models based on a *single* HTML page, it makes sense to name the page index.html. That way, the page will open directly when the URL that it is saved to is addressed in a browser.

# Step 2 – Inserting a jQuery Mobile "page"

As we saw in the previous chapter, the basic framework for jQuery Mobile content is the data-page. This jQuery Mobile object encloses everything else; including what might appear to be additional "pages." In this chapter, we will be employing different jQuery Mobile objects to present (and hide) content, but we still want to start with a jQuery Mobile "page".

To emphasize and expand on this point: jQuery widgets, objects that supply content, have to be inserted within jQuery Mobile pages. Otherwise, they lack framing code that makes them work.

Therefore, the second step in preparing to present jQuery Mobile objects is to insert a jQuery Mobile Page. Moreover, as we do that—in the form of the Dreamweaver jQuery Mobile Page widget, Dreamweaver CS5.5 will generate essential jQuery Mobile files in your defined Dreamweaver *site.*

If you try to skip this step, you won't have the essential jQuery Mobile framework installed, and the jQuery objects you try to install won't work. In fact, Dreamweaver (reasonably) won't *let* you embed jQuery Mobile objects outside of the framework of a jQuery Mobile page, with the attendant files.

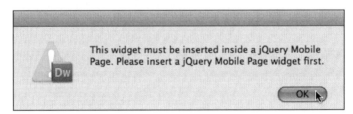

Generate the jQuery Mobile Page widget by choosing **Insert | jQuery Mobile | Page**. The **jQuery Mobile Files** dialog appears. The **Remote (CDN)** option links versions of the required files at the jQuery Mobile site, and the **Local** option links local versions of those same files to your pages. In the previous chapter, I explained the minor differences between these options for generating the CSS and other files required for jQuery Mobile pages. The short version is that the **Remote (CDN)** option attaches a remote CSS file maintained by jQueryMobile.com, while the

**Local** option attaches a local version of that style sheet file (a version that is installed as part of Dreamweaver CS5.5). The Remote (CDN) option only works if you are working with an Internet connection. If you elect to use the Remote (CDN) option, you won't be able to edit the CSS file until you download it, and save it in your site folder.

Three of the four boxes in the dialog are not really editable. Dreamweaver does indicate where it is getting the JavaScript files (files with .js filename extensions) and CSS file used in the widget, along with the folder on your own computer where Dreamweaver CS5.5 stores these files.

As we began to explore in the previous chapter, the jQuery development community periodically updates these jQuery Mobile files. If you wish, you can download these files yourself from jquery.com. In the previous chapter, we walked through how to download and replace the .css file that is part of the jQuery Mobile widget. If you have a compelling reason to do so, you can also download the latest version of the JavaScript files in the **jQuery Mobile Files** dialog, but in foreseeable circumstances, you can simply rely on Dreamweaver to download the appropriate files. The **jQuery Mobile Updates** link takes you to an Adobe page that includes some update information for jQuery files.

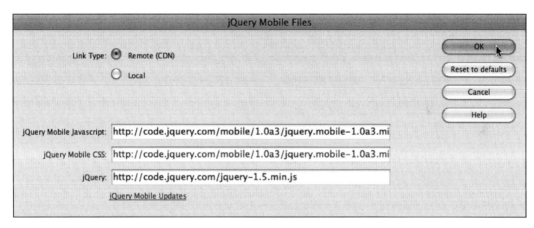

However, in short, you can choose the **Local** option in the **Link Type** area, and click on **OK** to generate a jQuery Mobile Page widget. When you do, the jQuery Mobile Page dialog appears. Naming the jQuery page "page" is default choice for the ID box. Later, as you customize and add content, you can change this, but the default option works fine to start with.

Normally you will want a header and footer on your jQuery Mobile page. You can elect to generate header and/or footer objects using the respective checkboxes. We explored these elements of jQuery Mobile pages in the previous chapter.

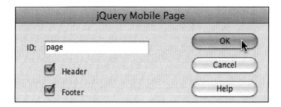

When you click on **OK** on the **jQuery Mobile Page** dialog, a basic, jQuery Mobile page is generated with placeholder text. This page is similar to the jQuery Mobile starter page you learned to generate in the previous chapter, but much simpler. It will be helpful to refresh your memory of techniques we explored in the previous chapter for viewing and editing the content of this page, including the nature and role of toggling **Live View** on and off, using the Window Size popup to size a mobile-sized Design view, and editing HTML in Split view with **Live View** on.

Also applicable is the discussion of replacing the default CSS file with your own (updated and safely backed up) jQuery Mobile CSS file, using the CSS Styles panel.

All the discussion of these techniques in the previous chapter applies to working with a custom-built jQuery Mobile page in Dreamweaver CS5.5.

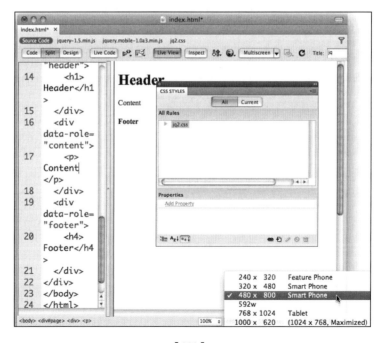

One thing that is immediately different from the experience of using a jQuery Mobile starter page is that there are, yet, no interactive or animated jQuery Mobile objects active on the page—just a basic page layout. We will add interactive, animated objects next.

# Inserting a Layout Grid

As we have discussed, columns play a greatly diminished role in pages designed for mobile devices. The reason is obvious: there isn't much width in the viewport of a mobile phone, and even tables have a narrower screen than laptops. Nevertheless, there are plenty of situations where it *is* useful to lay out content in columns in mobile-friendly pages. When that is appropriate, the tool is jQuery grids.

Can we use the good old `<div>` tags that served us so well in HTML to lay out page content in columns? Yes. What about using *tables* for layout? Well, that technique is actually supported within jQuery Mobile pages.

In addition, just to elaborate a bit, the only reason we don't use tables for page layout in jQuery pages is the same reason we don't use them anywhere else: they are clunky, hard to apply global styles to, hard to update, and don't support a lot of the attributes div containers support. That said, table design enthusiasts take note—you *can* design page layouts with tables in jQuery Mobile pages.

Moreover, again, regular divs can be used to create columns in jQuery Mobile pages.

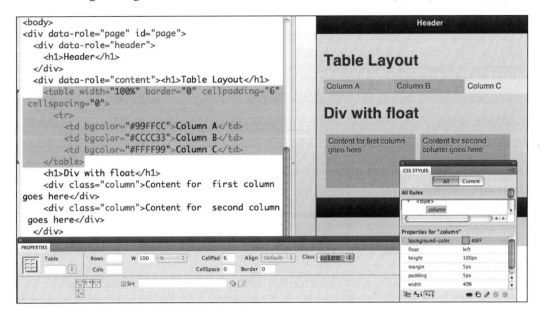

However, there is a more flexible, standard way to design column layouts within a jQuery Mobile page: The standard jQuery Mobile CSS file comes with a set of defined class styles called ui-block and ui-grid. Moreover, there are two sets of these styles, one for two-column layouts, and one for three-column layouts.

Dreamweaver's jQuery Mobile widget for a Layout Grid does a very complete job of generating a wide variety of grids, with definable numbers of columns and rows. Remember, as you generate such grids, that you *are* designing for a relatively narrow viewport of one kind or another and will want to be restrained in how many columns (and rows) you generate.

However, as you are vigilant from a design standpoint, you can relax on the technical front. The Layout Grid widget in Dreamweaver strings together fairly complex combinations of the 2-column and 3-column grids to create grids of 4, 5, 6, and more columns if you choose to do that.

In order to generate a layout grid in a jQuery Mobile page, make sure your insertion point is in the content div data-role. An easy way to do that is to select the text "content" in the code that is generated when you create a jQuery Mobile "page", and replace it with the layout grid, or, to place your cursor *after* the "content" placeholder text.

Then, choose **Insert | jQuery Mobile | Layout Grid**. The jQuery Mobile Layout Grid dialog opens. Choose a number of rows and columns, and click on **OK** to generate the layout grid.

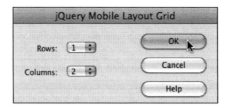

# Defining styles for Layout Grids

The jQuery Mobile Layout Grid uses two class styles— `.ui-grid-a` for two column grids, and `.ui-grid-b` for three column grids. Dreamweaver, as noted, will generate HTML from the jQuery Mobile Layout Grid dialog to string together combinations of these two grids to create grids of more than three columns. In addition, Dreamweaver CS5.5 generates `.ui-grid` class styles to define specific block formatting.

The point? By editing the properties of `.ui-grid` and `.ui-block` class styles, you can define the appearance of elements of layout grids.

As you do that, avoid editing the widths of the grids or blocks, or the margins, padding or border dimensions. Changing those properties will destroy the generated layout. However, you *can* edit background colors and images.

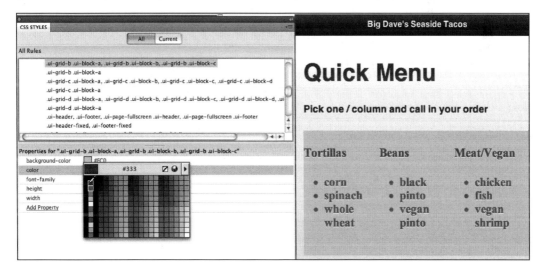

# Designing mobile pages into a collapsible block

jQuery Mobile Pages, as you saw in the previous chapter, essentially create the sense of navigating from page to page while relying on JavaScript to actually display and hide content. That is the technique used in the sample jQuery Mobile pages generated in Dreamweaver CS5.5.

Expandable blocks operate on a similar principle—they show and hide content depending on a visitor's actions. However, with expandable panels, this takes place through sections of the page appearing to expand or shrink.

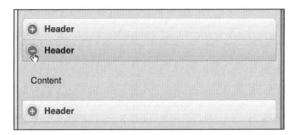

# Building a collapsible block

Like other jQuery Mobile objects, collapsible panels require the framework of a jQuery Mobile page. Therefore, the first step in implementing them is to create a jQuery Mobile page. This is done by choosing **Insert | jQuery Mobile | Page**. We explored the options for generating jQuery Mobile pages in Dreamweaver a bit earlier in this chapter.

Once you have generated a jQuery Mobile page, with all the attendant CSS and JavaScript files that make that work, you can define collapsible panels. Do that by setting your insertion point (this is most easily done in the code side of Split view, with **Live View** turned on).

Choose **Insert | jQuery Mobile | Collapsible Block**. No dialog appears; Dreamweaver CS5.5 generates HTML code for a set of three collapsible sections within the block.

After our experience with starter pages in the previous chapter, and Layout Grids in this chapter, and with your background in HTML5 and CSS, you have already conceptualized how we will customize the look and content of the collapsible block. We can change the formatting by using a combination of jQuery Mobile data-theme sets and customized CSS styles. Moreover, we can change the content by editing the HTML, including by copying and pasting collapsible blocks.

# Changing initial block state

The entire set of collapsible elements is defined by this code:

```
<div data-role="collapsible-set">
```

In between the opening and closing `<div>` tags for a collapsible set are individual expandable blocks:

```
<div data-role="collapsible" data-collapsed="true"> </div>
```

Alternatively, blocks that are expanded by default when the page opens, are defined with this code:

```
<div data-role="collapsible">
```

By default, the first of the three expandable sections is expanded when the page opens, and the other two are collapsed. Adding the parameter `data-collapsed="true"` to the initially open panel changes it to collapsed when the page opens.

Conversely, removing `data-collapsed="true"` from a panel changes it to display expanded when the page opens.

# Changing block data-themes and styles

We can add a data-theme parameter to any data block. For example, changing `<div data-role="collapsible">` to `<div data-role="collapsible" data-theme="e">` applies data-theme e (a yellow and red color scheme) to that block.

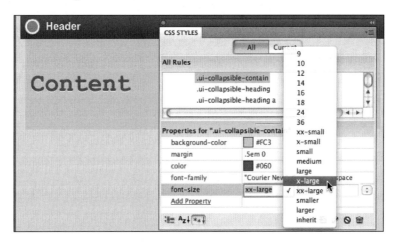

I won't rehearse the whole discussion / rant about the limitations of themes, but clearly to achieve any level of uniqueness, you will want to combine customized CSS with themes. The CSS styles associated with the collapsible panels, styles generally starting with `.ul-collapsible`, can be customized in the CSS Styles panel.

You will want to be cautious in changing dimensions; including padding, margins, and borders, as messing with these parameters might wreck the collapsible columns. However, you *can* customize fonts, colors, font sizes, background colors, and other properties.

The `.ui-collapsible-contain` style, for example, controls many of the properties of the content of an expanded block.

# Editing Collapsible Block HTML

Depending on your inclinations, you can edit the *content* of collapsible blocks in Design view, with Live View turned either off, or in Live View, by editing the content on the Code side of Split view. In either case, you just add HTML tags (like headings, paragraph tags, ordered or unordered list), and text, images, and media.

If you edit content in the Code side of Split View, click the Refresh button in the Document toolbar periodically to update the Design side of the view.

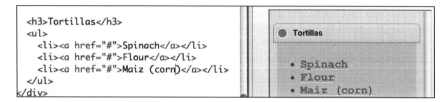

At this stage of the game, you have figured out on your own how to add a collapsible block to a set: just copy, paste, and edit an existing block.

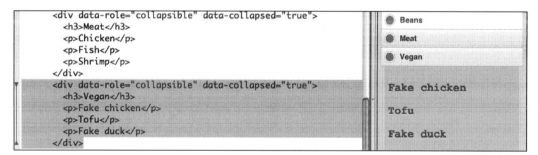

Moreover, since you asked (I read your mind), yes, you can embed collapsible blocks *within* a collapsible block. But the point, remember, is to keep mobile page layouts fairly simple, so—as the saying goes—when organizing content for mobile, less is more.

# Adding jQuery form objects

The experience of filling out a form in a mobile device environment is substantially different from filling out a form on a laptop or desktop. There is no mouse, or even (often) a *Tab* key to navigate between form fields. Big fingers and tiny options in popup menus make for a bad match. A form that might work fine in a full-sized browser may well be terribly uninviting and inconvenient in a mobile device.

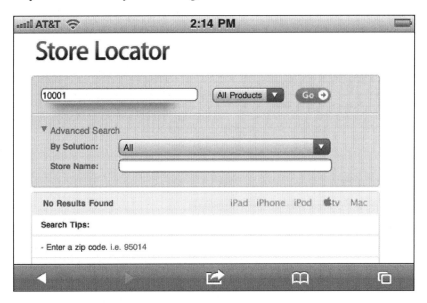

Part of the solution to that challenge is that mobile devices often convert form fields to more accessible elements. For example, options in a select menu might display much larger when tapped, making it easier to make a selection.

The other part of the solution for making forms accessible and inviting in mobile devices is to implement new form fields, such as sliders (where visitors can choose from a range of values by sliding a thumb on a bar) or flip toggle switches (with easy to use "on" and "off" switch options) to make filling out forms online more functional and more fun.

# Forms in Dreamweaver

Dreamweaver has historically provided three methods for creating forms. You can, of course, define forms and form fields using HTML in Code view. You can generate forms by choosing **Insert | Form**, defining a form, and then—within it—inserting form *fields* (like a text field) and the requisite buttons (like a Submit button to make the form do something). Recent versions of Dreamweaver have added Spry Validation form fields that first test data (for example, to see if it looks like an e-mail address) before allowing a visitor to submit the form. I note this history because a) you can't get where you are going if you don't know where you have been, or whatever that saying is; and b) all these techniques still work in mobile devices, so if you know any or all of them, you can supplement the *new* jQuery Mobile form tools in Dreamweaver CS5.5 with those tools.

Here, however, we will focus on the jQuery Mobile form tools that are geared to create mobile-friendly forms, and include form fields like the slider, and the toggle switch, that until now have not been easily accessible in Dreamweaver.

Before diving into those tools, here is the world's most compressed course in creating forms in Dreamweaver (in general, not just using jQuery Mobile form tools):

1.  All form *fields* (like a text field, or a Submit button) have to be enclosed within a *single set* of `<form>` tags.

2.  In order to work, forms must have a defined action. For forms that connect to server side scripts (scripts written in programming languages like PHP or Perl, and reside on a server), the action is a link to post the data to the location of that script at a server. There are many free, fairly intuitive online resources for generating such scripts, with directions for how to upload them to your server and connect them to a form. A very simple, but functional action is to simply e-mail form content to an e-mail address using the action `mailto:xxx@xxx.xx` where xxx@xxx.xxx is an e-mail address. This simple solution then launches an e-mail client (program) and prompts the user to e-mail the form content to the provided e-mail address.

With those two basic rules in mind, let's examine new tools in Dreamweaver CS5.5 for creating forms with particularly mobile-friendly form fields.

# Creating a jQuery Mobile form

Like the other jQuery Mobile objects we have examined in this chapter, jQuery Mobile form elements can only be inserted into an already generated jQuery Mobile page. However, beyond that, it is also necessary to create both a *form* and a submit button using more traditional form features in Dreamweaver. Therefore, the process of setting up a form that will enclose jQuery Mobile form elements is:

1.  Create a jQuery Mobile Page
2.  Insert a form inside that jQuery Mobile Page with a Submit (button)
3.  *Then* you can add specifically mobile-friend jQuery Mobile form fields to that form

That three-step process is not the only way to create jQuery Mobile forms, and it does not incorporate every possible option for such forms. However, it is a basic foundation for making it possible to implement jQuery Mobile form elements.

Let us work through an example, creating a basic form that, when submitted, will send content to an e-mail address through an e-mail client. These steps assume—of course—that you are working in a defined Dreamweaver *site*, and that you have created an HTML5 page with a jQuery Mobile Page. With those pieces in place, the following steps flesh out the "three-step process" outlined in rougher strokes above:

1.  Inside the jQuery Mobile Page (you can select the placeholder "content" text in either Code view or Design view to make sure you are doing this right), choose **Insert | Form | Form**. The **Tag Editor – form** dialog appears. Only the options in the **General** tab are essential to creating a form.

2.  In the **Action** field, enter `mailto:[an email address]` using, of course, a real e-mail address. If you were working with a form linked to a server-side script, you would enter the URL of that script here.

3.  Choose **Post** from the **Method** dropdown, this is the method almost always used to send form data to a location.

4.  The **Encoding Type** parameters are defined by the script that is managing the data. If you are uploading via e-mail, enter `text/plain`

5.  Enter a name for your form in the **Name** box.

6.  The Target dropdown allows you to choose **_blank** if you want to open the linked form script in a new browser window — generally that is not necessary.

7.  After completing the **Tag Editor – form** dialog, click on **OK** to generate the form.

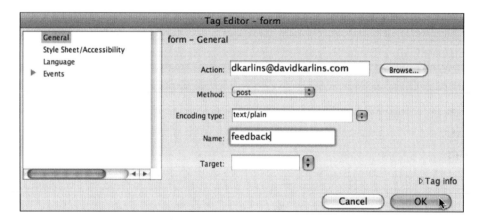

The set of steps above simply defined a form. There are no form fields in that form yet, so nothing in Live View indicates there even is a form. You can see the form code in Code view of course, and you can see the form itself, indicated by a red outline, in Design view with Live View turned off.

Remember "rule #1" from earlier in this section: *All form fields have to be inside a form.* So make sure you are clear on where your form is on your page, even though it has no content as of yet.

With your cursor *inside your form*, choose Insert > Form > Button. We are not (quite) yet at the stage of integrating special jQuery Mobile form fields, so this option is available simply from the **Insert | Form** submenu. When the **Input Form Accessibility Attributes** dialog appears, you do not need to enter anything in any of the fields, simply click on **OK** to generate a **Submit** button.

You now have the basic elements of a form: the form itself with a defined action, and a Submit button. *Now* it's time to add jQuery Mobile form fields.

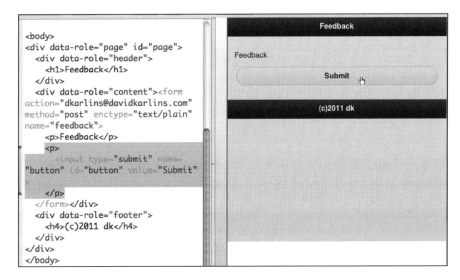

# Special mobile form fields

I noted earlier that mobile devices often have built-in interface tools to make form content more accessible. So does jQuery Mobile. When you place standard HTML form fields, like text boxes, checkboxes, and buttons, jQuery Mobile substitutes custom form fields that are more accessible in mobile devices. Checkboxes are made larger, select menus pop up lists of large buttons, form field labels and field names are resized to maximize screen real-estate.

So, some of the "special" form fields available from the jQuery Mobile submenu are simply adaptations of standard HTML form fields. Others are new to the HTML form field set. In either case the jQuery Mobile form fields include, as noted, special formatting that makes them more mobile-friendly.

Let us examine three of these form fields, and based on those examples, you will be able to work with additional form fields in the jQuery Mobile set. In *each* of these examples, *be sure that you are inserting the jQuery Mobile form fields within the set of* <form> *tags*.

# Inserting a text input field

Text fields are the most flexible way of collecting data in forms. They are used to collect user names, passwords, e-mail addresses, shipping addresses, and more.

To insert a jQuery Mobile text input field in a form, choose **Insert | jQuery Mobile | Text Input**. (If you want to allow multiple line input, choose **Text Area** instead). The jQuery Mobile text input field is automatically sized, but you have to replace the label placeholder text (**Text Input**) with your own text. You can do this in Design view (with Live View off) or in Split view.

You can also replace the input name by changing the default field name for the text field by editing the code `name="textinput"` with another field name inside the quotes. However, avoid spaces and special characters (stick to letters and numbers). So, for example, to rename a text input field "email" you would change this code to `name="email"`

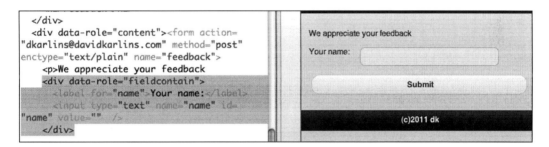

# Inserting a slider

Everybody is rating everything these days. You might not have read much physics, but how would you rate Bosonic string theory on a scale of 1-100? Well, OK... there *are* valid reasons to include rating options in a mobile form. Moreover, if you are going to including a "rate this ... (whatever)" in your form, you should make it easy for people to do that.

Enter the *slider*—a particularly handy way to input values in a mobile form.

To insert a slider in a jQuery Mobile form, choose **Insert | jQuery Mobile | Slider**. Customize the slider as follows:

1. Replace the **Slider** label text with your own text.
2. Replace the `value="0"` code with a value that will display by default
3. Replace the `min="0"` code with a value that will be the minimum value

4. Replace the `max="100"` code with a value that will be the maximum value

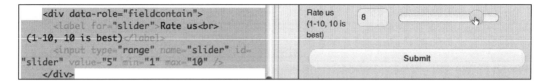

# Inserting a toggle switch

Toggle switches provide a handy way for large fingers to easily choose "yes" or "no"; "in" or "out"; or make some other two-option choice in a mobile device.

To insert a toggle switch in a jQuery Mobile form, choose **Insert | jQuery Mobile | Flip Toggle Switch**.

Customize the toggle switch as follows:

1. Replace the **Option** label text with your own text.

2. Replace Off (not in quotes) in the code `<option value="off">Off</option>` code with your own text

3. Replace On (not in quotes) in the code `<option value="on">On</option>` code with your own text

```
<div data-role="fieldcontain">
    <label for="flipswitch">Get on our
list?</label>
    <select name="flipswitch" id=
"flipswitch" data-role="slider">
        <option value="off">Nope</option>
        <option value="on">Yup!</option>
    </select>
</div>
```

# Formatting jQuery Mobile Form Fields

As you have seen in the preceding three examples, inserting jQuery Mobile form fields is pretty intuitive. And, in addition to adjusting field parameters (like labels, or values for fields like sliders) in Code view, you can also adjust some of the field properties in the Properties panel.

That said, the less you mess with the parameters of these jQuery Mobile form fields the better. Some work has gone into configuring them so that they fit well in, and work well with mobile devices. Avoid, for example, tweaking the display width of the fields—something you would probably do if you were designing for laptops and desktops. The jQuery Mobile form fields do a nice job of fitting themselves, and their associated labels, into mobile viewports.

You *can* customize the look of jQuery Mobile form fields by using data-theme settings, and by customizing CSS—using the same basic approach we have used throughout this chapter to identify CSS classes and tweak or radically redesign them in the CSS Styles panel.

Without reviewing that in detail, you can apply a data theme by inserting the code `data-theme=(x)` (where x is a letter, at this writing a-e, that defines a jQuery Mobile data theme) after the <div> tag, that opens the form area of the page. Moreover, you can simply define an appropriate class style, and apply it to some or all of the form elements.

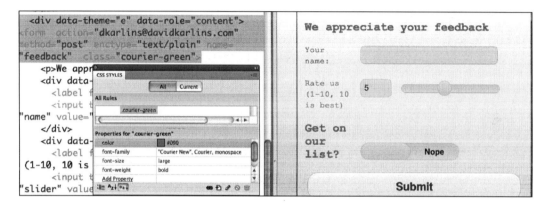

# Recipe: Build a page with collapsible blocks and a form

In this recipe, we will use a specific example to make the experience a bit more real. Surveys tell us that a huge percentage of people looking to grab a taco somewhere search online for a place to get one—on their mobile devices. So let us use my non-existent taco stand at Coney Island as a model for this recipe, and you can easily adapt it to your own needs.

The mobile page we build will have four collapsible blocks: menu, location, place orders, and a bit about the taco shop. In the course of building it, we will walk through creating four collapsible blocks, and embedding a form within one of the blocks. Here we go:

1. Of course, we are assuming you are working within a Dreamweaver site. If not, create a new one or open an existing one. Then choose **File | New** and in the **New Document** dialog, choose **Blank Page** in the **Category** column, **HTML** in the **Page Type** column, **<none>** in the **Layout** column, and **HTML5** from the DocType popup. Then click on Create.

2. Choose **File | Save**, and save the file as `index.html`. As this is going to be a one-page site, the `index.html` filename will open the page when the site's URL is addressed in a browser. Assign a page title of "Mobile Tacos".

3. At this stage of the process, by default, your cursor is in between the set of `<body>` tags. That is right where it should be. Insert a jQuery Mobile page by choosing **Insert | jQuery Mobile | Page**. As we are going to be keeping this project relatively simple and standard (but not *too* simple, or standard – don't worry), you can choose the **Remote (CDN)** Link Type option, and we will avail ourselves of the online version of the jQuery Mobile CSS file. With **Remote (CDN)** selected, click on OK.

4. The jQuery Mobile Page dialog opens. Click on **OK** with the default settings.

5. Replace the original `Header` placeholder text with "Coney Island Tacos". Alternatively, you can depart from my recipe right from the start, and freelance your own content from here on in. Replace the footer text with the imaginary website of Coney Island Tacos – `www.coneyislandtacos.com`. Use the **Insert | Hyperlink** menu option if you wish to define the hyperlink.

6. Define a work environment: Select Split View and choose 480x800 from the Window Size popup at the bottom of Design view. Turn on Live View.

7. Start with applying one of the jQuery Mobile themes for formatting. In the code side of Split view, enter the code `data-theme="e"` – or experiment with other themes (try a, b, c, d, or e).

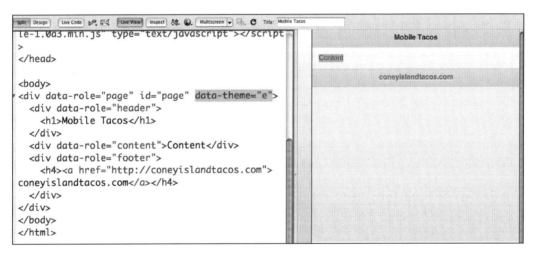

8. Next, let us create four expandable panels. Select the placeholder `content` text, and choose **Insert | jQuery Mobile | Collapsible Block**. Copy and paste one of the sets of collapsible block code to create a forth block. That code is:

```
<div data-role="collapsible" data-collapsed="true">
      <h3>Header</h3>
      <p>Content</p>
   </div>
```

9. Customize the headers for all four blocks. You will find the headers enclosed in `<h3>` codes. I am going with: Menu; Email Order; Find / Call Us; and About Coney Island Tacos as headers, but feel free to improvise.

10. Customize the content of all the collapsible blocks *except* the Email Order block—we will create a form for that next.

11. In the Email Order block (or whichever block you are using in a custom project for an input form), select the placeholder `content` text and choose **Insert | Form | Form**. In the **Tag Editor – form** dialog, make the action `mailto:youremail@youremail.xxx` (substituting your own e-mail address). Change the method to Post. Enter `text/plain` in the Encoding Type field and click on OK in the dialog. Here, it might be helpful to pop out of Live View to create the input form. Enter text "Order Form" inside the form and press *Return* or *Enter* to create a new line.

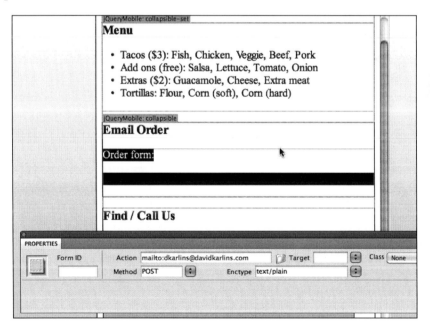

12. Making sure your insertion point is *inside the form,* choose **Insert | jQuery Mobile | Select Menu**. Change the label to **Taco**. Click on the **Select** menu itself, and use the List Values button in the Properties Inspector to open the List Values dialog. Enter labels (which appear in the form) and values (which are sent via e-mail when the form is submitted), using the **+** button to add new rows, and the up and down arrows to reorder items as necessary.

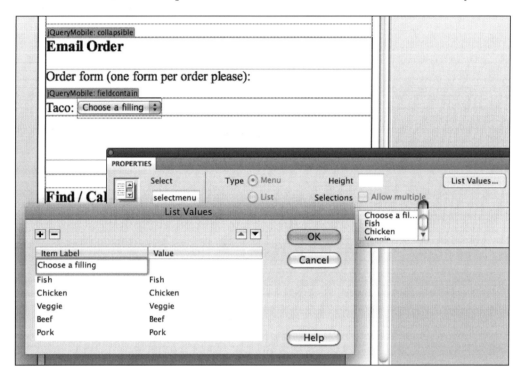

13. Add additional select menu to allow people to choose a taco shell.

14. Still within the form, choose **Insert | jQuery Mobile | Checkbox**. In the **jQuery Mobile Checkbox** dialog, enter **Sides** in the **Name** box, and choose 4 checkboxes and a horizontal layout, and click on **OK**. Edit the labels right in Design view in the Document window, and use the Properties inspector to define values for each checkbox that match the labels.

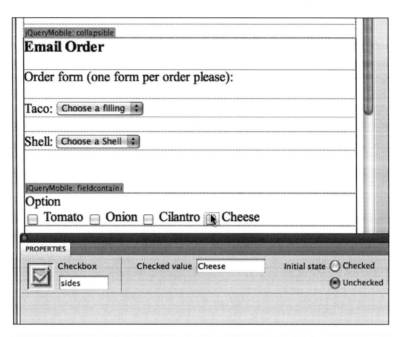

15. Complete the form by inserting a **Submit** button. Again, *make sure your insertion point is inside the form,* and choose **Insert | Form | Button**. Click on **OK** in the dialog without making any selections as a **Submit** button is the default.

16. To customize the look of the page, create a new class style. Use the New CSS Rule at the bottom of the CSS Styles panel to create a new CSS rule. Name the class style **Format**. As we are using a remote version of the associated CSS file, and as this is a one-page site, we can break the rule of relying exclusively on linked, external style sheets, so choose **(This Document Only)** from the popup at the bottom of the New CSS Rule dialog, and click on **OK** in the dialog. Define some custom properties, like font family, font size, and font color. Use the **Properties** inspector to apply the class style to selected elements on your page.

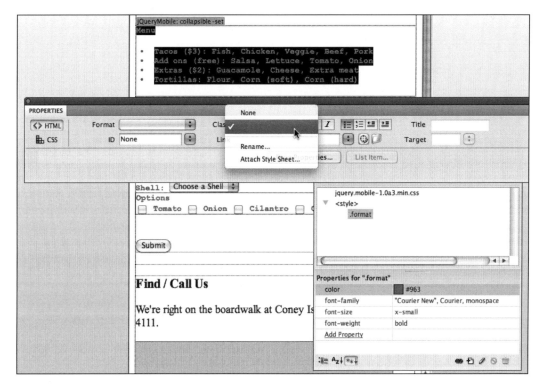

You can further customize the project by creating additional class styles, and applying them.

You can test the order form in a browser.

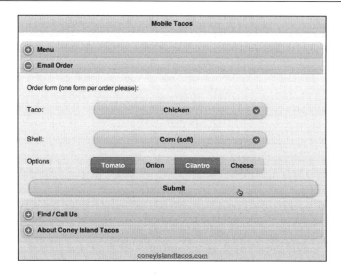

# Summary

In this chapter, you learned to create jQuery Mobile content from scratch by creating a regular HTML5 blank page, and then using a jQuery Mobile Page as a foundation.

Inserting a jQuery Mobile Page connects the page to jQuery Mobile JavaScript and CSS – either at a remote or local location.

With the jQuery Mobile Page generated, you can use additional page layout techniques, beyond the "pages" approach that comes with the sample jQuery Mobile pages we built pages from in the previous chapter.

One of those page design techniques is a Layout Grid, which is essentially div style columns, but with special properties that make the columns display effectively in mobile devices. We also learned, incidentally, that tables and regular divs work in jQuery Mobile pages as well.

The two most important jQuery Mobile techniques we introduced in this chapter are collapsible blocks, and jQuery Mobile form objects. Collapsible Blocks expand and collapse, and provide a very comfortable way to present content in a small viewport. Adding jQuery form objects creates more mobile-friendly versions of familiar input form objects (like text boxes), but also enables new form fields like sliders and Toggle flip switches. You will find a detailed exploration of every available jQuery Mobile form object and their properties at `http://jquerymobile.com/test/docs/forms/index.html`.

To customize the look and feel of jQuery Mobile-based pages, we can utilize the broad brush formatting of data-themes, supplemented with custom CSS.

# 11
# Generating Apps

Up to this point, we have covered every dimension of creating iOS and Android apps in Dreamweaver CS5.5, except... creating the apps themselves! We will do this now.

Particularly in the last two chapters, we have explored the design dimension of Dreamweaver CS5.5 for mobile, using jQuery Mobile tools. In this chapter, we won't review the entire journey we took to get here; I will assume that you can build a mobile-ready jQuery Mobile-based web page.

What we will cover here is the following:

- Generating apps from Dreamweaver—an overview
- Configuring application framework(s)
- Customizing mobile application settings
- Building apps
- Emulating mobile apps
- Recipe: Build and emulate a mobile app

## Generating apps from Dreamweaver—an overview

Let's return to a question we have explored in other chapters: What is the difference between a mobile-friendly web page, and an app? There is an ongoing debate over the answer to this question, and the general trend is that apps are getting to be more like well-designed mobile-friendly websites, and vice versa.

# Advantage: App vs web page

However, there are differences, beyond the underlying technology (apps are written in Objective-C programming language, not HTML5, JavaScript and CSS).

Among the advantages of packaging mobile web content as an app:

- Apps run on mobile devices even when the device is offline
- Related to the preceding point, apps load more quickly, particularly when there is a slow Internet connection
- Once installed, apps are easier to access on mobile devices — they display on the device desktop and do not require going through a browser
- Apps run in mobile devices without the encumbrance of a browser interface that takes up viewport space and distorts the presentation of the content
- Last and not least, you can sell apps online through Apple and Android's online stores

Apps have other advantages over mobile web pages, but generally, they involve programming techniques that are beyond the scope of features that can be easily generated from Dreamweaver CS5.5.

However, not every web presence needs to have an app version, and there are arguments for web pages over apps. As we have seen in the two previous chapters, mobile-friendly web pages with HTML5, CSS3, and JQuery Mobile objects run quickly and smoothly in mobile devices compared to "regular" web pages. Moreover, even with Dreamweaver CS5.5's new capacity to generate apps, it is still easier to develop and much easier to post a website than it is to submit an app.

# PhoneGap and Dreamweaver CS5.5

Apps for iOS and Android mobile devices are written in the Objective-C programming language. For some time, developers have been working on technology that would convert HTML5, CSS, and JavaScript to Objective-C apps.

The most widely supported and advanced technology for doing this is **PhoneGap**. The apps that result from PhoneGap conversion do not have all the functionality of apps written from scratch in Objective-C. Apps developed with PhoneGap are allowed by Apple for distribution through iTunes.

In addition, Dreamweaver CS5.5 relatively seamlessly integrates PhoneGap, with one major caveat: You can generate Android apps—for Google Android mobile devices—with Dreamweaver CS5.5 for Windows or on a Mac. However, you can only generate apps for iOS using Dreamweaver CS5.5 on a Mac. This limitation is not something inherent in Dreamweaver CS5.5. It is a product of the fact that Apple does not make the required tools for converting web pages to apps available for Windows computers. However, it does mean that if creating iOS apps is important to your web development work, you are constrained to, or stuck with, using Dreamweaver on a Mac.

# Configuring application framework(s)

Before you can use PhoneGap with Dreamweaver CS5.5 to generate mobile apps, you have to download, install, and connect Dreamweaver with the **SDKs (software developer kits)** for each operating system. This takes a couple of hours, but most of that time can be spent stir-frying vegetables, jogging, or watching a basketball game—the time involved is taken up by downloading rather massive files. This is particularly true if you install the iOS SDK, which—remember—is only available for Macs.

While downloading the Apple SDK files takes time, the process overall is very simple. Moreover, you only do it once. Once you install these tools and connect Dreamweaver to them, they stay ready to use.

# The App toolkits

Our exploration of using the respective toolkits for generating iOS and Android apps is constrained by two things. First, we are not high-level professional coders and second, these toolkits operate behind the scenes in Dreamweaver CS5.5, and for most of us, that is just fine.

However, it is worth taking a moment to identify what will be going on behind the scenes when we use Dreamweaver CS5.5 to generate Android and (on Macs) iOS apps.

The Xcode suite of tools was developed and is distributed by Apple. The entire set of tools can be used to write software for Mac OS X and iOS. The subset of these tools applicable here creates iOS apps—we are not going to be using Dreamweaver to write applications for desktops and laptops. Xcode 4 is the current version of Xcode. Apple sells it and it can be downloaded directly from Apple. However, Dreamweaver CS5.5 is configured, so that Mac users can install the Xcode4 seamlessly.

Eclipse is the toolset for creating apps for Google's Android mobile operating system. Like Xcode, it can be used for applications beyond mobile devices. It can be downloaded independently from Google.

As alluded to earlier, the third piece of the puzzle is PhoneGap, an open source set of tools supported by Adobe that uses the preceding toolkits (and others) to convert web pages to apps.

With this as a minimalist conceptual background, let's see how all this works in Dreamweaver CS5.5 to generate apps from web pages.

# Installing the frameworks

To configure the application framework(s) available for your system, choose **Site | Mobile Applications | Configure Application Framework**. You do not have to have any Dreamweaver files open, nor do you have to have a Dreamweaver site defined to do this. You do have to be connected to the Internet, as you will be downloading files.

When the **Configure Application Framework** dialog opens, click on the **Easy Install** button to download and install the SDK files for Android. This process really is easy, simply follow the prompts to download, install, and define the path to the Android SDK files.

If you are using Dreamweaver CS5.5 on a Mac, then you can use the provided link in the dialog to the **Apple iOS Dev Center**. You need to have an Apple account to do this, but they are free and you can sign up for one on the spot if you don't have one. Follow links to download the newest available version of Xcode and the iOS SDK. Once the download is complete, double-click on the installer on your computer. Download the SDK from there, and install it on your Mac the same way you install any application—double-click on the .dmg file and accept all installation defaults. After you install the programs, return to Dreamweaver's **Configure Application Framework** dialog (you should just leave Dreamweaver and this dialog open while you download the Apple SDK). Use the **Browse for file** next to the **iOS Developer Tools Path** text box and navigate to and select the OS X 10.6.x / Developer folder.

When you finish either or both of these processes, links will appear in the boxes in the **Configure Application Framework** dialog. Click on **Save** and Dreamweaver will be able to access these programs to generate apps for the applicable operating system, as shown in the following screenshot:

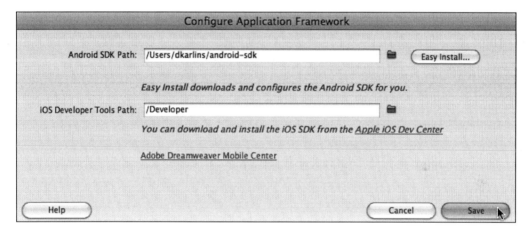

# Defining mobile application settings

Dreamweaver CS5.5 has conveniently packaged all the various settings required to define an app in a single dialog. These, range from technical information required by Apple and/or Android to choosing which image to use as an application icon, or in the startup screen (those images are optional).

Of course, the actual content of the app is defined by the mobile-friendly web page you design. However, the properties in the **Mobile Applications** dialog define elements of the app beyond the page content.

> Before launching the **Mobile Application Settings** dialog, you must have the page open that is to be exported to an app. Yes; I said the page, not the pages. As I think will be clear at this stage of the process, all the content that is to be exported into an app has to be on a single HTML page, even though that page can have multiple jQuery Mobile "pages" within it.

1.  So, with your page open and saved select **Site | Mobile Applications | Application Settings**. The dialog opens.

2.  The **Bundle ID** field satisfies technical requirements for both Android and iOS apps. Read the instructions in the dialog carefully and be sure, as you replace the template content with your own, not to delete the periods. The format is com.company.appname with your own company with your company name in the company space, and your own app name in the appname space. This information is not accessible to the public.

3.  Enter the application name in the **Application Name** field, and your name in the **Author Name** field.

4.  You can define an application icon to display on the mobile desktop by using the browse for file icons next to that field to select files on your computer. The file does not have to be embedded in your open page and it will automatically be scaled to the appropriate dimensions. The file does have to be in PNG format. Moreover, for iOS, you can similarly select a **Startup Screen PNG**.

5.  In the **Target Path** field, use the **Browse for File** icon to navigate to and select an output folder.

6.  Unless you have reasons not to, accept the default settings in the **Select Target OS Version** area of the dialog.

7.  When you have defined these settings, click on **Save**, as shown in the following screenshot:

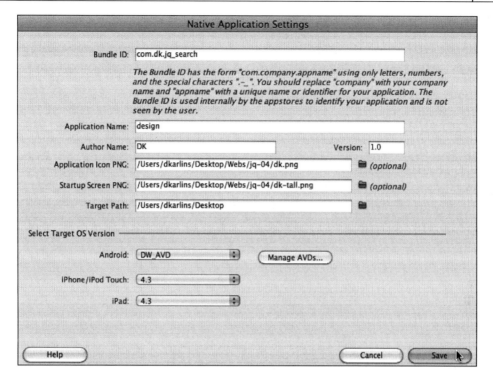

Don't rush out to call Steve Jobs (or his counterpart at Google) just yet to pressurize them to approve your app quickly. First, you don't have Steve's number and second, your app is not packaged (exported) yet.

What you have done is defined the settings that will be applied when your app is packaged. Moreover, you added a file named `phonegap.js` to your Dreamweaver site. You can see that file in your **Files** panel. You will need it when you take the next step and package your page as an app.

# Building and emulating apps

Having defined Native Application Settings, you can now package your open (and saved) page as an Android app. Moreover, if you are on a Mac, as an iOS app for either iPhone, iPad, or both.

When you installed the SDKs for Android and/or iOS, you also installed emulation software that replicates how apps will run in the target environments. It is hard to imagine a situation where you will not want to emulate and test your app immediately after generating it. In addition, you can (by choosing **Site | Mobile Applications | Build and Emulate**).

If you don't want to emulate your app(s), then you can simply choose **Site | Mobile Applications | Build**, to build, but not emulate the app.

When you select **Site | Mobile Applications | Build and Emulate**, a submenu provides options for each SDK you installed. If you installed the full set, on a Mac, then that set of options is iPhone, iPad, and Android, as shown in the following screenshot:

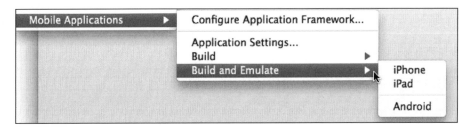

Choose one of your available apps. Packaging the app and launching the appropriate emulator takes some processing time and resources.

# Testing mobile apps on your computer

After an app is generated, a dialog appears displaying the path to your application, as shown in the following screenshot:

You can preview and test it in the emulator that is launched from Dreamweaver (but is a distinct, different application running on your computer).

Obviously, unless you have a touch screen on your laptop or desktop computer, you cannot fully simulate the experience of navigating the app in a touch screen environment.

1. Click and drag with your mouse to simulate that same experience with a finger on the screen.

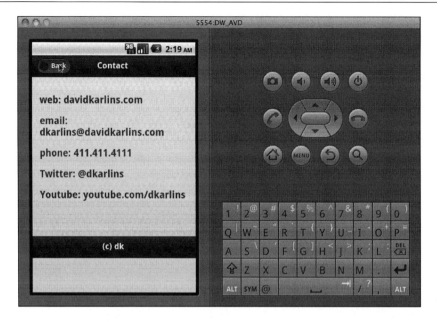

2.  After you test your app, you can change it in Dreamweaver, resave it, and rebuild the app. If you choose **Build and Emulate**, then the updated app will appear in the emulator

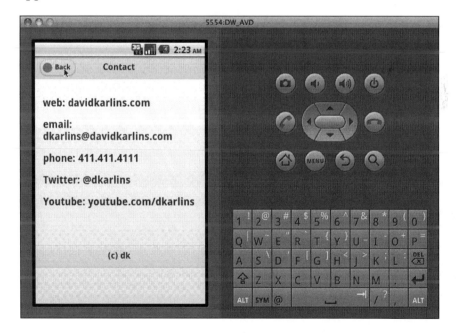

3. Again, the settings you defined in the **Application Settings** dialog apply to all apps you package. Therefore, if you are on a Mac and installed the iOS and Android SDKs in the **Configure Application Framework** dialog, then you can—one-by-one—package and test iPhone, iPad, and Android apps from the same Dreamweaver HTML page.

What remains is to sign up as a developer with Android and/or Apple and follow their rules for registering and submitting apps for sale at their respective online stores.

# Recipe: Building and emulating a mobile app

For this recipe, we will start with the assumption that you have:

- Created and are working within a Dreamweaver site
- Generated a single, mobile-ready HTML5 page using only HTML5 (including images and media); CSS (CSS3 effects are OK); and jQuery Mobile JavaScript (other JavaScript works, but the jQuery Mobile library has scripts specially configured to work well in mobile devices)

- Saved your page

- Created an application icon—an image saved in a PNG format (it can be of any size)

Given that the process is very similar for Android and iOS apps and that half of you cannot install the Apple iOS SDK (it is not available in Windows), we will package our page into an Android app for this recipe. However, you can follow almost the exact same steps with minor substitutions to package the page as an iPhone or iPad app as well.

1. Configure the Android Application Framework by selecting **Site | Mobile Applications | Configure Application Framework**. In the **Configure Application Framework** dialog click on the **Easy Install** button in order to download and install SDK files for Android.

2. If your HTML5 page is not open, and saved, open and save it now. Select **Site | Mobile Applications | Application Settings**. The **Native Application Settings** dialog opens. Define the following settings:

   - In the **Bundle ID** field, replace com.company.appname with your own company name in the company space, and your own app name in the appname space. Do not delete the periods.

   - In the **Application Name** field, enter the application name.

   - Enter your name in the **Author Name** field.

   - Use the browse for file icons next to the **Application Icon PNG** field to select an image file from your computer.

   - In the **Target Path** field, use the **Browse for File** icon to navigate to a select an output folder.

   - Accept the default settings in the **Select Target OS Version** area of the dialog and click on **Save**.

3. Select **Site | Mobile Applications | Build and Emulate | Android**. Wait while the app is built and opened in the Android emulator.

4. Test the app in the Android emulator. Note any changes you wish to make. Close the emulator, and edit the page in Dreamweaver. Re-build and emulate the app and test it again.

# Summary

Not all mobile web presences require an app. However, some do. Moreover, you can build apps from HTML5 pages right in Dreamweaver CS5.5.

Building and emulating apps is simple. The hard part was designing a mobile-friendly web page that will become the app.

Once you use Dreamweaver's tools for downloading and hooking up the Android and/or Apple iOS SDKs (software development kits), you can define Native Application Settings for any page, and use the same settings to build an app for Android and/or iOS devices.

You will almost certainly want to both build and emulate apps. Emulation allows you to test the app in a program supplied as part of the SDK that simulates how the app will run in the target device. Once you have tested the app in an emulator, you can edit it in Dreamweaver and re-build the app to apply changes.

The apps generated and saved by Dreamweaver use the **PhoneGap** framework, which is approved by both Google Android and Apple for developing apps. From a technical standpoint, the apps are ready to distribute and you do that by submitting them to the distribution networks for the respective systems — Android Market and/ or iTunes.

# Index

## Symbols

.box
  hover style  153
.sidebar1 element  62
.ui-collapsible-contain style  228
.ui-grid class  225
-moz-transform  130
&lt;/head&gt; tag  78
&lt;/title&gt; tags  118
&lt;/video&gt; tags  182
&lt;address&gt; element  92
&lt;aside&gt; element  90
  about  90
  CSS Float attribute  90
&lt;audio&gt; tag  165
&lt;body&gt; tag  44, 115, 185
&lt;div&gt; tags  65, 227
&lt;embed&gt; tag  169
&lt;figure&gt; element  99
&lt;footer&gt; element
  using  91
&lt;h2&gt; tag  37
&lt;head&gt; tag  78
&lt;header&gt; element
  about  6, 38
  adding  87
  content organizing, with hgroups  87, 88
  navigating  87
&lt;hgroup&gt; element
  adding  87
&lt;nav&gt; element  74
&lt;object&gt; tag  170
&lt;section&gt; elements  63
&lt;section&gt; tag  40
&lt;source&gt; tag  181

&lt;title&gt; tag  118
&lt;video&gt; element  185
&lt;video&gt; tag  182
3-column HTML5 page
  creating  27-29
  saving  27-29

## A

Add Property link  68, 130
Adobe's Flash Video. *See* FLV
Adobe Media Encoder CS5
  HTML video, creating  176-178
All tab  215
animated CSS3 effect
  creating  148-153
  settings  150
animated transform effect
  creating  148-153
  settings  150
Apple i-Gadgets
  troubleshooting  109, 110, 117, 118
Apple iOS Dev Center  249
application framework
  configuring  247
Application Settings dialog  254
Apply button  46
apps
  building  251
  emulating  251, 252
  generating, from Dreamweaver  245
  mobile apps, computer-testing  252-254
apps generation, Dreamweaver
  overview  245
  packaging mobile web content as app,
    advantage  246, 247

# W

# X

# Y

# X

**Thank you for buying
Dreamweaver CS5.5 Mobile and Web
Development with HTML5, CSS3,
and jQuery**

## About Packt Publishing

Packt, pronounced 'packed', published its first book "*Mastering phpMyAdmin for Effective MySQL Management*" in April 2004 and subsequently continued to specialize in publishing highly focused books on specific technologies and solutions.

Our books and publications share the experiences of your fellow IT professionals in adapting and customizing today's systems, applications, and frameworks. Our solution based books give you the knowledge and power to customize the software and technologies you're using to get the job done. Packt books are more specific and less general than the IT books you have seen in the past. Our unique business model allows us to bring you more focused information, giving you more of what you need to know, and less of what you don't.

Packt is a modern, yet unique publishing company, which focuses on producing quality, cutting-edge books for communities of developers, administrators, and newbies alike. For more information, please visit our website: www.packtpub.com.

## Writing for Packt

We welcome all inquiries from people who are interested in authoring. Book proposals should be sent to author@packtpub.com. If your book idea is still at an early stage and you would like to discuss it first before writing a formal book proposal, contact us; one of our commissioning editors will get in touch with you.

We're not just looking for published authors; if you have strong technical skills but no writing experience, our experienced editors can help you develop a writing career, or simply get some additional reward for your expertise.

## jQuery Mobile First Look

ISBN: 978-1-849515-90-0         Paperback: 216 pages

Discover the endless possibilities offered by jQuery Mobile for rapid Mobile Web Development

1. Easily create your mobile web applications from scratch with jQuery Mobile

2. Learn the important elements of the framework and mobile web development best practices

3. Customize elements and widgets to match your desired style

3. Step-by-step instructions on how to use jQuery Mobile

## HTML5 Multimedia Development Cookbook

ISBN: 978-1-849691-04-8         Paperback: 288 pages

Recipes for practical, real-world HTML5 multimedia-driven development

1. Use HTML5 to enhance JavaScript functionality. Display videos dynamically and create movable ads using JQuery

2. Set up the canvas environment, process shapes dynamically and create interactive visualizations

3. Enhance accessibility by testing browser support, providing alternative site views and displaying alternate content for non supported browsers

Please check **www.PacktPub.com** for information on our titles

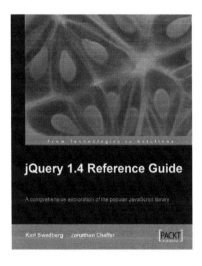

## jQuery 1.4 Reference Guide

ISBN: 978-1-849510-04-2          Paperback: 336 pages

A comprehensive exploration of the popular
JavaScript library

1.  Quickly look up features of the jQuery library

2.  Step through each function, method, and
    selector expression in the jQuery library with
    an easy-to-follow approach

3.  Understand the anatomy of a jQuery script

4.  Write your own plug-ins using jQuery's
    powerful plug-in architecture

5.  Written by the creators of learningquery.com

## Learning jQuery, Third Edition: RAW

ISBN: 978-1-849516-54-9          Paperback: 468 pages

Create better interaction, design, and web
development with simple JavaScript techniques

1.  An introduction to jQuery that requires
    minimal programming experience

2.  Detailed solutions to specific client-side
    problem

3.  Revised and updated version of this popular
    jQuery book

Please check **www.PacktPub.com** for information on our titles

Printed in Great Britain
by Amazon.co.uk, Ltd.,
Marston Gate.